THE ACTIVITY OF PHILOSOPHY

A Concise Introduction

FRED A. WESTPHAL
University of Miami (Florida)

PRENTICE-HALL, INC., Englewood Cliffs, New Jersey

13-003608-0.

Library of Congress Catalog Card Number: 68-19996.

Printed in the United States of America.

Current printing (last digit):
10 9 8 7 6 5 4 3 2 1

Prentice-Hall International, Inc. *(London)*
Prentice-Hall of Australia, Pty. Ltd. *(Sydney)*
Prentice-Hall of Canada, Ltd. *(Toronto)*
Prentice-Hall of India Private Ltd. *(New Delhi)*
Prentice-Hall of Japan, Inc. *(Tokyo)*

For Awanda, Eric, and Kevin

PREFACE

The purpose of this book is to acquaint the reader with some aspects of the activity called philosophy. The problems selected for treatment are among those that have occupied the minds of reflective men since the first glimmerings of wonder and inquiry touched the dark corners of ignorance and unexamined belief. Philosophy, perhaps the oldest of intellectual enterprises, has been a virtual vanguard in man's ancient (and oftentimes anguished) quest for a valid view of himself and his place in the world. It is with the work of the philosopher, therefore, that we shall be concerned—his problems, his methods of dealing with them, and the difficulties he and all of us encounter when engaged in the activity of philosophy.

No book, least of all one of this size, can adequately cover all or even most that is of significance in philosophy. Choices concerning which issues and which proposed solutions to them are most suitable for the beginner in philosophy to pursue must inevitably be made. Yet the decisions can be made with meaningful and defensible criteria in mind. (1) The problems should be those which can be expected to be of most relevance and interest to the non-professional philosopher. (2) They should be issues which have been sufficiently significant to stimulate and sustain serious thought not only in the past but in our own day as well. (3) The proposed solutions to the problems selected should be capable of being understood without having to presuppose an unrealistic amount of technical and historical background on the part of the reader. (4) The philosophical arguments as they appear in the writings of the philosophers themselves should be easily accessible so that they may be explored firsthand. This book is not intended as a *substitute* for pursuing primary sources but rather, it is meant to *supplement* readings which contain the very arguments we have attempted to simplify and explain. Philosophical writing, however, is not the easiest to comprehend, even for the most gifted student, and it is for this reason that a supplementary, expository work of this nature can be helpful if properly used. Undoubtedly there will be some who will succumb to the temptation to avoid the oftentimes difficult primary source readings but by doing so they will cut themselves off from an indispensable source of sound philosophical training.

There are many anthologies available which were designed as introductory reading in philosophy. What follows is a partial list of such readers, all of which are arranged around the topics explored in this volume. Notice that the titles in the list are abbreviated so as to make references to them throughout the book less cumbersome.

AB　—W. P. Alston and R. B. Brandt, eds., *The Problems of Philosophy* (Boston: Allyn and Bacon, Inc., 1967).

BKW　—D. J. Bronstein, Y. H. Krikorian, and P. P. Wiener, eds., *Basic Problems of Philosophy* (3rd ed.) (Englewood Cliffs, N.J.: Prentice-Hall, Inc., 1964).

EP   —P. Edwards and A. Pap, eds., *A Modern Intro-duction to Philosophy* (rev. ed.) (New York: Free Press, 1965).

F   —J. Feinberg, ed., *Reason and Responsibility* (Belmont, Calif.: Dickenson Publishing Co., 1966).

MGAS—M. Mandelbaum, F. W. Gramlich, A. R. Ander-son and J. Schneewind, eds., *Philosophic Prob-lems* (2nd ed.) (New York: The Macmillan Co., 1967).

SA   —M. G. Singer and R. R. Ammerman, eds., *Intro-ductory Readings in Philosophy* (New York: Scribner's, 1962).

ST   —E. Sprague and P. W. Taylor, eds., *Knowledge and Value* (2nd ed.) (New York: Harcourt, Brace & World, 1967).

TBO —F. Tillman, B. Berofsky, and J. O'Connor, eds., *Introductory Philosophy* (New York: Harper and Row, 1967).

TH   —H. Titus and M. Hepp, eds., *The Range of Phi-losophy* (New York: American Book Company, 1964).

An attempt has been made in this book to present the arguments of *other* philosophers rather than to make philosoph-ical proselytes of its readers. However, it would be the height of naïveté to claim that one was *wholly* successful in such an attempt and it will become clear before too long where the au-thor's philosophical sympathies lie. I sincerely believe, how-ever, that my philosophical persuasions (and who is devoid of them?) have been kept suppressed for the most part in spite of an urge to let them loose. My only aim has been to present inter-esting and important philosophical arguments with clarity, accu-racy, and fairness. This book will be a success if only some of its readers acquire a better understanding of the activity of philos-ophy and gain greater facility in wielding the tools for intelligent evaluation of competing viewpoints.

ACKNOWLEDGMENTS

In a sense, no person can justly claim to be the sole author of a book. He owes so many debts to those from whom he has learned (both formally and informally) and from whom he has received stimulation and encouragement. I am certainly no exception. Special thanks are due my brother, Dale, and his colleagues at Western Michigan University who read the manuscript and provided helpful suggestions. My good friend and colleague, Howard Pospesel, has been especially generous with his time in helping detect blunders in the manuscript which only an author, it would seem, could miss. Finally, my wife Awanda deserves some sort of medal for service above and beyond the call of wifely duty. Her constant encouragement and the expertise with which she prepared the manuscript at its various stages beginning with translations of somewhat hieroglyphic early drafts were more than a husband had a right to expect.

CONTENTS

MIND AND IMMORTALITY: III
Will I Survive Death? page 79

THE PROBLEM OF FREE WILL IV
AND DETERMINISM:
Am I Ever Responsible for My Actions? page 117

THE PROBLEM OF MORALITY: V
Can I Know What Is Morally Right? page 161

THE PROBLEM OF KNOWLEDGE: VI
When Can I Say That I Know? page 205

WHAT IS PHILOSOPHY?

I

There is a story told about two college students who, after having completed an introductory course in philosophy, were in the throes of confusion and frustration. Instead of having all of their questions answered and their problems clarified, they found themselves with even more difficulties and bewilderment than when they had embarked upon their search for truth. Then one day the unhappy pair chanced to hear a report concerning the existence of a 156-year-old wise man living in the mountains of Tibet who was purported to have attained the "secret of life." The two students managed to get more precise knowledge of the old gentleman's location and, after acquiring the necessary supplies, set out in search of the truth which they hoped lay somewhere halfway around the world. The journey was torturous and rife with danger, but finally the young men, suffering from starvation and exposure, dragged themselves into the old man's village. They managed to state their intentions to several of the natives and were slowly ushered into the presence of a decrepit, ancient man seated at the front of a small, dimly-lit room. The students' eyes widened with anticipation as they told of their intense desire to know the "secret of life" and of how they had risked their very lives to hear the wise man's answer. The old man spoke slowly and falteringly. "Life . . . life . . . is . . . a deep well," he said.

The young truth-seekers waited for more words of wisdom but all they could hear were the long, deep, scratchy sounds of the old man's breathing. One of the students broke the silence and in a tone of disgust mingled with disappointment exclaimed, "We have gone through a virtual valley of death for thousands of miles seeking the secret of life, and all you can say is that life is a *deep well?*"

This seemed to rattle the heretofore complacent, motionless figure seated before them. He laboriously lifted his head and said with a pained look of disbelief in his sunken eyes, "Do you mean it *isn't?*"

CORRECTING SOME MISCONCEPTIONS

Whether our young heroes eventually found what they were looking for and whether the old wise man managed to survive the shock of someone's questioning his solution to the riddle of life are not known. In retrospect, however, we may point out several things which might have spared the young men considerable effort and disillusionment had they known of them.

(1) A first course in philosophy should not be expected to solve every problem completely or to provide ready-made solutions which can be reproduced merely by rote. The discipline of philosophy is more like designing and building your own

house than it is like buying a dwelling already made. The individual who wants a home which truly fits his needs might well consider doing the job on his own (provided he has the time and talent required). If such is the case, one would presumably think through every aspect of the design carefully, critically, and creatively. He would most likely acquaint himself with the various alternatives open to him and would, if time permitted, study examples of work which others had done before him. It would be a wise move on his part if he were to seek advice from experts in the areas of architecture and interior design before making his final decisions.

The would-be philosopher should proceed in roughly the same way in constructing his answers to the fundamental problems perplexing him. He should proceed with the clear understanding that philosophy is primarily an *activity*, something to be *done* by the individual himself. Yet in stressing the fact that one must do philosophy for himself rather than merely parrot positions adopted by this or that philosopher, we are not implying that the activity of philosophy is to be carried on in an arbitrary way or that one's philosophic beliefs are a matter of personal taste. It is an activity which, in order to be done well, must be approached thoughtfully, critically, and methodically, just as one would if he were building his own home. After all, if a person's house is something he plans to live in for an extended period of time, its design and construction had better be the result of careful and intelligent thinking. How much more important it is that one's philosophy, which presumably is something a person intends to live with and by, be put together with careful, critical consideration to detail.

Although the activity of philosophy must be done by the individual, it may, like the activity of designing and constructing one's own home, be guided and inspired by the work of others. The beginning philosopher would do well to consider carefully the work that has already been done on a particular problem before he rushes in with his own "solution." It might very well be that someone before him has taken the approach which he is about to offer, and that a number of crucial difficulties with it have already been pointed out. Perhaps after having acquainted yourself with the various difficulties with a particular position you believe to be essentially correct, you might attempt either to restate or refute these criticisms. Keeping one's eyes open for weaknesses not only in the arguments one advances but in those which run counter to them as well are important aspects of the activity of philosophy.

Another similarity between building your own home and constructing your own philosophy suggests itself. The greatest satisfaction and sheer enjoyment that this discipline can afford lies in the actual activity of *doing* philosophy, and not in the dubious belief that you have reached an irrefutable position on a given issue. The pleasures of philosophy await those who will regard the actual *activity* of philosophical thinking as a valuable experience in itself, even apart from its ultimate goal which ought to be the resolution of philosophical perplexity.

(2) On the other hand, the first outing in philosophy should not completely confuse and frustrate the serious, inquiring student. The two young fellows in our story could very well have been suffering from an acute case of "intellectual indigestion." That is, they had probably been expected to clarify too many problems, follow too many arguments, and keep a large flock of theories and names straight, all the time trying to understand philosophers' sometimes obscure uses of language.

Rather than spending their time juggling jargon and matching philosophers' names with the theories they held, the students should have been learning how to use various tools for doing philosophical analysis. They should have learned, first of all, what philosophical problems are and how to state them so as to avoid misunderstanding. Then some of the major arguments which have been advanced as ways of answering key philosophical questions should have been carefully examined. Above all, their introductory course in philosophy should have helped

4

them develop methods for fair and intelligent evaluation of these arguments so that they could get involved in philosophical dialogue for themselves. A person cannot be expected to engage in the activity of philosophy unless he is provided with and learns how to handle the necessary tools for such an enterprise.

(3) A right approach to philosophy should teach us to be suspicious of hollow profundity. A good deal of what goes by the name "philosophy" can be about as hollow and superficial as the Tibetan wise man's remark, "Life is a deep well." People who are impressed with "deep" sounding statements mistakenly think that philosophy in general is a very "deep" subject and that the more mysterious a philosopher's pronouncements are, the more profound he must be. For one reason or another many people picture the philosopher as a poor unfortunate who locks himself in his study in order to spin elaborate theories about "reality," and who then occasionally enters the public arena to utter or publish paradoxical profundities beyond the understanding of ordinary mortals.[1]

The first task of a person doing philosophy is that of making himself understood. If a particular thinker believes he has come across an item of truth about which he desires to convince others, what could be more important to him than to speak or write in the clearest possible manner? Yet it is often the case that philosophers use words in extraordinary ways and coin new words when old ones do not suit them, without saying clearly how these words are being used. It is a mark of philosophical maturity and not mere verbal quibbling to demand that philosophers explain what they mean by a particular use of words when their meaning is obscure. If it is some sort of resolution of

---

[1]You should hear some of the reactions a philosophy professor gets when he admits what he does for a living. "Oh, that must be terribly deep stuff," is the one most commonly encountered. Then there are the responses of more "informed" individuals who say things like, "Oh, I enjoy reading philosophy a great deal. I think that Will Rogers was the greatest American philosopher, don't you?"

philosophical problems which is desired, then we cannot stress too much the importance of couching philosophical arguments in understandable terms. For no progress can be made in determining the truth or falsity of a particular statement unless that assertion is meaningful. The question, "What does that statement mean?" is always prior to the question, "Is that statement true or false?"

(4) A right approach to philosophy should teach us to be wary of authorities who are supposed to have all the answers. It makes no difference how ancient or how reputed an authority on philosophical matters may be; neither of these qualities is a guarantee that his opinions are correct. It would be convenient (however dull) if we *could* solve every problem by simply checking things out with a keeper of wisdom somewhere. But how would we go about locating such a person? By what marks are we to recognize him? Sooner or later we discover that the claims of *rival* "authorities" on a given philosophical issue have to be weighed. And the only way of doing this is to analyze critically each of their arguments.

Philosophical issues are in a sense great levelers because when it comes to resolving them, no one's opinion is worth more than the next person's unless it is backed up by good arguments.[2] Argument, after all, is the stock in trade of the philosopher. It is his major (if not his sole) *modus operandi,* and the philosopher who tries to go on his merry way without using it is like the carpenter who goes to work without his hammer and saw. Neither one is likely to accomplish anything constructive. In

---

[2] The word "argument" is commonly taken to mean a "heated quarrel or wrangle." Although philosophical discussions can become quite hot at times, we have a different sense of the word in mind. In our use of the term, a person presents an argument by making statements which he takes to be support or evidence for some conclusion. The statements or considerations he appeals to as support for his conclusion are to be regarded as reasons why he holds his position. Ideally at least, philosophers should not resort to passionate, persuasive ploys to make their points.

short, you have a logical right to ask those philosophers you come across not only "What do you *mean* by that?" but also "What *reasons* do you have for saying that?"

THE NATURE OF THIS BOOK

(1) *We shall deal with only five philosophical problems, each of which is a fairly live issue in contemporary philosophical discussion.* In addition, the problems selected are those which should be most significant for the non-professional philosopher. Care has been taken to avoid those philosophical issues which are of such nature that extensive training in the discipline would be necessary in order to appreciate their significance. Very little would be accomplished if a person were expected to have a firm grasp of a dozen or more philosophical problems in his initial acquaintance with the subject. Confusion rather than clarification would probably be the consequence of such a course.

After completion of the present chapter, which includes an important section on differing conceptions of the philosophic task, we shall treat our problems in the following order (although one could just as profitably adopt another sequence since each chapter is fairly self-contained):

The problem of God: Does a perfect personal being exist?

The problem of Mind and Immortality: Will I survive death?

The problem of Free-will and Determinism: Am I ever justly held responsible for my actions?

The problem of Morality: Can I know what is morally right?

The problem of Knowledge: When may I say that I know?

(2) Since the activity of philosophy is almost wholly composed of the presentation of arguments for or against a given position, *the statement of various arguments proposed as solutions to the problems we have selected makes up the major part of this book.* We shall leave such things as accounts of the historical development of a particular problem or theory for more advanced courses in philosophy. We shall also omit for the most part discussions which compare one philosophical argument with another, or one particular position with another. Studies which do this sort of thing can indeed be helpful in understanding more fully a given philosopher's viewpoint, and most useful in showing how a specific approach in philosophy came about. But it might be better for the student in his initial contact with philosophical arguments to learn how to follow and criticize them intelligently rather than to trace their genealogy and shirt-tail relations.

Every attempt has been made to present the most interesting and significant arguments for a given position in a fair, accurate, and convincing manner. Furthermore, they will be stated in familiar, everyday terms as far as the argument under consideration permits. Any cumbersome and confusing jargon which some philosophers occasionally feel impelled to use will be explained if not omitted outright.

(3) *A most important feature in our treatment of philosophical problems involves the suggestion of various difficulties with the arguments advanced for a particular viewpoint.* Every effort should be made to become involved in the critical evaluation of the arguments encountered. Ordinarily, difficulties or weaknesses in a given argument will merely be suggested and not spelled out in great detail. This leaves room for the reader to pick up the suggested criticism and carry it on for himself. Undoubtedly, additional problems will be found with some of the arguments, and this is just what should happen as one acquires philosophical skills. The beginner in philosophy should be under no delusions regarding the fact that the advancement of a

philosophical thesis is no easy matter; he should be thoroughly aware that regardless of how plausible a given argument may appear on first glance, there will be points of weakness in it which should be given attention. Yet the difficulties which we shall point out in regard to a given argument are not equally crucial; some are more telling than others but all of them should serve at least as springboards for thought and discussion.

A careful, critical reader may spot difficulties in our suggested difficulties! That is, the criticism of a given philosophical argument may get the same treatment as the arguments in favor of a particular viewpoint. It may be that a suggested criticism betrays some misunderstanding of the position under review, or perhaps the weak links in a given argument can be strengthened so as to save the conclusion of that argument. It might be well to remember that where arguments are concerned, "Difficulties do not always a refutation make."

(4) *The relatively short length of the book should leave more time to think through the problems involved and to participate in the activity of philosophical analysis and criticism for yourself.* The conciseness of the book and its emphasis upon critical thinking are intended to assist the reader in his study of the actual writings of the philosophers whose arguments we have summarized and, hopefully, simplified. There can be no substitute for reading the primary sources, and although philosophical writing is not by any means the easiest type of literature to follow, some acquaintance with it is strongly encouraged. To guide you along the most fruitful lines in this regard, suggestions for further study are included at the end of each chapter.

DIFFERING CONCEPTIONS OF PHILOSOPHY

To say that philosophers do not often see eye to eye on any given issue would be to make a gross understatement. However, they differ not only concerning their proposed solutions to philosophical questions, but even as to what the task of philosophy is. In fact, one of the most important problems facing the philosopher is that of determining precisely what his job is and how he ought to go about it. In the remainder of this chapter we shall discuss a number of differing conceptions concerning the nature of philosophy. Some of these notions are more in vogue nowadays than others, and we shall take note of these as we proceed. A word of caution is in order before we start, however. We should not think that a particular philosopher must regard the role of philosophy in only one way. In fact, it is probably the case that most philosophers believe their job involves a number of different, but related activities.

Philosophy Should Uncover Truths Which Are Inaccessible Through Sense Perception and Scientific Verification.

A good many philosophers have regarded themselves as discoverers of special kinds of facts which elude our perceptual faculties and the procedures of scientific inquiry. The philosopher's task on this view is roughly that of the scientist's, namely to come up with truth (even though their methods are quite different, as we shall soon see). We shall pose three questions for ourselves and in answering them attempt to clarify what is involved in this conception of the philosophic task. The questions are: (1) What sorts of discoveries do philosophers claim to make? (2) What methods does the philosopher use in arriving at his alleged discoveries? (3) How do these alleged discoveries differ from scientific discoveries?

WHAT SORTS OF DISCOVERIES DO PHILOSOPHERS CLAIM TO MAKE? There seem to be two different ways of viewing the claims to discovery which philosophers have made. First, a philosopher will often claim to have come up with some truth

10

regarding the existence or nonexistence of certain imperceptible entities. For example, a philosopher might advance some argument for the existence of a personal being without limitations (i.e., God as traditionally conceived), or he might believe that because of certain reasons a person's mind should be considered a special sort of entity and therefore distinguishable from the body. Both of these claims, of course, have been denied by other philosophers, but the assertions that God does not exist and that the mind is identical to certain states and processes in the body are still rightly classified as alleged discoveries of particular truths. A large part of our investigation of philosophical problems will be concerned with various claims and counterclaims concerning the existence or nonexistence of entities which are not observable by means of our senses.

But there is another side of the philosopher as discoverer, although not all those who believe that their task is to uncover truth about what exists engage in this form of activity. The history of philosophy abounds with examples of thinkers who claimed to have discovered systems of categories or concepts which would correctly interpret or explain the whole of reality. Philosophers who have viewed their job along these lines are after something like an overall view of the way things are. They attempt to take data gained from scientific inquiry, and along with their own observations and reflections construct a general view of everything that can be regarded as real. In working out such a general view of reality, a thinker may also find himself making claims about particular entities he believes to exist. But he would normally consider his most important task to be that of framing a conceptual system capable of unifying and explaining in a general way the facts he encounters.

In order to understand what philosophers who do this sort of thing are up to, it might be helpful to liken them to political commentators who attempt to assess the significance of a certain groups of facts and provide a general framework of thought by which seemingly disordered and diverse events may be interpreted. For example, a commentator often attempts to assess or interpret the "political climate" of the country in the light of certain facts gathered from voting statistics and the results of public opinion polls. He presumably tries to see the political situation as a whole and he might utilize certain general explanatory concepts in the process.

WHAT METHODS DOES THE PHILOSOPHER USE TO ARRIVE AT HIS ALLEGED DISCOVERIES? Ordinarily the philosopher who regards himself as a discoverer of either the existence of particular entities beyond the reach of our perceptual capacities or a system of categories which correctly interprets or accounts for the way things are uses the only tools open to him—arguments. He attempts to show that because of various reasons it was necessary for him to arrive at the conclusion he drew, and that anyone else who follows the arguments he advances should come up with the same result. Ordinarily the philosopher does everything possible to avoid the charge that his position is merely arbitrary or based upon his feelings or wishful thinking.

One method employed by some prominent figures in the history of philosophy involved (1) isolating those propositions whose truth is regarded as "self-evident" and then (2) making use of these propositions to arrive at other truths which logically follow from the former. The notion of "self-evident truth" does not mean precisely the same thing to all those who employ the expression, but for Descartes[3] (perhaps the leading practitioner of this method) a proposition was self-evident if its truth could not be doubted without one's landing himself in a contradiction. For example, one of the propositions he regarded as self-evident was "I think, therefore I exist." He argued that if you doubted

---

[3] René Descartes (1596-1650) is regarded by many as the "father of modern philosophy" since (1) his method in doing philosophy departed so dramatically from earlier, more traditional methods, and (2) philosophers after him inherited a whole group of problems which his conclusions seemed to open up. His most important works are *Discourse on Method* (1637) and *The Meditations* (1641).

the truth of this proposition, you would still be thinking (since doubting is a form of thinking). And in order for a person to think, a person must necessarily exist. A person contradicts himself if he sincerely claims to doubt that he exists, since the very fact that he doubts requires that he exist in order for him to be capable of doubting. Consequently, Descartes maintained that "I think, therefore I exist" is a proposition whose truth is self-evident. By using this somewhat meagre item of knowledge and other propositions he took to be self-evidently true, he maintained that we could uncover even more truths if the rules for valid reasoning were adhered to at every step. (We shall discuss Descartes's alleged discoveries in later chapters in order to see how far this particular method can take us in doing philosophy.) [4]

There are some philosophers, however, who have regarded themselves as discoverers of what is real but who lack a proper respect for reasons. There has been a tendency on the part of some philosophers simply to present their views on little more than a "take-it-or-leave-it" basis without defending their alleged discoveries with arguments. Their approach could be described as the "I'm telling you" method as a recent historian of philosophy so aptly put it. [5] The systems they construct may well have a profound atmosphere about them, but such men are often short on reasons why they believe what they do and why anyone else should view things in a similar way. If a philosopher presents us with arguments which are couched in fairly understandable terms, we are at least given a fighting chance of determining whether or not some philosophical discovery has indeed

---

[4] A different notion of self-evidence is held by G. E. Moore, an outstanding twentieth-century philosopher. He regards as self-evident any proposition which can not be proved true by any evidence but which upon due reflection we seem rationally compelled to accept as true nevertheless. Examples of such self-evident truths would be mathematical propositions and various statements concerning what is morally right. We shall deal more fully with the latter in Chapter Five.

[5] John Passmore, *A Hundred Years of Philosophy* (London: Gerald Duckworth and Co., Ltd., 1957), p. 343.

13

been made. The philosopher who ignores the tools of argument in his trade is roughly comparable to a scientist who, while investigating nature, refuses to use his powers of sense perception.

How Do the Alleged Discoveries of Philosophers Differ from Scientific Discoveries? We should be careful not to locate the differences between the scientist and philosopher in the wrong place. Contrary to what one might think, both of them to some degree utilize data gained from sense experience in their work. Even those philosophers who place little stock in the senses as reliable guides to knowledge sometimes make points which *rely* upon sense perception in one way or another. Plato, for example, observed that the physical world constantly undergoes change and therefore could not be considered "real" in the fullest sense of the term. In spite of his depreciation of data gained through the senses, he obviously thought the latter were reliable enough to reveal the fact of change in the physical world.

Furthermore it is not true that only scientists are interested in affecting the course of future events (which of course they do by understanding and manipulating certain processes of nature). Philosophers as well have attempted to shape the future by changing people's beliefs and habits of thought, which in turn affect their actions. Neither is it true that only the philosopher theorizes or speculates while the scientist simply sticks to digging up facts through observation. The really famous figures in the history of science did provide theories which were designed to explain *why* the facts were as they found them. Both the scientist and the philosopher attempt to "make sense" of what they take to be facts by providing explanatory theories of some sort.

What then is the distinctive difference between the philosopher as discoverer and the scientist? It seems to boil down to differences in the ways in which their respective theories are confirmed or refuted. An important part in the testing of a scientific hypothesis involves the making of predic-

14

tions which will come true if the hypothesis is correct. Ordinarily, the scientist sets up an experiment so that he can observe whether or not the predictions which he believes follow from his hypothesis come true. If the predictions come off as expected, then the hypothesis has some confirmation. The important thing is that something of an observable nature must be able to count either for or against the hypothesis in order for it to be classified as empirical or scientific.

Now the case is quite different when it comes to testing a philosophical theory or hypothesis. One does not go about confirming or refuting it by setting up experiments and seeing whether or not some specific predictions come about which are implied by the hypothesis. A philosophical theory does not, in short, have "predictive power" at all and, consequently, to "test" such a theory, one must content himself with analyzing and evaluating the arguments which have been advanced by the philosopher in support of his position.

It might be helpful to suggest some criteria for evaluating philosophical arguments if this is the only test open to us. You might keep the following questions in mind as you encounter any philosophical argument:

1. Does the philosopher in question define key terms upon which his argument hinges?
2. Is the philosopher in question consistent in what he says? Does he avoid making contradictory or logically incompatible statements?
3. Are the statements the philosopher uses in support of his conclusion true?
4. Does the theory which the philosopher proposes adequately explain what it was intended to explain? Does his theory avoid the generation of new problems and perplexities of an even more difficult nature than the ones his theory is supposed to solve?

If we carefully and honestly apply these criteria and find that an affirmative answer should be given to all four questions, we may conclude that we are justified in regarding the theory under review as tentatively confirmed. We must exercise caution here, however. It may be that we have over-looked or misunderstood something of a crucial nature in the argument we are analyzing. Furthermore, we must always be on guard against two ever-present tendencies on our part—to be over-cordial to those viewpoints with which we already agree, and to be unfair toward those with which we disagree. It is a curious fact that it is such a simple matter to find opposing points of view full of flaws while at the same time it is so difficult to spot any fallacies in arguments which support our own positions.

We should not underestimate the difficulties involved in weighing an argument fairly, disinterestedly, and dispassionately when we might already have formed an opinion or begun to lean in some direction on the issue under review. By the same token, these obstacles should not discourage us from making careful, concerted attempts to analyze and evaluate the arguments of those who purportedly have uncovered some truth.

Philosophy Should Elucidate Linguistic Expressions Employed in Everyday Experience.

CURING PHILOSOPHICAL PERPLEXITY: THE PHILOSO-PHER AS THERAPIST. Some philosophers take their task to be that of applying treatment or "cure" for philosophical problems by showing how they originate through philosophers' (usually unconscious) misuse of language. They picture the role of the philosopher, therefore, as that of a *therapist* who ought not to offer new solutions to the problems of his troubled patient or confront him with more alleged discoveries of a non-scientific nature. Rather, he ought to help the perplexed philosopher to see for himself how he gets to the point where he asks certain philosophical questions. The aim of the philosophical "therapist" is to cure philosophical perplexity which has the understanding so tied up in knots that no way out of the difficulty seems possible. The ultimate aim of this philosophical therapy is to check the tendencies on the part of philosophers to produce various sorts of odd-sounding statements and to propound theories which simply lead to more (and worse) perplexities than originally beset them.

Ludwig Wittgenstein (1889-1951) was the leading exponent of the therapeutic approach to philosophy, and he attracted a number of other philosophers (mostly in English-speaking countries) to his view. His book *Philosophical Investigations* has been one of the most discussed works in twentieth-century philosophy, and it continues to exert considerable influence in contemporary philosophical circles. Wittgenstein compares the traditional philosopher to a fly who has become trapped in a fly-bottle. The latter was an old-fashioned device which trapped flies by luring the unsuspecting insect through the narrow opening in the neck of the bottle. Access into the trap was easy but once inside the confused fly had extreme difficulty in finding his way out. The philosopher in Wittgenstein's view is likewise lured by certain expressions used in everyday speech to generate philosophical perplexities from which he cannot extricate himself. The only cure for him is to retrace his intellectual steps and discover how he became trapped.[6]

Let us sit in on a typical therapeutic session and see how a particular philosophical perplexity is diagnosed, treated and, hopefully, "cured." The case is that of "chronic" doubt concerning the existence of mental states in others — a malady which has bothered more than a few philosophers.[7] The same type of

---

[6] Ludwig Wittgenstein, *Philosophical Investigations* (New York: Crowell-Collier & Macmillan, Inc., 1953), Sec. 309 — "Your aim in philosophy — to show the fly the way out of the fly-bottle." Sec. 123 — "A philosophical problem has the form: 'I don't know my way about.'" Sec. 255 — "The philosopher's treatment of a question is like the treatment of an illness."

[7] John Stuart Mill, for example, seemed to doubt his belief in the existence of mental states in others. *An Examination of Sir William Hamilton's Philosophy*, 6th ed. (London: Longmans, Green & Company, Ltd., 1889), pp. 243-44. Bertrand Russell was also bothered by this philosophical "illness." See his *Human Knowledge* (New York: Allen and Unwin, 1948), p. 193.

doubt plagues those who ask "Can we ever know that there are material things or must we be content with having only various sensations?" Since the latter problem is dealt with in Chapter Six, we shall here attempt to show how the philosopher as "therapist" would treat the former, that is, chronic, philosophic doubt whether other people have mental states similar to our own. The cure for this problem (as well as for other philosophical perplexities) would take the form of getting the philosopher to see for himself how he got into his fix.

Ordinarily, the philosopher who raises doubts concerning the existence of mental states in others ends up by denying outright that we can ever know the mind of another. It is the extremely paradoxical nature of such a position which serves as a symptom of something having gone wrong somewhere. No normal person (including the philosopher when he is outside his study) seriously believes that he is the only one who has thoughts and feelings. The attempt to maintain such a position and act upon it would involve such a radical intellectual reorientation as to be practically impossible, even though one could always *say* that he doubted whether other minds existed. The philosophical therapist believes his task is to cure philosophical problems before they result in strange and misleading statements of which "We cannot ever know the mind of another" is an example.[8]

What is the first stage of philosophical "illness" in general and the initial cause of the "chronic" doubt concerning the existence of other minds in particular? Probably the most important thing a philosopher does when he generates a philosophical puzzle is to make some slight but crucial departure from the ordinary, everyday meaning of a word or expression. He takes a word which has a standard use or meaning in familiar, everyday contexts and (usually unwittingly) assigns it a new and extraordinary job to do in his statements. The particular word which

---

[8] The following discussion of the "other minds" perplexity has been influenced by, and reflects somewhat the work of, Norman

gets this kind of handling in the "other minds" puzzle is the word "know." Philosophical doubt concerning other minds begins with a linguistic move which on the surface seems quite harmless and even fairly plausible. It is *so tempting* to say something like the following:

I know when *I* am in pain or thinking or being sincere, and I know what these experiences are by being acquainted with them in myself. But I can't know the pains or thoughts of *another* person in the way that I know my own. All I can observe about other people is their behavior and what they say. When my friend moans and rubs his elbow, I assume or *believe* he is in pain, but I never do directly *know* his pain. If he has mental states, only he can know them. But haven't we all made mistakes about other people's mental states when we try to determine what they are on the basis of how others act? A person can pretend to be happy when deep inside he may be extremely sad, or one can look as though he is thinking about what he is doing at the moment and really be "miles away." But if on some occasions we can be so wrong when we try to know what another is thinking or feeling, maybe we are wrong in thinking that other people have mental states and experiences *at all*. Can we ever really know the mind of another? Maybe our belief that there are other minds is not a correct one, that the behavior of others is not really connected with any mental states in them at all.

This is roughly the case history of the typical "chronic" doubt concerning other minds. Look especially at how the philosophical perplexity gets a foothold. The philosopher says, for example, that he *knows he is in pain* or that he is thinking. Then he contrasts this supposed knowledge of his own mental states with the knowledge we claim to get of the contents of other people's minds. The "knowledge" the philosopher has of his

---

Malcolm and John Wisdom, two contemporary practitioners of the therapeutic approach to philosophy. Norman Malcolm, "Wittgenstein's *Philosophical Investigations,*" *Philosophical Review,* LXIII (1954), 530-39. Norman Malcolm, "Knowledge of Other Minds," *Journal of Philosophy,* LV (1958), 969-78. Both of these articles are reprinted in *The Philosophy of Mind,* V. C. Chapell, ed. (Englewood Cliffs, N.J.: Prentice-Hall, Inc., 1962), pp. 74-100, 151-60. See also John Wisdom, *Other Minds* (Oxford: Blackwell, 1952); and John Wisdom, *Philosophy and Psycho-Analysis* (Oxford: Blackwell, 1953).

own pain, for example, strikes him as being a genuine case of knowing something, but he is not quite so sure about his claims concerning anybody else's pain. He can't make mistakes about the existence of his own pain but he can make all sorts of errors in making judgments about other people's mental states. The problem the philosopher set for himself when he doubted the existence of minds outside his own would probably never have arisen had he not misused the word "know" in his very first statement. Who ever says in ordinary contexts, "I know I am in pain"? What would it mean to say this except perhaps, "I *am* in pain"?[9] We do say on occasion that we *are* in pain or *have* a pain of such and such a type, but not that we *know* our pains. Had the philosopher been more sensitive to the way the word "know" is actually used in our everyday contexts, he would have found that we say "I know" only in those contexts where it would make good sense to say instead, "I believe. . . . " We use the expression "I know" when something could meaningfully be brought forward to show that we were mistaken.[10] But when we are in pain, what sense would it make to say, "I believe I am in pain," or "I suspect I have a pain in my back but I am not sure"? The question of being mistaken about the presence of a pain in ourselves simply does not arise, and consequently it is improper to use the expression "I know" in the philosophical statement, "I know I am in pain." Only philosophers make such statements anyway, and because they violate the ways in which words are used in ordinary, everyday language, the philosophical problem concerning other minds gets a foothold in their minds.

If the philosopher would not think that he has "knowledge" of his own mental states and that this supposed knowledge is so different and so superior to the knowledge we claim to

---

[9] "It can't be said of me at all (except perhaps as a joke) that I *know* I am in pain. What is it supposed to mean—except perhaps that I *am* in pain." Ludwig Wittgenstein, *Philosophical Investigations*, Sec. 246.

[10] "One says 'I know' where one can also say 'I believe' or 'I suspect'; where one can find out." *Ibid.*, p. 221.

have of other people's experiences, knowledge of the latter would probably not strike him as so poor a relation as it does. If he had not mistakenly concluded that he "knows" his own mental states in a unique and unmistakable way, he would probably not lament the fact that we can't know other people's minds. After all, what would it be like to *be* face to face with someone else's thoughts and feelings? What the philosopher seems to be lamenting when he points out that knowledge of other minds is so limited and unreliable (if not outright impossible), is that *we* don't *have* other people's thoughts and feelings. But what is this to complain about? Does the philosopher really think we could *be* someone other than ourselves?[11]

If the patient does not respond to this sort of treatment, something else might be tried. The philosophical perplexity concerning the existence of other minds might be so advanced that a number of cures would have to be suggested. Besides his misuse of the word "know" another mistake has been made by the philosopher, and this sort of error is so prevalent in philosophy that pointing it out can help cure other perplexities besetting the philosopher. In ordinary, everyday language we often say things like "I'll keep that piece of advice in mind" or "His mind is cluttered with all sorts of nonsense," and for non-philosophers no problems result from hearing or making such statements. But along comes the philosopher, who places the strangest interpretation on expressions like these.[12] It is so tempting for him to picture the mind as a place, as a special kind of theatre in which images, thoughts, and feelings are flashed on a peculiar sort of internal, private screen. Each person has his own private theatre and no one else can get in to see what picture is playing.

---

[11] Wisdom, *Other Minds.*

[12] "When we do philosophy we are like savages, primitive people, who hear the expressions of civilized men, put a false interpretation on them, and then draw the queerest conclusions from it." Wittgenstein, *Philosophical Investigations*, Sec. 194.

Misapplication of statements like the ones above (i.e., statements employing the word "mind" and terms related to mental conduct) contributes to thinking of the mind according to this model or analogy. Perplexities about mind (and particularly that of showing how we can know *another's* mind) begin to assert themselves only when a person starts *philosophizing* about mind; when one asks what kind of *thing* or entity it is and how it is to be compared to the body, philosophical perplexity is just around the corner. The philosopher, in short, presses the analogy or model which pictures the mind as a peculiar sort of place in which various kinds of "spiritual" acts and processes take place. He generates his problems concerning the nature of minds because he is held captive by a picture or model suggested to him by certain expressions in everyday language. As long as the picture is not taken too literally or seriously, no perplexity results. But as soon as someone tries to classify the mind (and its contents) for the purpose of comparing it with other *things* in his experience, the production of deep and perplexing puzzles is inevitable. One cure, then, for a good many philosophical perplexities is this: If you find yourself trapped in a perplexity and can't find your way out, retrace your intellectual steps. Chances are that somewhere along the line you have unconsciously allowed some picture, analogy, or model to capture (or at least affect) your thinking. Do not press these pictures or models which abound in our everyday speech about the world and ourselves. Take them for the analogies they are and do not allow yourself to become bewitched into regarding them as literal representations of some thing or entity.[13]

Yet another "drug" could be used to cure not only the philosophical perplexity concerning other minds, but a number of other problems as well. The philosopher often does not have a clear view of the ways in which language actually functions, and he can be particularly confused about the uses of various kinds

---

[13] "Philosophy is a battle against the bewitchment of our intelligence by means of language." Wittgenstein, *Philosophical Investigations*, Sec. 109.

of words. It is so easy to think that all nouns, for example, function in only one way, that being to *name* some person, place, or thing. In fact, in their incurable passion to find unity among things which are actually quite different, some philosophers have tried to think of *all* words as being *names*. They have attempted to isolate the *essence* of language and what it is for words to mean something by regarding the meaning of an expression as that for which the expression stands. In this view, then, all words are construed as labels for various sorts of things, and the meanings of words are known when one knows what the word or expression stands for.

This is a plausible view of language and meaning at first glance, but it will not stand critical scrutiny. First, if every word were a name, then a sentence composed of four words such as "The sun is shining" would be merely a list in the way that "flour, apples, sugar, and milk" is a list. But surely such a list is not a sentence, since it is neither true nor false. A sentence is more than any set of things for which each of the words composing the sentence stands.

A second difficulty with the "name theory of meaning," as we might call it, is this: all sorts of descriptive phrases can be coined which stand for nothing that exists. Yet these descriptive phrases have meaning which they could not have, if the meaning of a word or group of words is what is named by those words. For example, the phrase "the present king of America" has meaning, though we are quite certain no one is designated by these words.

Third, if the meaning of an expression is what that expression stands for, then we should have to admit that the meaning of the expression "the first man to stand on the top of Mt. Everest" wore an oxygen mask, grew a beard, and was born in New Zealand. When did we last see a meaning wearing an oxygen mask over its bearded face?[14]

---

[14] See Gilbert Ryle, "The Theory of Meaning," in *The Importance of Language*, ed. Max Black (Englewood Cliffs, N.J.: Prentice-Hall, Inc., 1962), pp. 151-53.

It is not too difficult to understand what can happen philosophically if all words are taken to be names which stand for or label some particular thing or entity. The word "mind" would have to be viewed as being the name of some type of thing and terms like "thought," "decision," and "feeling" must also be considered to stand for different kinds of inhabitants of the mind. Since we can't seem to locate the mind and its contents in the *physical* world, we feel forced to adopt the model which pictures the mind as a peculiar, private, non-material thing or place. Since each person's mind is non-material, it cannot be observed by anyone else, although everyone can know perfectly what is going on in his own private theatre or "mind." Now, when such a model or picture of the nature of mind gets hold of a philosopher, there is really no way of avoiding the philosophical perplexity concerning the existence of other minds. If I treat another person's "theatre" as necessarily closed to me, then I cannot know what is going on inside him. But I'm even worse off than this because I cannot even know whether there *is* a theatre inside, since no one can get by the door. It could be just an empty shell of a building or a clever façade. It would not help to *ask* another person about his own private theatre, his mind, because all I will get from him is a bunch of words. I have no way of knowing that there is *meaning* behind them; he may be a cleverly designed robot programmed to behave the way he does.

The philosopher, in addition to guarding his thoughts against misleading and captivating analogies or models suggested to him by certain expressions used in everyday language, ought to become familiar with the ways language actually functions. Instead of being tempted to seek for *the* meaning of a word or expression, he should determine for what purposes or tasks specific words are used in various kinds of everyday contexts. Words and expressions are not used in vacuums but rather in connection with different kinds of behavior for a variety of purposes. If the philosopher would cultivate a sensitivity to the many functions of language, he would spare himself considerable philosophical perplexity and extricate himself from entanglement in the thickets of his own theories.

For example, instead of immediately jumping to the conclusion that every time a person uses the word "mind" (or some variation thereof) he *must* be referring to some private, inner place or entity in which peculiar, ghost-like events occur, the philosopher should try to discover the *actual* job to which the word is put in non-philosophical contexts. If Aloysius says, "Barney's mind is cluttered with all sorts of nonsense," we should try to determine what such an expression is doing for the person who utters it. We would probably find that Aloysius hears Barney often make statements which seem false or possibly absurd. In the opinion of Aloysius, Barney can be expected to speak and write nonsensically in most matters. Upon hearing Aloysius's assertion we might also have good grounds for expecting Barney's future opinions on certain matters to be given little weight by Aloysius. And the latter could be using his statement about Barney to recommend that *we* be on our toes if we have any dealings with him which require clear and correct thinking.

It is important to notice that at no point is it necessary to regard the statement about Barney as referring to or describing some secret, spiritual substance encased within his body which only he can know first hand. In fact, if statements like the one Aloysius made *were* interpreted this way, the perplexity concerning the content of Barney's mind would become irresolvable. No sort of investigation or argument could possibly prove to a philosopher's satisfaction that anyone else had mental states and processes similar to his own.

If philosophers would take the trouble to get a clear view of the way people actually use words and expressions in everyday contexts, they would not be so quick to isolate any single use of a word and regard it as the sole meaning of that word. Once the philosopher is cured of this bad habit, he will find that a good many (if not all) of his perplexities can be dissolved, since he will then see them for what they are—the products of his own confusion concerning the role of language in everyday life.

MAPPING THE "GEOGRAPHY" OF OUR CONCEPTS: THE PHILOSOPHER AS CARTOGRAPHER. A considerable number of contemporary philosophers maintain that the task of philosophy is the elucidation or clarification of concepts which are employed by everyone in everyday contexts. These philosophers compare their work to that of mapmakers who plot the relationships which exist between different areas of land and illustrate the salient features of a given area. In roughly the same way, philosophers who engage in "logical" or "conceptual" cartography attempt to map the areas or categories to which various kinds of concepts belong and show the relationships between the concepts we employ in everyday language.

If we are going to understand what is involved in this approach to philosophy, some preliminary questions need attention. First, what are concepts? We are all well acquainted with concepts since we use them in all of our thinking and talking, but difficulties can arise when we attempt to say what a concept in general is. Perhaps the best path open to us here is to use an example. Suppose we wanted to analyze and elucidate a concept which we all employ and which has been very important to philosophers over the years, that of "cause." How do we isolate this concept in order to subject it to rigorous examination? Somehow we are able to fasten on the general idea or concept of cause by being acquainted with a wide range of statements in which the word "cause" or some equivalent expression is used. We notice, for example, a similarity or common feature between a number of statements which all employ "cause-words," and then we abstract the feature which is shared by this range of statements. The common feature we are able to isolate or abstract is called a concept. What we have isolated, however, is neither some non-material entity or thing nor a single word or expression in any particular language such as English. The concept of cause is the feature which statements employing "cause-words" or

26

their equivalents in any language have in common. "Concepts are not things, as words are, but rather the functionings of words, as keeping wicket is the functioning of the wicket-keeper."[15]

But there are so many concepts; which ones are of special concern to the philosopher? For the most part, the conceptual cartographer elucidates and maps the relationships between those concepts which all of us employ in our thought and speech. He centers his attention on concepts which are found in "ordinary" language as opposed to those which are parts of esoteric, technical, or specialists' vocabularies. Concepts used in "ordinary" language are, so to speak, in the public domain; they are not the property of any specialist, and consequently they should be distinguished from concepts like "positron," "intermezzo," and "electolyte." Just a few of the concepts which are used by all of us and which the philosopher regards as crucial for his discipline are "know," "perceive," "cause," "free," "choice," "feeling," "motive," "good," "right," "real," "person," and "meaning."

It should be kept in mind that the philosopher as cartographer is not claiming that only *he* knows how to use these and other concepts properly. On the contrary, people ordinarily know when and when not to use the concepts at their disposal. But knowing *how* to use them and stating the relationships and crossbearings between these concepts are not the same thing. It is here that the analogy between the work of the philosopher and that of an actual cartographer comes into the picture. A person may know his way around a particular area of the countryside but nevertheless be hard-pressed to make a map of that area or give directions. Furthermore, once a map has been constructed for a given area of land, there is no guarantee that no revisions or reconstructions will ever be called for. Actual geography is not static, and neither is conceptual geography, because features of our language undergo changes of various sorts. Again, the

---

[15] Gilbert Ryle, *Dilemmas* (London: Cambridge University Press, 1954), p. 32.

procedure of an actual cartographer must not be arbitrary; he may not draw boundaries where he pleases. In the same way, the philosopher as cartographer cannot draw distinctions among our concepts if such distinctions are not actually present in our language. Admittedly, the mapmaker does not literally and in detail describe a certain area; he rather gives a synoptic view of the salient features of the area under consideration. But this feature of the cartographer's task does not give him license to draw his map any way it suits him (unless, of course, he does not intend to share his work with others).

Having discussed the nature of concepts and particularly those which are of special concern to the philosopher, we may now more profitably examine the methods of conceptual cartography. Gilbert Ryle, one of the leading exponents of this approach to philosophy (and also one of the most important figures in contemporary philosophical circles) has described what is involved in "logical geography." He says,

> To determine the logical geography of concepts is to reveal the logic of the propositions in which they are wielded, that is to say, to show with what other propositions they are consistent and inconsistent, what propositions follow from them and from what propositions they follow. The logical type or category to which a concept belongs is the set of ways in which it is logically legitimate to operate with it.[16]

What Ryle and other conceptual cartographers want us to see is that understanding a language involves a knowledge of the implicit, unwritten rules which govern the uses of expressions in everyday language.

> To know what an expression means involves knowing what can (logically) be said with it and what cannot (logically) be said with it. It involves knowing a set of bans, fiats and obligations, or, in a word, it is to know the rules of the employment of that expression.[17]

---

[16] Gilbert Ryle, *Concept of Mind* (New York: Barnes and Noble, Inc., 1949), p. 8. See also Ryle's important article entitled "Ordinary Language," *Philosophical Review*, LXII (1953). Reprinted in V. C. Chapell, ed., *Ordinary Language* (Englewood Cliffs, N.J.: Prentice-Hall, Inc., 1965), pp. 24-40.

When a person uses a certain expression, that person implicitly commits himself to saying and doing certain other things, and his use of that expression prohibits him from speaking and acting in other ways. When, for example, a person says, "I know such and such," he is logically committed by the meaning of the phrase "I know" to say (or be prepared to say) more. He should be prepared to say, among other things, *how* he came to know and be ready to defend his claim with reasons. To use the expression is to put your reputation on the line; we should be able to bank on such a statement just as though it were a promise. But saying "I know such and such" prohibits your saying certain other things because of the implicit rules regulating uses of the expression "I know." You would demonstrate ignorance of the meaning of the expression, "I know such and such" if you went on to say, "But what I know is not true," or "I have serious doubts about what I know."

It is important to note here that to determine the logical geography of a given concept, one must pay close attention to the way that concept is used in propositions; one must observe how the concept normally behaves, so to speak, when it is employed in ordinary, non-technical contexts.

What are the criteria for correct conceptual cartography? What is to keep a philosopher from mapping our concepts in an arbitrary way? In the first place, the mapping of a particular concept should not generate irresolvable philosophical perplexities. If we end up with a conceptual map which lands us in absurdities and contraditions or which, if accepted, would make it impossible to account for the ways we do in fact think and act, then we can be assured that we have made some crucial mistakes somewhere. Some philosophers, for example, have maintained

---

[17] Gilbert Ryle, "The Theory of Meaning," in *British Philosophy in the Mid-Century*, C. A. Mace, ed. (London: George Allen and Unwin, Ltd., 1957), pp. 239-64. Reprinted in C. A. Caton, ed., *Philosophy and Ordinary Language* (Urbana, Ill.: University of Illinois Press, 1963), pp. 128-53). (Also in anthology TBO; see preface for key to symbols of anthologies referred to throughout the book.)

that knowing is a certain kind of act, that the concept of knowledge belongs under the category of action. But look what happens if we so regard the concept of knowledge — various kinds of perplexities and absurdities result from this bit of conceptual cartography. If knowing something is an act, then we must be performing thousands of acts simultaneously, since at a given moment we know a host of facts and have a great many skills which involve "knowing how" to do certain things. Furthermore, actions are usually classifiable in terms of how successful they are; some of our actions succeed in carrying out what we intend, and others fail. But what sense does it make to ask if a person's *knowing* something was successful or not? This question *should* make sense if we are to classify knowing as a certain kind of acting. Yet another absurdity results from regarding knowledge as an act. Ordinarily, if we say that a person *did* something, we would think that there was a reason behind the act or that the agent did the act with some intention in mind. We would hesitate to call some bodily movement an action unless this factor were present to some degree. Yet what would be the reason or motive behind knowing that $8 \times 7 = 56$, for example? Surely many of the things we know are useful and it makes sense to ask a person why he is *seeking* knowledge in a certain field, but once that person *has* acquired an item of knowledge, it seems absurd to ask him what his motive or intention is for knowing what he does. Since all of these difficulties are traceable to placing the concept of knowledge in a wider logical area called "action," we had better take another look and map out both of these concepts and their relationships to each other in a more acceptable way.

There is another criterion for correct conceptual cartography. The philosopher should not construct his conceptual map in such a way that it clashes significantly with the way words are used in everyday contexts. He should seek to discover the distinctions embedded in "ordinary" or non-technical language and reflect these distinctions in his conceptual map rather than ignore and distort them. If there are distinctions found in the everyday language, we should adopt the working principle that they are there for a purpose and that they have stood the test of time, serving well our varied needs. Philosophers have a tendency to be intolerant of ordinary language and seem to think that it is both easy and desirable to improve upon it. However, J. L. Austin, another well-known conceptual cartographer, warns,

> Tampering with words in what we take to be one little corner of the field is always *liable* to have unforeseen repercussions in the adjoining territory. . . . There is certainly no reason why, in general, things should be left *exactly* as we find them; we may wish to tidy the situation up a bit, revise the map here and there, draw the boundaries and distinctions rather differently. [italics mine][18]

It might be added, however, that there ought to be good reasons in every case for drawing boundaries and distinctions in ways which are different from those found in the normal, ordinary uses of language. Such departures and liberties with words which already have assigned jobs to do should be taken only after intensive investigation of these tasks has been completed (and remembered by the philosopher as he devises his theories). Furthermore, the first criterion for correct conceptual cartography should be kept in mind—a proposed philosophical revision on a given term or centering down upon a single use of that term as its sole meaning must not generate perplexities and absurdities which would not otherwise have existed.

Philosophy Should Challenge the Individual to Make Decisions Concerning What He Is and What He Shall Do Even Though There Are No Rational Grounds for Those Decisions.

A relatively new conception of philosophy which goes by the name of existentialism has come into its own particularly

---

[18] J. L. Austin, *Sense and Sensibilia* (New York: Oxford University Press, 1964), p. 63.

since World War II.[19] Like the two conceptions of philosophy just discussed, it is a special kind of revolt against traditional ways of doing philosophy. The existentialists are generally agreed that the whole drift of Western philosophy from the Greeks onward has been radically mistaken. The traditional approach overemphasizes the rational or intellectual side of man to such an extent that philosophers have been virtually preoccupied with questions like, "What is knowledge?", "What can we know?", "What is the relationship between the mind and the body?" and so on. Philosophy tended to lose sight of the individual existing human being by trying either to explain the nature of "ultimate reality" or to state the conditions under which man can acquire knowledge of the world and his moral obligations. The "decision-making" and "feeling" sides of man's existence were given only scant attention, and as a result non-existentialist philosophers were charged with turning out distorted accounts of man as he actually exists.[20]

The existentialist proposes that philosophy take into account the *whole* man and attempt to throw light on the question, "What does it mean to be an existing human being in view of the unique status of man when he is compared with the rest of,

---

[19] Some of the major existentialists are Soren Kierkegaard and Friedrich Nietzsche in the nineteenth century and Jean-Paul Sartre, Gabriel Marcel, Martin Heidegger, and Karl Jaspers in the twentieth. There are several inexpensive paperbacks which contain selections from their works. Two of these are *Existentialism from Dostoevsky to Sartre*, Walter Kaufman, ed. (New York: Meridian Books, 1956), and *Essential Works of Existentialism*, H. J. Blackham, ed. (New York: Bantam Books, 1965). The brief account of existentialism which follows is intended merely to acquaint the reader with several tendencies in this philosophic approach.

[20] Because of the wide differences which exist among the existentialists, it is difficult to characterize their view of the purpose of philosophy. It might not be too far off, however, to call the existentialist a kind of *activist* and *moral prophet* who attempts to "shake people up" by calling for them to reexamine their status as human beings and accept the implications regarding certain features of human existence which a person might have overlooked.

nature?" What the existentialist finds so unique about human beings is that they are the only beings in whom "existence precedes essence." If we can make fairly clear what is meant by this existentialist slogan, a giant step toward understanding this philosophical approach will have been made.

Consider, if you will, any particular thing in the non-human realm, such as a desk. What a desk is (its various properties) is determined by something outside that object itself. When the desk was manufactured, its nature (or essence) was fixed once and for all. The possibilities of its being anything but a desk are virtually non-existent, though it might on occasion be used for purposes other than those for which it was designed. Its nature was, of course, determined by the individual or individuals who designed and assembled it. This fairly obvious fact about things like desks should come as no startling revelation. But the existentialist sees a radical difference between things like desks, on the one hand, and human beings on the other. The difference is not one of *degree* such that a human being could, in principle, be completely described by the various sciences when they are sufficiently refined to unravel the complicated structure of man. The difference between man and every other thing in nature is one of *kind*. Whereas the nature or essence (defining characteristics) of things like desks *precedes* their coming into existence, the nature or essence of human beings comes *after* they have begun to exist.

What a human being is and the kind of being he will be are not fixed for him prior to his inglorious entrance into the world. He first of all begins to exist, and then *he* determines as time goes by what he is or shall be. Human beings have no defining characteristics by means of which they can be described in the way that the properties of a desk can be enumerated. The properties which make an object a desk and only a desk are given to it, and consequently its nature is settled or fixed. With human beings, however, the case is radically different, claims the existentialist. No adequate description of any given individual is possible simply because the possibilities of radical change in what that person makes of himself are so immense. Man is something like a qualityless, indeterminate, self-moving "fluid" which can assume any state or shape it desires so long as what it desires is physically and logically possible.

Once this general way of viewing human existence is adopted, certain other existentialist doctrines seem to follow. To the question as to how a person becomes something with definite qualities, the existentialist responds that the individual himself must *decide* what he shall be. That is, he determines that he will be the kind of person who does such and such and regards such and such as worthwhile. Nothing governs or determines one's decisions as to what he will regard as worthwhile to have or strive for in his life: they are absolutely free choices. And because they are the individual's own choices, he must accept full responsibility for what he is and does. He cannot blame his heredity or the society of which he is a member for what he is, because they do not determine his nature the way a desk designer determines what properties his product will have.

It seems obvious that many people do not look at their existence along these lines. Many people do not see themselves as the shapers of their destinies and natures, but rather passively take on those qualities which they think others will approve. So few people really regard themselves as isolated individuals wholly responsibile for the type of persons they are. The usual tendency for most people is to seek some kind of refuge from responsibility by losing themselves in the anonymity of the crowd or by becoming absorbed in the details of day-to-day living. The existentialists acknowledge that most people do not particularly like the emotional by-products of living each moment as though it were their last, of realizing full well that a person's own decisions make him what he is, and that those decisions are wholly without any justifiable grounds. It would help us immensely if we *could* prove that a given style of life or a significant personal decision was based on good reasons. But the existentialist would like us to see that none of our decisions concerning what we should value in life and accomplish in our deeds can be justified by appealing to any standard outside our own desires. We are left utterly alone to decide what we shall be and do, and more importantly, after we decide we must face the consequences of our choices knowing full well that we could just as well have chosen something other than what we did. The necessary by-products of honestly facing these truths about the human condition are "dread" and "anguish," as the existentialists put it.

The existentialists place before individuals the two options of "authentic" and "inauthentic" existence. One may choose to be "authentic" by sincerely acknowledging (1) that he creates his own values by decisions which have absolutely no grounding, and (2) that he must bear the brunt of the consequences for what he decides. Furthermore, the "authentic" person does not seek illusory places of refuge from the project of creating himself. He does not seek assurance or assistance from any quarter (such as God or Reason or Science) when he chooses what sort of being he is and shall be.

The "inauthentic" person is the one who, as Kierkegaard put it, lives "thoughtlessly" or "distractedly." He exists through the support of all sorts of delusions. He does not take seriously his unique status as a creator of his own nature. He allows himself to become a "mass man," without individuality or independence of thought and decision. The "inauthentic" person is a great rationalizer, because he tries to justify in one way or another what he is and does. He runs away from the responsibility of making his own nature and may try to convince himself that he is made in the "image of God"; or he may claim that he is "doing the will of God" when he requires some foundation for his behavior. He may resort to any distraction in order to squelch the anguish and dread which would certainly come to him if he honestly faced up to the fact that he must choose, without any assurance whatsoever that his choice is the correct one.

35

The "inauthentic" person is most anxious to escape from the thought of and the fact that his own death is certain and possibly just around the corner. Death, because it is the end of all possibilities for the individual and the ultimate sealer of one's past decisions and actions, is the most dreadful of all experiences to man. But the certainty and possible imminence of death can be the most helpful aid to an authentic existence, because it calls the individual to reexamine the meaning of his existence and the challenges him to genuine creativity and independence in the brief moment allotted him.

CONCLUDING INTRODUCTORY REMARKS

It is not easy to make an intelligent choice from among differing ways of doing something until the various methods have been observed in operation and one has tried them for himself. The same could be said when it comes to determining how one should proceed in the activity of philosophy. A major purpose of this book is to show how various philosophical methods have been applied to a number of key problems by those considered to be experts in the ways they handle their respective philosophical tools. At the same time, you are encouraged to take each of the conceptions of philosophy just discussed and go as far as you can with each of them. Try each of them on for size and see which one fits philosophically. That is, try to determine which method leads to increased clarification of philosophical perplexity and which approach makes the greatest contributions to the solution of significant philosophical problems. Remember that no philosopher is bound to adopt just one way of doing his job and that you need not confine yourself to one *modus operandi* either. The important thing is that a beginning be made in your exploration of the problems — and hopefully the pleasures — of philosophy.

SUGGESTIONS FOR FURTHER STUDY

Anthologies

BKW, Chaps. 1 and 9; MGAS, Chap. 1; SA, Part 1; ST, pp. 1-23; TBO, Chaps. 8 and 10; TH, Chap. 1, 6, 7, 16, 17, 18, 28.

Others

Ayer, A. J., ed., *The Revolution in Philosophy*. London: Macmillan and Company, 1956.

Kaufmann, Walter, ed., *Existentialism from Dostoevsky to Sartre*. New York: Meridian Books, 1956.

Malcolm, Norman, "Wittgenstein's *Philosophical Investigations*," *Philosophical Review*, LXIII (1954), pp. 530-59. Reprinted in V. C. Chappell, ed., *The Philosophy of Mind*. Englewood Cliffs, N.J.: Prentice-Hall, Inc., 1962.

O'Connor, D. J., ed., *A Critical History of Western Philosophy*. New York: Free Press, 1964. See especially A. M. Quinton's "Contemporary British Philosophy" and Alasdair MacIntyre's "Existentialism."

Russell, Bertrand, *The Problems of Philosophy*. New York: Oxford University Press, 1959.

Ryle, Gilbert, "Ordinary Language," *Philosophical Review*, Vol. LXII (1953). Reprinted in V. C. Chappell, ed., *Ordinary Language*. Englewood Cliffs, N.J.: Prentice-Hall, Inc., 1964, pp. 24-40.

Warnock, G. J., *English Philosophy Since 1900*. London: Oxford University Press, 1958.

THE PROBLEM
OF GOD

II

Does a Perfect Personal Being Exist?

There was a time in the history of Western thought when philosophy and religion walked hand in hand through life sharing one another's problems, forming a united front on a number of important issues. However, through the years they have slowly drifted apart, and the marriage has broken up. It has become apparent that the enterprises of religion and philosophy are quite distinct both in their aims and methods of operation. Beliefs in the area of religion are ordinarily supported by appeals to an ultimate authority which is taken to have divine origin. A person who believes, for example, that Jesus was "God in the flesh" would cite either what the individual accepts as divinely inspired writings or the pronouncements of divinely commissioned persons as authority for his belief.

The philosopher, on the other hand, tends to regard with suspicion *any* appeal based solely upon authoritative writings or persons to back up beliefs. He advocates instead that we use our natural powers of observation and reason both to search for truth and to evaluate the credentials of "authorities" to whom some people appeal for support.

The aims as well as the methods of religion and philosophy differ. The major goal of religious activity seems to be to assist people in attaining what is thought to be a correct relationship with a divine being or beings. There are differences, of course, concerning the correct path to pursue in realizing this goal, and this fact accounts in large part for the variety of religious beliefs and practices in the world. Religion, in other words, seems to place great emphasis upon urging the individual to commit himself wholeheartedly to a being (or beings) regarded as worthy of worship and obedience.

Although it is extremely difficult to state *the* aim of philosophy, it at least seems clear that it is primarily an *intellectual* enterprise; its goal is either clarification of some aspect of human experience or the discovery of truths which are not within the bounds of scientific inquiry. Only in an incidental way does the philosopher appeal to people's *wills*, exhorting them to devote themselves completely to some being, divine or otherwise.

The religious man may choose to retreat to the high ground of faith whenever his beliefs are challenged, and such an approach is very frequently employed. But it is hard to believe that a reflective, intellectually honest religious person could forever ignore the question, "*Why* believe in the existence of a perfect personal being?" Regardless of what a person's commitments on this issue happen to be, this problem rarely fails to stimulate and challenge one's critical and analytic capacities.

THE CONCEPT OF GOD

Before we can hope to tackle any problem, we must be sure that we have a clear idea of what the question is all about.

To ask, "Does God exist?" without first clarifying the concept of God presupposed in the question is merely to invite confusion. We simply must get straight on the meaning of the term "God" before we can even begin to determine whether some particular being called "God" exists or not.

Philosophers who have concerned themselves with proving or disproving God's existence are in surprising agreement as to the kind of being about whose reality they are debating. By the term "God" these philosophers (and I suspect most people who have been trained in a Catholic, Protestant or Jewish tradition) seem to mean something close to the following: God is a unique being who is similar to human beings in certain respects but unlike them in others. This being is *like* humans in that he has knowledge, is capable of causing changes in things, and regards certain acts as morally right or morally wrong.

The important respects in which this being is supposed to *differ* from humans are these: his knowledge is not derived piecemeal nor with varying degrees of success; rather he knows *everything* all at once (or "intuitively" as some people would put it) without ever making mistakes. Furthermore, his ability to effect changes in things is not limited by fatigue, weak muscles or the necessity of being in one place at a time. He has no such limitations because he is not composed of anything material; he does not occupy a certain specifiable space at a specific time. Lastly, his moral judgments do not have any personal bias or error in them since he *knows* perfectly what is right, and always *does* what is right because nothing can hinder the execution of his decisions.

It seems that the theist,[1] in order to make his concept of God meaningful, has merged two basic concepts, that of "perfection" and that of "person." God is like a person with all the human limitations left out. To the theist, the most significant

---

[1] That is, a person who believes that there is a personal being who is distinct from everything which is physical or has limitations.

limitation of man is his having a body, so God must be thought of as *not* having a body. Another important defect in human beings is their proneness to make mistakes in reasoning, observation and judgment. Consequently, if God is to be regarded as the perfect personal being, he could not be the kind of being who makes mistakes of any sort.

It is admitted that this definition of the term "God" will not satisfy everyone (or anyone, perhaps) *completely*. Some will complain that it includes too much and others that it includes too little: In spite of inevitable defects in such a definition, there does seem to be enough agreement by those who have advocated and by those who have attacked theistic arguments to allow meaningful discussion to proceed.

Difficulties with the Traditional Theistic Concept of God

It should be remembered that at this stage we have not concluded that a perfect personal being exists or does not exist. We are simply trying to get clear concerning what is being asked in the question, "Does God exist?" Unless we can comprehend the concept of God, no amount of argument concerning the existence or non-existence of such a being will have much point. There are some important difficulties which need attention before we can proceed.

(1) In giving content to his concept of God, why does the theist select certain qualities of human personality when there are many other kinds of things with which we are acquainted?

(2) Why does the theist select just a few qualities of human beings to help compose his concept of God? Man does not simply know certain things, create various objects and make judgments about what is morally right and wrong; he can also be angry, afraid, hopeful, despairing, disappointed, anxious and much more. On what grounds does the theist refuse to attribute these capacities to God?

42

(3) In what sense can God be said to "know"? What does the phrase "perfect knowledge" mean? How can we understand what a claim to factual knowledge would be that could not be mistaken? The traditional theist maintains that God has complete knowledge of everything that happens, and that he did not come to know or find out because he always knew all that was to transpire. In addition, God cannot forget anything nor does he use what he knows to increase his store of knowledge. There is nothing about the past, present or the future which he has not always known.

In spite of all the qualifications he places upon his original claim concerning God's knowing what takes place, the theist insists that we can, nevertheless, meaningfully assert that God knows things. He admits that God's knowledge of facts about the world is quite different from *our* knowledge of those same facts. But to the theist this does not seem to pose an insurmountable obstacle to making his concept of God understandable. Unfortunately, however, it is not enough for someone to tell us that God knows what takes place in the world but that such knowledge on God's part is not like our knowledge of factual matters. We are entitled to ask why the theist says God *knows* such things at all when he obviously seems to be using the word "knows" in an extraordinary and novel way.

Isn't there a striking similarity between the approach of the theist and that of A in the following conversation?

A: I bought a skluff yesterday.

B: What's a skluff?

A: A skluff is like a football.

B: Oh, you mean it is inflatable like a football?

A: No.

B: Then you mean it is *shaped* like a football?

A: No.

B: You must mean it is used in a game where the players throw and kick it to one another?

A: No.

B: Then why do you say a skluff is like a football?

A, in this imaginary conversation, has so qualified the phrase "like a football" that bewildered *B* cannot understand why it was said in the first place that a skluff was like a football. A could rightly be charged with a violation of the standard or stock use of the expression "like a football." The theist could be accused of doing roughly the same thing in his talk about God when he says, "God knows such and such, but his knowing does not involve coming to know nor can he fail to know everything that is the case."

When we mortals use the word "knows" in a statement like "Jim knows what happened yesterday," surely an important part of what we mean to assert is that questions about *how* and *when* Jim came to know, whether or not he is likely to forget what he knows, and what he can be expected to do with his knowledge make perfectly good sense. They make good sense because these considerations are part of what is meant when a claim is made concerning someone's knowing some specific factual matter.

The theist who talks about God's knowledge in the terms we have laid out may be charged with violating the informal rules governing the use of the word "knows," rules which a person learns as he acquires familiarity with his language. He seems to be trying to give the word "knows" a use or meaning in a context which changes the usual meaning of the word into something unrecognizable and bewildering. It might be suggested, therefore, that if the theist wants to claim that the perfect personal being knows what takes place in the world, then the theist must adjust his concept of God in such a way that it makes sense to say of him that he acquired knowledge at a certain time, that could forget some of what he came to know, and that he uses his knowledge to predict the future and increase his store of knowledge.

The traditional theist, of course, is horrified at such a suggestion. How could God be a most superior being and have all the limitations which this view ascribes to him? Is it not a contradiction to say that you have a concept of a perfect personal being and then proceed to elucidate your concept by pointing out how such a being would have to be limited?

Perhaps this suggested way out of the woods will be less alarming to the traditional theist if he keeps two things in mind. First, if a person claims to have a concept of a being who is supremely perfect or without limitations, he certainly cannot mean that he has a concept of a being so great that it is *beyond* thought. But does not the theist come dangerously close to saying this when he ascribes knowledge to God but means by this something quite different from our normal attribution of knowledge to human beings? Why should the theist call a being the perfect personal being simply because the latter is supposed to be capable of "knowing" things in such a unique and extraordinary way that we are unable to understand what is being asserted about him?

There is a second consideration that might make the traditional theist more amenable to a concept of God which is more understandable in terms of our ordinary uses of words. Many traditional theists already admit certain limitations in the perfect personal being. They maintain, for example, that God cannot make a round square, and that to say that God *could* do this violates the logic of the terms "round" and "square." But must it not also be admitted that to say God knows but neither comes to know nor increases his knowledge, etc., violates the logic of the word "knows" just as surely as the expression "a round square" abuses the meanings of those two words? The limitations which we suggest the theist might consider ascribing to the perfect personal being (if such a being exists) turn out to be of the same variety as those already ascribed to him by traditional theists, viz., the "limitation" of logical consistency.

If it were maintained that God *could* make a square circle or did know events in our world as the traditional theist supposes he knows them, then the theist by this act pushes his concept of the most superior being beyond the reach of understanding. And on what grounds could he then claim to have a *concept* of a most superior being?

(4) Another difficulty emerges when we are told that God is "morally good" or, more correctly, "morally perfect." What is meant by saying that someone is a moral person if at the same time it is maintained that that person *could not* possibly do anything ethically wrong? We would be inclined to say that if a person has a built-in safeguard so that he *could* never do anything wrong, his actions and character should not be described in moral categories at all. The adjectives "good," "bad," "moral," and "immoral" simply do not make sense if applied to such a being. If a person had been drugged in such a way that all his actions were the direct result of his treatment, we would most likely say that such a person's actions should not be judged in moral categories at all. It seems fairly clear, then, that it must be at least *possible* for someone to engage in unethical behavior if we are to call that person moral or immoral.

The difficulties just discussed should not be regarded as necessarily insuperable. Although various problems with the concept of God as it has come to be accepted in traditional theistic circles have been pointed out, the purpose has not been to advocate its abandonment altogether. Perhaps reexamination of its meaningfulness is called for along with some attempt to clear up difficulties like the ones mentioned above. It seems obvious that no amount of argument for the *existence* of God will make up for lack of adequate clarity in the *concept* of God itself. This, however, is not to demand exhaustive comprehension of the nature of God (if there is such a being). It is simply to acknowledge that when we speak about a being we take to be a person, we must utilize the language we have, the one with which we operate in everyday life. *Understanding* words and expressions is knowing how to operate with them or knowing how to use them. When words are taken from circumstances and contexts where their use is understood and are assigned tasks that clash with their familiar roles, as seems to occur in religious discourse, we should be aware of this move and prepare ourselves for the problems this procedure creates. Remember: one does not necessarily understand a certain group of words simply because he *thinks* he does or feels confident that he does.

STATEMENTS ABOUT GOD

Even if it should be granted that the theist can make his traditional concept of God intelligible, he is still not ready to begin the defense of his belief in the existence of God. When the theist incorporates his concept of God into statements like "God created the world" or "God loves man," we may rightly inquire into the meaning of such utterances. That is, we may raise the question, what sort of statements are these? Are they factual in nature like the assertion "Jones made a new bookcase for his study" or "Smith loves his children very much"? The theist's assertions have an apparent similarity to the statements about Jones and Smith, but is the likeness anything more than apparent? Surely when it comes to giving evidence for his statements, the theist cannot use the same kind of approach as we would employ to back up assertions like the ones about Jones and Smith. If someone required us to verify our statement about Jones's new bookcase, we would reply that we observed him sawing the lumber, pounding the nails, and applying the finish to his creation. And if we were asked how we know that Smith loves his children so much, we would point out how he treats them, what he says about them, and how he reacts to their happiness and unhappiness. But if the theist claims to be making factual statements about God and his relation to human beings, what sort of evidence could be produced to verify what he says? We wouldn't expect the theist to say that he *saw* God making the

47

world, nor can he check God's reaction to the fortune and mis-
fortune of his "children" because on the theist's own definition,
God and his actions are not observable.

Considerations such as these have led some philosophers
to argue that theological utterances are not factually meaningful,
that no statement about God can be regarded as an assertion
about what is actually the case. If these philosophers are right,
if theological utterances are not statements about any factual
state of affairs, then what sort of statements are they? Should
they be considered statements or assertions at all if they really
say nothing that can be verified in the usual sense of that term?
And if theological utterances are not *factually* significant, what
meaning do they have, if any? We must now state some arguments which purport to answer these questions concerning the
status and role of such utterances. The issue is utterly crucial
because to ask whether the statement "a perfect personal being
exists" is true or false without first determining whether this
utterance itself is meaningful is to put the philosophical cart
before the horse. For if we find that a particular statement does
not make sense, then the question of its truth or falsehood cannot
even arise. Any arguments for the truth of the proposition ("a
perfect person being exists") in order to be meaningful must
first establish the meaningfulness of the statement to be proved.

"Theological Statements Are Meaningless Because They Are Not Verifiable."

One view of the nature of religious statements, held by
A. J. Ayer,[2] an influential British philosopher, is that they are
devoid of literal meaning because they are incapable of being
verified. His position relies heavily on what has come to be
known as the "verifiability criterion of meaning" which states

---

[2] A. J. Ayer, *Language, Truth & Logic*, 2nd. ed. (New York:
Dover Publications, Inc., and London: Victor Gollancz, Ltd.), pp.
114-20. Reprinted in *The Existence of God*, John Hick, ed. (New York:
Crowell-Collier & Macmillan, Inc., 1964), pp. 217-24.

that an assertion is literally meaningful if and only if some possible sense experience could be specified which would count for or against the truth of the statement in question. It should be noted, however, that a statement need not have been *verified* already in order for it to be meaningful. All that is required by the verifiability criterion of meaning is that the assertion be *capable* of verification — if not now, then at some future date when technical advances may provide the means of verification. For example, the utterance "There are living forms on the planet Jupiter" is meaningful even though it has not yet been determined whether or not this is true. One can specify how such a claim *could* be verified through sense experience, and therefore it is a genuine, meaningful assertion.

When we say that a particular statement is true, we could mean that it is true in one of two senses. It may be true in the same way as the following statements are: "All squares have four sides," and "Either Hugo is in Hot Springs or he is not." We can determine that these statements are true simply by analyzing the meanings of the terms composing them. If we know what the word "square" means, we know the statement "All squares have four sides" is true. There is no need to begin counting the sides of every square we encounter to tell whether that statement is true or not. The statement concerning the whereabouts of Hugo is likewise true even though it does not tell us much. It doesn't say where Hugo is — it only says that he is at a particular location or he is not. We know statements taking this form to be true because of a rule of logic called the law of "non-contradiction," which may be stated as follows: It cannot be that statement S is true and statement S is false at the same time. Consequently, it cannot be that Hugo is in Hot Springs and that he is also not in Hot Springs. One or the other is true but not both of these assertions, and hence we know that Hugo either is in Hot Springs or is not.

We may call statements which have the same form as the ones we have just discussed "analytic" because their truth or falsity can be determined merely by analyzing the meanings of

49

the terms composing them. Could theological utterances like "God loves man" and "God created the world" belong to the analytic camp? It is difficult to see how they could. There is the initial difficulty of specifying what the terms in these utterances mean, especially the term "God," and then there are more problems in determining what it means for God to "love man" and "create" the world. There does not appear to be any general agreement as to what these words mean, so it is hard to justify the claim that utterances like these are analytic. Furthermore, it would always make sense to deny that "God created the world" even if and provided that one understood the terms in this utterance. If this were an analytically true statement, one would be uttering a logical contradiction if he said "God did not create the world." Yet it does not appear contradictory to say the latter whereas it does appear contradictory to say that "All squares have five sides" or "Hugo is in Hot Springs and Houston." Since it is not contradictory to say "God did not create the world," it cannot be that the utterance "God created the world" is analytic. If it is true, it must be true in some other sense than analytic.

However, there is another group of statements which we could call "synthetic" or "empirical." This sort of statement does claim that something is actually a matter of fact; it asserts that some particular thing or group of things did exist, is existing or will exist and had, has or will have certain properties. They also are used to make claims concerning the occurrence of events in the world. Examples are so numerous and come so readily to mind that it would be superfluous to list any. The important features of synthetic statements are, first, that their truth or falsity cannot be determined merely by analyzing the meaning of the terms composing them but that some possible reference to sensory or perceptual evidence is required to confirm or refute them.[3] The second mark of synthetic statements is that one may

---

[3] This is controversial; some philosophers maintain that there are some true synthetic statements whose truth is arrived at independently of any data derived through the senses. See page 210 in Chapter Six for further treatment.

deny or negate them without thereby landing oneself in a logical contradiction. For example, the rain may be literally pouring down and you may still say, "It is not raining"; you would, from a factual or empirical standpoint, be wrong, but you would not be contradicting yourself as you would be if you said, "It is raining and it is not raining." The statement "It is not raining," therefore, belongs to the synthetic or empirical camp.[4]

Now, the theist's statement, "God created the world," seems on the surface at least to be an assertion which belongs to the empirical variety. But it only looks that way. We can expose the statement's non-empirical status when we ask, "What possible sensory experience could we have in order to determine whether or not this statement is true?" The answer must be that no possible sense perceptions could even begin to help us decide whether it is true or not. The problem is not that no one was present at the construction site of the universe. The point is that even if someone *had* been present, the "event" of God's creating the world would not have been perceivable. At no point could a would-be observer have said, "Look: there is God creating the world." By the theist's own admission God is not perceivable, so no one *could* watch Him doing anything.

Since statements about God cannot be true in either the analytic or the synthetic (i.e., empirical) sense, they must be considered to be factually or literally meaningless. A statement can be literally or factually meaningful only if some possible sense experience could serve as decisive evidence for its truth or falsity. Theological statements are by their very content incapable of verification through perceptual means even in those cases where something is asserted about God which is purported to be taking place in the present, i.e., God's ever present action guiding and controlling the course of nature. Here again, it would be absurd to claim that one actually is *observing* the actions of God. What is observable is only the behavior of natural

---

[4] A more complete explanation of the distinction between the two groups of statements discussed above may be found in the first section of Chapter Six. It could be read with profit at this point.

things, and the theist's contention that he "sees" God in nature is a purely figurative use of the word "sees." He makes no *factual* assertions in his statements about God, and consequently they are literally meaningless. His statements are *neither* true nor false and the same must be said of the atheist's statement "God does not exist." It too is unverifiable and hence, meaningless.

Theological statements may perhaps serve some purpose for the theist, nevertheless. They may be used to express certain feelings of awe and wonder at the universe and man's place in it. They may on occasion be used to comfort and reassure the bereaved and anxious as well as to regulate people's conduct by reminding them of the divine punishments and rewards they may expect for their actions. But since expressions of feeling of any sort cannot be true or false because they really don't assert or claim anything, theological statements, since they are expressions of certain kinds of feeling, can be neither true nor false.

"Theological Utterances Are Without Meaning Because They Are Not Falsifiable."

A slightly different view from the one advocated by Ayer is the one which maintains that because there is no way to show that the statements "God exists" or "God loves man" are false, they are not really assertions at all. The argument proceeds like this:[5]

If we are in doubt as to what a person means by a particular sentence, "one way of trying to understand (or perhaps it will be to expose) his utterance is to attempt to find out what he would regard as counting against, or as being incompatible with,

---

[5] Antony Flew and Alasdair MacIntyre, eds. *New Essays in Philosophical Theology* (London: The Student Christian Movement Press; New York: Crowell-Collier & Macmillan, Inc., 1955). The argument which follows, presented by Flew, is reprinted in *The Existence of God*, Hick, ed., pp. 224-28. Also anthologies AB, F, ST, TBO. See preface for key to symbols.

its truth."[6] Suppose the statement we would like to understand is, "God loves man." If we ask the person who says this (presumably a believer in God) what would make him say, "God does *not* love man," he would most likely reply, "Nothing." No matter what facts you were to point out to the devoted theist, he would persist in his belief that God loves man. You might mention the great natural calamities which have befallen mankind, the ravages of disease or the brutality of man against man and think that these familiar facts would surely count against the belief in a perfect personal being. But for every fact, no matter how harsh and seemingly damaging to the theist's position, he will simply say, "God would not let these things happen if he didn't have some greater good in view; he must have good reason for permitting the suffering that takes place in the world." What the theist does by such a maneuver is to retreat to an invulnerable position where nothing can count against his belief. Admittedly, it is a seemingly secure perch for the theist.

There is just one drawback. If one says something which is compatible with *any* possible fact or facts you care to mention, then that person is not really making a synthetic or empirical assertion at all. For an assertion to be of this type there must be something which could possibly count *against* your claim, even if there actually is no such counter-evidence. To be a genuinely empirical assertion, in other words, a statement must be *falsifiable*. If I assert that there is a new automobile in my garage, there are a number of things which could count as evidence against my statement. If a person with normal vision were to look in the garage and see only a beat-up rattle-trap standing there, my statement would be falsified. And even if no one were actually to check the car in my garage, we all know what sorts of facts *could* falsify my original claim.

The theist's utterances, on the other hand, are incapable of being falsified since no conceivable fact *could* count against

---

[6] *The Existence of God*, Hick, ed., p. 226.

them. His utterances, therefore, do not really *say* anything at all, and because of this cannot fulfill the role for which they were designed by the theist. They cannot, for example, serve as statements of explanation for the existence and structure of the universe, nor can they draw our attention to certain "facts" concerning the "unseen world" beyond the reach of scientific discovery.

"Theological Statements Are Meaningful Because They Have a Use."

The last viewpoint on the question concerning the meaningfulness of theological statements rejects the two preceding positions on the ground that a statement is meaningful if it can be shown to have a use.[7] Religious statements are used by people to accomplish a certain task, and consequently it would be philosophically narrow to reject them out of hand as meaningless. The argument proceeds: When we study the actual job done by religious assertions, we see that they are used in much the same way as moral assertions. If I say, "People ought to assist others who are in distress," what I am doing is announcing my intention to act in a certain way if I should find myself in a situation where someone needed my help. I am saying that I intend to help people who need assistance. It is much the same with religious statements. If someone says, "God loves man," it may not be apparent at first glance how this could be an announcement of an intention to conduct his life in a certain way. But ordinarily a person making such a statement would place himself within a religious tradition which incorporates stories or parables to teach its ideals of conduct. If the person is a Christian, for example, he would point out that God commands us to love our fellow men and that Jesus by his life and teaching is the

---

[7] R. B. Braithwaite, *An Empiricist's View of the Nature of Religious Belief* (Cambridge, England, and New York: Cambridge University Press, 1955). Braithwaite's argument is reprinted in Hick, ed., *The Existence of God*, pp. 228-52.

supreme example of selfless regard for others. So, after questioning a person using the statement "God loves man" or by observing his life, we may rightly conclude that this statement is really being used to announce the speaker's intention to follow a certain moral policy in his conduct. This use of the statement "God loves man" is its primary meaning, and consequently statements about God are not without meaning.

We must not draw the erroneous conclusion that every indicative sentence in our language is made with the intention of stating a fact. Rather, we must study the way people actually use various kinds of statements in order to arrive at their use or meaning. The religious person is not using his statements about God primarily to point out certain facts about anything. He thinks of life in a theological way because he believes that this standpoint serves as a basis for his commitment to a certain way of behaving in the moral sphere. His theological utterances reflect this close connection between religious belief and moral policy.

Difficulties with These Arguments

(1) With regard to the first argument, what should be said about the meaningfulness of the verifiability criterion of meaning ("A statement is literally meaningful if and only if some possible sense experience could help us to determine its truth or falsehood") itself? Are there any sensory experiences that could verify *this* statement? If not, does it rule itself meaningless just as it does theological statements?

Furthermore, it does seem that we can think of some possible situations which could tend to confirm the theistic hypothesis. It is not claimed that events of the sort we shall sketch shortly have taken or will take place, but only that it makes sense to say that they could occur and could rightly be taken by a reasonable man as evidence for the proposition that a perfect personal being exists. Suppose every person in the world at precisely the same moment hears in his own particular language a voice from the sky claiming that what he was hearing was from the perfect personal being. The message contains detailed predictions concerning the occurrence of a great number of unusual but harmless events around the world. One prediction is that whenever any person makes an effort to cause physical harm to another person, he will be prevented by a mysterious paralysis in his body which will last as long as he attempts to cause evil. Suppose all over the world every prediction comes true precisely as stated. Would not a reasonable man consider these combinations of events preceded by the universal experience of hearing the prophetic voice from the skies as having some evidential value for belief in the existence of a perfect personal being?

(2) The second argument states that nothing counts against theological statements because nothing could happen which would lead people who make them to disbelieve them. However, are there not people who have asserted at one time that a benevolent God exists but then, because of personally tragic experiences of one sort or another, later denied that such a being exists? Might not the existence of suffering in the world count as evidence against the statement, "God loves man" at least for *some* people?

Furthermore, couldn't we specify certain experiences in a *future* life which would tend to falsify at least some theological utterances? If, for example, we were to experience various sorts of discomfort in a future state, then we would have some evidence to count against the religious assertion, "In the next life, God will provide everyone with complete and eternal happiness." Whether or not there will be a personal survival of death is beside the point here. All we have tried to do is to point out what *could possibly count* as evidence against a religious utterance.

(3) Finally, regarding the third argument, we might ask how the following religious statements could be construed as announcements of an intention to behave in a certain specific

way: "God created the universe," "God is a non-material Being," "Help me, dear God!"

What if a person who would make these statements does not associate himself with any religious tradition, but classifies himself as a non-sectarian theist? Would he not be making theological statements even though they would not be made against a background of religious stories or parables? Is it correct to say that theological statements have any one primary use? If one is acquainted with the actual ways in which people use religious language, he might tend to think that the view expounded in the third argument is an over-simplification although, on the whole, probably on the right track.

GROUNDS FOR BELIEF
IN THE EXISTENCE OF GOD

The first argument for the existence of a perfect personal being, or at least for a being far surpassing the limitations of human personality, will now be considered. It differs from other theistic arguments because it proposes to prove with logical certainty that God exists. Its advocates claim to demonstrate its conclusion with the same logical certainty that characterizes proofs in geometry, for example. It claims that there can be no room for doubt about the existence of God if the argument is properly understood from the beginning to the end, from its premises to its conclusion.

The Ontological Argument: "The Non-Existence of God is Unthinkable."

The ontological argument, devised by St. Anselm (1033-1109),[8] goes like this: I have the idea of a being "than which

---

[8] Anselm, *Proslogion, 1-4* (various editions). Relevant sections reprinted in anthologies AB, BKW, EP, F, MGAS, SA, ST, TBO.

none greater can be thought." That is, I have the concept of a being who is perfect (without limitation) in every conceivable way. This being of whom I have formed an idea cannot be thought of as being surpassed by any other thing. If I begin by thinking of beings which are limited in various degrees, I can gradually arrive at the concept of a being who is least limited of all, i.e., without any limitations in his nature whatsoever.

But *in what respects* is this being of which I am thinking superior to all other beings? The being of which I am thinking (which as yet has not been proved to exist or even assumed to exist outside my mind) must have these qualities which we cannot think of as inferior in any way.

Now, if we think of two possible beings, one which exists *only as an idea* in someone's mind and another being who exists *independently* of someone's thinking it, we would conclude that the latter type of being is superior to the former kind of being. It is clear then that a most superior type of being must have the most superior kind of existence, namely existence as an actual being, and therefore must not be dependent upon someone else's thinking him. Therefore, it is impossible to think of a perfect being and at the same time *deny* that such a being exists independently of anyone's thoughts of him. One cannot think the idea of a perfect being without also thinking that such a being must enjoy the best kind of existence, that is, existence which does not depend upon anything else.

The argument in summary is this:

1. People conceive God to be a being "than which none greater can be thought" (i.e., a perfect being).
2. Therefore, God exists at least in people's minds.
3. A thing is more perfect if it exists in reality as well as in people's minds.
4. Since a perfect being would have all perfections, the perfect being must have the best kind of existence, namely existence which does not depend upon someone's thoughts.
5. Hence, God exists in reality.

Difficulties with This Argument

(1) Anselm seems to assume that the term "existence" stands for some special kind of property which things may have. Before we go any further, perhaps we should do a bit of "conceptual cartography" along the lines mentioned in Chapter One. Let us ask ourselves, what kind of term is "existence"? To what area of our conceptual "map" does it belong? Should we follow Anselm and continue to think that existence is a peculiar property or quality? It might seem plausible to regard the term "existence" as standing for a certain sort of property because we do on occasion say things like "Mr. Pickwick does not have existence but Sue Schlunk does." It certainly *looks* as though we are saying in this statement that Mr. Pickwick lacks something which Miss Schlunk has. Yet if we stop for a moment and think through what the statement is actually claiming, we can avoid being trapped into regarding existence as a property. What this misleading statement is really saying is that "Mr. Pickwick is a fictional character but Sue is not (she is a flesh-and-blood human being)." It is not necessary, you see, to talk about things having or *not* having existence.

But what's the harm done if we map out the term "existence" as Anselm did and regard it as standing for a special sort of property? Well, let's take this point of view for the sake of argument and treat existence as a property to see what happens. We immediately bump into some very perplexing puzzles. For example, we know how to detect properties like "red," "heavy," and "round," but how do we come across the property "existence"? Even if we could know how to go about looking for it, how would we recognize it if we found it? Furthermore, if we regard existence as a property, how are we to treat fictional characters and imaginary ideas? Do *they* "have" existence? Suppose you were asked to describe the character Mr. Pickwick. Wouldn't it seem odd if after the completion of your description you added, "Oh, I forgot one property of Mr. Pickwick. He had fictional existence"? Or suppose you were listing the properties of this book and after you had pointed out its color, weight and size, etc., you topped off your list with the property of existence? Wouldn't your addition at the end be superfluous if not meaningless?

(2) Besides regarding existence as a *property* Anselm seemed to regard it as a *perfection*. That is, he maintained that simply because a thing exists, it is good, and it is therefore better if something of which we can form an idea exists in actuality than if it does not exist in actuality. The crucial question, however, is this: How can it be determined outside any specific context and without reference to any properties which a thing might have whether or not that thing is "perfect"? If we were asked to consider two things, *A* and *B*, which were identical in every respect except that one existed in actuality and the other was a fictional thing, why should we conclude that one was more perfect than the other? I suspect that before we could make an intelligent judgment in the matter, we would want to know more about what *sort* of properties the real thing was supposed to have. The mere fact that one was fictional and the other actually existed would not help one bit in rating the two for superiority. Some things might be good because they exist (and have desirable qualities) and some things might be bad because they exist (and have undesirable qualities). By asserting merely "*X* (some particular thing) exists" you are neither ascribing a property to *X* nor are you saying something about the value or worth of *X*.

(3) Anselm's argument presupposes that there are two "levels" of existence, existence as an idea and existence in reality. From the statement "people have an idea of a perfect being," he concludes "God exists at least in the understanding." By means of this simple little move he thought that everyone would have to admit that a perfect being had *some* sort of existence. But if we allow this maneuver by Anselm to go unchallenged, we seem obliged to go all the way with him, for to say that a perfect being exists but he is confined to someone's mind is clearly contradictory. What a confining, dependent way

60

to exist—to be only an idea. However, when Anselm's statement "people have an idea of a perfect being" is taken in its ordinary sense as "people mean so-and-so when they use the term 'God'," it is easy to see that nothing follows from this concerning the existence of such a being. To say that you have an idea of God does not mean that God exists in your mind; it means merely that you interpret the word "God" in a certain way.

A Cosmological Argument: "God Is Necessary to Account for the Origin of Physical Things."

Several "cosmological" arguments were devised by St. Thomas Aquinas[9] (1224/5-1274), a leading figure in the history of Christian thought. We shall consider one of these arguments which intends to prove the existence of God on the grounds that anything which is limited or finite cannot adequately account for its existence. Furthermore, the whole class of things which have limitations of one sort or another cannot account for or explain its beginning to exist.

The argument may be summarized as follows:

1. Everything we are aware of is "contingent" (i.e., could once have not existed).

2. If time had no beginning, everything which *could* have happened, *would* have happened at some point in the past.

---

[9] St. Thomas Aquinas, *Summa Theologica*, Article 3. Relevant sections reprinted in anthologies AB, BKW, EP, F, MGAS, SA, ST, TBO. For excellent commentary on this and other Thomistic arguments consult F. C. Copleston, *Aquinas* (Baltimore, Md.: Penguin Books, Inc., 1961), pp. 117-27. Relevant selection reprinted in anthology F. Arguments of the type advanced by Aquinas have been referred to as "cosmological." because they attempt to prove that the universe or cosmos as a whole requires a cause for its existence which is distinct from the universe itself. His arguments draw attention to certain features which he believed were to be found generally throughout the whole of reality.

3. It could have been that nothing contingent existed.

4. Therefore, it is true that at some point in the past nothing contingent existed.

5. But since contingent things do exist and nothing can originate from nothing, there must have always been a being who brought contingent things into existence. Such a being necessarily exists and is called "God."

Now let's go back to the beginning of the argument and examine each step.

STEP 1. Stop for a moment and consider the things with which you are acquainted. All of them come into existence, undergo various changes while they are around, and then are destroyed or die. Natural things like plants and animals, manufactured items and even ourselves (at least as far as our bodies are concerned) all share these characteristics. Let us refer to these features common to all things in our experience by the term "contingency," because we need not say that these things *had* to be. As a matter of fact they exist, but they *could* just as well have not come into being at all.

STEP 2. If time had no beginning, then everything which could have happened, did happen. Everything which was logically possible would have become an actuality if it had enough time. The only reason why some possibilities do not become actualities in our lifetimes is that there simply isn't enough time for it. But if a *few* possibilities are realized in a limited or finite amount of time, then *all* possibilities would be realized in an *unlimited* or infinite amount of time.

STEP 3. We must remember that it *could* have been that nothing contingent ever existed. It is a possibility that at one point in the remote past nothing of a contingent nature existed.

STEP 4. By putting steps two and three together we must conclude that at some point in the past nothing of a contingent nature existed. If *all* possibilities become actualized in an infinite amount of time and it is a possibility that nothing contingent existed at some point in the past, then we know that this possibility became a reality. At one point in past time, nothing contingent existed.

STEP 5. But contingent things of various kinds do in fact exist at the present. How can this be explained in view of the fact that we discovered in Step Four? If at one point in the remote past nothing contingent existed, how did contingent things get their start? It doesn't make sense to say they caused themselves, because in order for one thing, A, to produce another thing, B, the first thing must already exist. And contingent things could not have originated literally out of nothing because in order for a thing to be regarded as a cause, it must be a real being. We could say that "something cannot come from nothing." The only satisfactory way of accounting for the fact that contingent things began to exist is to say that there must have been a being which always existed and who is not capable of either beginning to exist or of ceasing to exist. This being must be considered a "necessary being," therefore, since he had to have always existed and must continue to exist.

Difficulties with This Argument

By using the criteria we suggested in Chapter One for analyzing and evaluating philosophical arguments, let's see what can be done with Aquinas's argument.

(1) Isn't his very first statement open to question? Is it true that everything with which we are acquainted comes into being and stops existing at some time? Even if this is so for large-scale things like trees and cars, it wouldn't have to be the case for the elements which compose these things. For all we know, the basic elements of matter always existed and always will, and if this is actually the case, then Aquinas's argument is faulty in its first step.

(2) The second step of the argument requires more attention. It is said that "Time had no beginning" and that "given

enough time, all possibilities will be realized." Now in thinking about time it is easy to be taken in by some rather tempting metaphors or models. Unless we are on our toes, we will most likely talk about time as if it were some sort of peculiar entity which we measure but never directly experience. In an attempt to understand this mysterious entity we call time, we find it convenient and natural to use certain metaphors. It may seem to us that time is like a river without a source or a mouth, without beginning or end. But this metaphor or analogy is especially out of place and extremely misleading, because a river is something spatial in which other things may take place and exist. If we adopt this way of talking about time, it then becomes natural to think that time is something in which certain things take place. We are then faced with the puzzle as to what kind of thing or entity time is.

Furthermore, the question, "Did time have a beginning?" appears to be a legitimate one if we continue to think of time according to the model of a mysterious stream in which events take place. But the very nature of this question ought to be a signal to us that something has gone wrong in our thinking; somewhere we have been led astray. What sense does it make to say that time either had or did *not* have a beginning? We know what it means to say "Physics class began at 11:00 A.M." or "The Mississippi River begins in Minnesota," but what does it mean to say "Time began" or "Time did not begin"? We can specify a time at which the class began and a place where the river begins, but we are hard put to specify any such things concerning time. We don't even know what it would be like for time to begin in the first place. However, if it makes no sense to say "Time began," then it likewise makes no sense to say "Time did not begin" as Aquinas does. One cannot get a meaningful statement out of a meaningless statement simply by negating the latter. If it makes no sense to say "the glumpfs are canniffiring," it likewise is meaningless to say "The glumpfs are *not* canniffiring."

(3) Suppose the sentence "Time did not begin" is taken to be a short-hand (but misleading) way of claiming that there

never was a time when events were not taking place. On this interpretation, there would be temporal relationships between one event and another, since one event would take place *before* another and so on. Could we adopt this approach and thereby save Aquinas's argument? It doesn't look as though this will help, because if we admit that events have always been taking place, we shall have to deny that all things with which we are acquainted are "contingent," i.e., come into existence and therefore could have not existed. Aquinas is faced with a dilemma: if he does not adopt the view that events have always been taking place, then his statement "time did not begin" is meaningless. But if he adopts the view that events *have* always been taking place then he has to give up the first premise in his argument. Whichever way he takes, his argument turns out to be invalid as stated.[10]

(4) Aquinas concludes, "There must exist something the existence of which is necessary." If by this he means to assert that there is a being who is "logically necessary," then he seems to have misapplied the word "necessary." Only *propositions* of a certain type can properly be said to be "necessary."[11] The assertion "$3 + 4 = 7$" is necessary in the sense that if we know the meaning of the symbols involved in it, then we can tell whether or not it is true. No perceptual experience or observation concerning facts in the world is required on anyone's part to determine its truth or falsity. The statement "$3 + 4 = 7$" is not making a claim about something which exists, so any data we would derive from sense perception is beside the point when it comes to determining whether or not this assertion is true.

---

[10] Aquinas might say that events were always taking place, but that these events were thoughts in the mind of God. He would, however, have difficulties with this as well, since for the theist, temporal distinctions are not supposed to apply to the perfect personal being. God's thoughts are supposed to be "eternal," which ordinarily is taken by the theist to mean "not characterized by temporal sequence such as 'before' and 'after.'"

[11] "Necessary" propositions are "analytic" propositions which we have discussed in a previous section in the chapter.

On the other hand, statements like "Sue is wearing a blue dress" and "Rain is falling in Rio" are examples of contingent[12] or empirical statements. When we inquire into the truth or falsity of such assertions, we must consult or be able to consult evidence gained through sense perception. Such statements *are* making claims about something that is the case in the observable world and are therefore properly regarded as contingent or empirical. The truth or falsity of the statement "Rain is falling in Rio" is not dependent merely upon the meaning of the words composing it; it is true or false depending upon whether or not there *actually is* rain falling in Rio at the moment. Its truth or falsity is contingent upon certain conditions being the case in the changing, observable world.

Now, if every statement which makes a claim about something which exists or is the case is a contingent statement, then the expression "logically necessary being" is a contradiction in terms. A statement may be "logically necessary" but *something which exists* cannot be spoken of in this way. When Aquinas says "God is a necessary being," he would have to be interpreted as saying, "The statement 'God exists' is logically necessary." But this is to imply that a logically necessary statement may on occasion be making a claim about what is supposed to exist in the world. Such a maneuver on Aquinas's part confuses the nature of logically necessary statements (i.e., analytic) with that of the contingent (i.e., synthetic) or empirical type.

The Teleological Argument: Natural Things Display Evidence of Their Being Designed by an Intelligent Being.

The so-called "teleological" argument for the existence of God differs significantly from the cosmological approach. The

---

[12] "Contingent" statements are equivalent to synthetic or empirical statements, the main features of which have already been discussed.

latter argument focused upon (1) the perishable nature of things around us and (2) the necessity of a being which always existed, without telling us much about the *kind* of being this might be. However, the teleological argument is intended to draw our attention to the orderly manner in which natural processes take place and the many ways in which parts of natural things seem to have a purpose or goal in what they do. A process is said to be "teleological" if it appears to be moving toward a specific end or goal, utilizing means at its disposal to bring about the seemingly "foreseen" result. The advocate of the teleological argument for the existence of God claims that instances of such processes in nature are plentiful, and that such behavior on the part of living things and their parts cannot be accounted for except on the supposition that a powerful, intelligent being originally constructed (and now oversees) the marvelously intricate mechanisms of nature.

The advocate of the teleological argument would proceed like this:[13] Look about you. What you see on the one hand are many different kinds of manufactured things like cameras, watches, automobiles, etc., and, on the other hand, various kinds of *natural* things like dogs, cats, birds and trees. When we examine a manufactured item closely we find it composed of parts, each performing a special function which contributes to the overall purpose of the thing in question. For example, a camera has a lens whose function is to refract light waves in a certain way so that ultimately an image will be captured and a photograph will result.

Now, compare the camera to the human eye, a part of a natural thing. Each part of the eye contributes to the final goal of being able to see. The similarities between the ways in which

---

[13] William Paley, *Natural Theology* (1802), Chap. III. (Selection in anthology EP.) For criticism of the theological argument see Hume, *Dialogues Concerning Natural Religion.* (Selections in anthologies AB, EP, F, MGAS, SA, ST, TBO.) This argument has undergone modifications through the years, and not all who are impressed with the teleological approach would accept every part of the following statement as their own.

the camera's parts function to contribute to the overall aim of the mechanism and the ways in which the eye's parts function to realize the purpose of the eye are quite striking.

But wouldn't you consider it highly irrational to conclude that the parts of the camera function as they do because of blind chance? We just don't find cameras growing on trees. They have been designed by beings who have *arranged* the parts of the camera so that the mechanism as a whole will do a certain job. Wouldn't it be just as irrational to suppose that the many intricate, delicately balanced parts of the eye came about by blind chance? If the existence of cameras (and, in particular, the first camera) depends on the mind which designed them, then the existence of eyes (and, in particular, the first eye) depends on a mind which designed them. Things which are alike in such significant ways require similar types of causes.

Suppose one objects that the existence and nature of organisms and their parts can be adequately explained by the principle of "natural selection" and the "survival of the fittest." How many creatures were there, you ask, which did not have eyes and similarly helpful parts to maintain their existence? The ones with eyes survived while the probably countless other species that were not fortunate enough to have eyes became extinct. There were probably many varieties of creatures which did not happen to be lucky enough to have such equipment so necessary to survive in a hostile environment.

But if you argue like this, you will still have a difficult time explaining why there were any species at all which just "happened" to get eyes. "The survival of the fittest presupposes the arrival of the fit . . . ."[14] The whole process of evolution which took place seems to have favored those creatures which could compete with their environment and preserve their existence. And it looks as though the process of evolution was especially partial to a being like man. Human beings not only

---

[14] F. R. Tennant, *Philosophical Theology* (Cambridge: Cambridge University Press, 1930), Vol. II. Chap. IV, 79-93. Reprinted in Hick, ed., *The Existence of God*, pp. 121-36.

have capacities which merely *preserve* their existence, but they also have faculties which *enhance* life with pleasurable and valuable experiences. The capacities I'm thinking about are those which make possible experience in the moral, aesthetic, intellectual and religious spheres. How can these be explained as necessary results of the struggle to survive on the part of human beings?

Difficulties with This Argument

(1) Since the teleological argument is based upon certain likenesses it sees between manufactured and natural things, we should inquire as to when it is permissible to use an "argument from analogy"? If I say that my wrist watch must have been made by a being who can plan and use various means to accomplish a goal, how do I know this? Simply because such persons have been *observed* working on watches, if not by myself, then by others. Has anyone ever observed God creating an eye on some occasion?

(2) Doesn't more than one person normally design and manufacture cameras and watches? Should we conclude that a *group* of intelligent beings designed and produced the first eye? And we know that makers of cameras and watches work with materials made by someone else; is it the same with God? Furthermore, should one conclude that God is not fully an expert because there are defects in the workmanship of nature? If God is not responsible for these imperfections, who or what is?

(3) Can't we think of man's *intellectual* capacities as coming about because of his drive to preserve his existence? If this is plausible, why can we not view the moral, aesthetic and religious capacities of man as a "natural" outgrowth of his abilities to think, acquire knowledge and plan for the future?

(4) Upon examination of a certain mechanism a reasonable man may be required to conclude that it was designed. But this would not prove the *present* existence of the mechanism's designer. Similarly, even if the canons of rationality compelled

us to conclude that the processes and products of nature were designed, we would not have proved the *present* existence of that original designer.

DOES THE EXISTENCE OF SUFFERING DISPROVE THE EXISTENCE OF GOD?

Statement of the Problem of Evil

Many people who might be inclined to believe in the existence of a perfect personal being are sincerely troubled by the presence of extensive suffering in the world. Disease, starvation, calamities and catastrophes like earthquakes, storms, and floods, together with the "inhumanity of man to man" are all too familiar facts. It is not the presence of a few of these conditions at certain isolated points in history, but the *overabundance* of these phenomena that concerns the believer and would-be believer in the reality of God.

The existence of such amounts of suffering at the hands of natural forces and the actions of other people poses a problem for the traditional theist. If indeed God is a perfect personal being, one who is all-powerful and all-good, why does he permit such widespread suffering? And even more basic is the question, if God created nature and man, why did he make them so that they *could* be the source of so much suffering?

The situation of suffering in the world provides ammunition for an outright denial of the existence of a being who is all-good and all-powerful. It is contended that the suffering with which we are acquainted *counts against* the theist's position. The argument is that one cannot hold all three of the following statements at the same time:

1. God exists and is all-good.

2. God exists and is all-powerful.

3. There is suffering in the world.

Any *two* of these may be held at the same time but not all three.

The problem for the believer in an omnipotent (all-powerful) and morally perfect being can be made more understandable by using the following example. Suppose we were to hear of a man whose child is desperately ill or has been injured seriously in an accident. Suppose further that the father is a competent practicing physician thoroughly capable of treating the sickness or repairing the damage caused by the accident. At the very least, he would be able to administer some badly needed first aid. However, suppose we learn that this father did not so much as lift a finger to aid his child whom he claims to love very much. Such a person would seem to us to have acted immorally by failing to help or even try to alleviate the suffering of his child. If he were *able* to help and didn't, we would be led to doubt whether he really cared for his child. The analogy should seem obvious. God is supposed to be *able* to prevent widespread suffering and is also supposed to have a sincere *love* for human beings. Is it not natural to doubt whether he is able to prevent suffering on the part of creatures or whether he really cares if they suffer?

Attempts to Reconcile Belief in a Perfect Being with the Existence of Evil[15]

THE "DISCORDANT NOTE" ARGUMENT. If there were no pain, no suffering, no hardships to overcome (in short, nothing we would call evil), then how could we recognize and appreciate good? What would it mean to say some experience or event was good if there were nothing with which to contrast what we called good? Everything would simply be as it is, but be neither good nor evil. We require evil in our world just as the musician needs

---

[15] Several clear and incisive discussions of the problem of evil may be found in *God and Evil*, Nelson Pike, ed. (Englewood Cliffs, N.J.: Prentice-Hall, Inc., 1964). Usually attempted solutions to the problem of evil are explained and analyzed in this provocative collection of essays.

to hear an occasional off-key or discordant note in order to keep his ear keen for and appreciative of beautiful music. Or, to alter the analogy slightly, the creation of a beautiful symphony requires the blending together of notes which if heard by themselves would be less than pleasing if not downright jarring to the ear. But blended with the other notes, the final product attains aesthetic value.

THE "BLESSING IN DISGUISE" ARGUMENT. Pain, rather than being entirely bad, is often extremely beneficial. We may not like having a toothache or a pain which accompanies an appendicitis attack when they occur, but they signal us that something needs immediate attention if we are to avoid further pain or even death. Furthermore, when we look back upon our lives, we can often trace many good things which resulted from events we took to be tragic or painful at the time they happened. Perhaps if we could see more of the long-range consequences of our own and other people's suffering we would not regard it as evil after all.

THE "BEST OF ALL WORLDS" ARGUMENT. Suppose it was in your power to produce the sort of universe or arrangement of nature you considered best for human beings. Would you not include in your scheme those things which would tend to develop moral qualities in man like affection and concern for others, patience, courage, and a sense of justice? To claim you had arranged the best of all possible worlds but left no room for the production of these highest qualities a person can display would be contradictory.

But how could these be developed in persons unless we had roughly the sort of universe we actually have? If no one suffered pain (either of a physical or mental nature) or faced hardship of any sort or ever failed to have all of his needs satisfied, everyone would be self-sufficient. Since no one would require another person's love or assistance, how could the important moral quality of concern for other persons' well-being be developed? If a person is to develop the moral side of his

72

nature, he must live in a kind of world that operates according to fixed natural laws so that he can learn from the past and predict the possible consequences of his actions. But we must accept *all* of the consequences of a law-abiding universe if such an arrangement is a necessary means for developing moral personality. To have a universe in which floods, earthquakes and disease were impossible might upset the whole order of things, thereby making moral development impossible.

THE "TRUE CULPRIT" ARGUMENT. Many of the evils which befall us are traceable to the fact that human beings have free will. The unimaginable amount of suffering which resulted from World War II, for example, is due in large part to the decisions and actions of men like Adolph Hitler and those who followed their orders. Why blame God for the acts of men? Surely God could have created a kind of creature which would mechanically obey every moral law. But such a creature would be more like a *puppet* than a *person*. God chose to create persons, and he chooses to respect their status as persons by allowing them the free exercise of their wills even if that results in suffering for other people. Furthermore, why blame God for evil conditions like poverty, disease, and ignorance? Their existence is the fault of people who are capable of eradicating these evils from the earth but who freely choose to devote their energies to more selfish endeavors.

Difficulties with These Arguments

(1) Doesn't the "discordant note" argument underestimate the amount and intensity of suffering in the world? It is easy to forget that for most of the people now inhabiting this globe and for a vast majority who lived here before, life is a daily round of misery. Wouldn't much smaller doses of suffering at less frequent intervals provide the contrast necessary for us to identify and appreciate what is good?

(2) With regard to the "blessing in disguise" argument

73

we might reply like this: because good sometimes results from tragic or painful events, should we conclude that the good in such cases couldn't be produced in a less costly and a more humane way? If God is all-powerful, then other means are at his disposal to accomplish the goal he has in view. Furthermore, an all-powerful being should have been able to devise a better system for signalling us concerning some malfunction in our bodies than that of pain, because in regard to many malfunctions it doesn't work at all. Why the malfunctions which require attention in the first place?

(3) The "best of all worlds" argument and the "true culprit" argument have common difficulties. How would the natural order be upset in any significant way if a hurricane or tornado were "guided" by God out to sea and disintegrated instead of being permitted to destroy life and property? What difference could it make to nature as a whole if certain viruses were destroyed just as they entered a human body so that their capacity to produce pain and death would be checked?

The same kind of direct interference by an all-powerful being could prevent to a great extent the immense amount of suffering which results from the free choices of men. Just a little interference by God in the mind of Hitler and his henchmen could have spared millions of lives and prevented unimaginable amounts of agony and sorrow. Such interference would not make *all* men or even any *one* man a puppet, since only those actions which would entail great suffering for other people would have to be prevented.

The Finite God Proposal

There is a way out of the problem of evil advocated by those who are known as "theistic finitists."[16] They maintain that

---

[16] E. S. Brightman, *A Philosophy of Religion* (Englewood Cliffs, N.J.: Prentice-Hall, Inc., 1940), Chaps. 8-10.

God should be regarded as a morally perfect being in the sense that he always *wills* what is right and *tries* to do what is right. But they deny that this being necessarily must be all-powerful. They point out that even the theistic "absolutist" (the person who claims God is all-good *and* all-powerful) does not hold that God can do literally everything. Most absolutists would admit, for example, that God can neither make a round square nor cease to exist.

It is argued by the finitist that a being who is all-powerful and refused to alleviate widespread suffering would be vastly inferior to a being who wants to help us in our plight but who is hindered from accomplishing his purposes. It is suggested that God could be hindered in fulfilling his aims by the properties of matter, both in its organic and inorganic forms. The finitist sometimes holds that elements composing physical things have always existed alongside God and that his shaping and ordering them through the long process of evolution to arrive at their present form is the best job that he could do under the circumstances.

The finitist is also quick to point out that his concept of God is an understandable one whereas the absolutist's way of thinking of God makes him so remote and obscure as to be unintelligible. If one is to speak sensibly about God and adopt an attitude of worship toward this being, it seems necessary to understand what this being is like. For without this understanding the theists are in danger of talking about, and to, something wholly unintelligible.

DOES IT MATTER WHETHER GOD EXISTS?

Aside from the value of exercising the mind with a difficult problem and being stimulated by the subleties of argumentation involved in its resolution, why is study of this problem worthwhile? Does it really make much difference whether a personal being without limitations exists or not?

Philosophers who have worked within the framework of theism have argued that the existence of an absolutely perfect being would have implications for many of the major problems in philosophy. It is claimed by these thinkers that, if it can be proved that a perfect being exists, a number of philosophic issues are thereby solved. To what answers do some theistic philosophers think they are committed in regard to the four problems with which we shall deal in the rest of the book?

(1) If an absolutely perfect being exists, then such a being must have perfect or unlimited knowledge. He must know everything, including what will happen in the future. He must, therefore, know what every person will do in any given situation. But if God *knows* that person A will do B at time T in the future, then it is *true* that A will do B and nothing else at that time. In fact, A *could* not do anything but B at time T, since if he did, it would have to be denied that God knows everything. The reason for this is that if someone knows that B will occur, then it is *true* that B will occur; it would be contradictory to say that someone *knows* B will happen and then say "but B will not or might not happen." God's knowing what will happen in the future makes it impossible for anything to happen other than what actually does. The believer in the existence of a perfect being is committed, therefore, to the view that each person's choices and actions are determined for him; no one can do anything other than what he actually does. Human beings do not make free choices, therefore, since no *genuine* alternatives are open to them when they deliberate concerning what they will do.

(2) Does a person survive his bodily death? The believer in a perfect being would most likely say "yes" for the following reason. If there is a perfect being, he would be unlimited in power and wisdom. Being the source of man's existence and faculties, God would not place within each person the desire to preserve his existence and attain happiness unless he made

76

some provision for preserving the existence of the human personality after death. If a perfect being allowed man to be completely destroyed with the destruction of the body, it would mean that God had given human beings desires which he (God) knew would be frustrated. This would imply that the perfect being acted deceitfully and without good reasons, something inconsistent with the nature of a perfect being. Therefore, argues the theist, human beings continue to exist after death.

(3) The last two problems—"Can I know what is morally right?" and "When can I say that I know?"—are not so easy for the theist to handle. According to the theist, there must *be* certain moral rules which ought to be adopted by everyone, since a perfect being would have to be morally perfect and it would be inconceivable that a morally perfect being did not *know* what is morally right. It would also be contradictory to say "There is a perfect being" and then say "there are no absolutely true statements," since a perfect being must have perfect knowledge, and what such a being *knows* has to be true.

However, it is one thing to know that there *are* certain moral rules which ought to be adopted by everyone and quite another to know *how* we are to arrive at a knowledge of them. On the latter score, the theist seems to be in no better position than anyone else. However, in regard to the question "When can I say that I know," a theist might argue as Descartes did, namely that a perfect being would not have given man faculties for sense perception and reasoning and constructed these faculties in such a way that they would continually lead us into error. As Descartes pointed out, we have a propensity to believe that things exist outside ourselves and that we can know the world around us, if we use our faculties in the right way. A perfect being would not have placed such capacities within man, if they were not reliable for acquiring knowledge. For the perfect being to have done so would mean that he was deceitful, which is inconsistent with the nature of a perfect being.

Admittedly, the assumptions made by a theist who would

argue in the ways just discussed are questionable, to say the least. Even if it could be shown that a perfect being exists, the theist might be wrong in his views concerning what follows from such a "fact." We shall not pursue the difficulties with his arguments further at this point but rather encourage the reader to analyze them for himself, either now or (what would be better) after he has become more familiar with the issues still to be treated in the remaining chapters. Our reason for raising these arguments at all was merely to show that the question with which we have occupied ourselves in this chapter is one which a number of respectable thinkers have regarded as pivotal for the activity of philosophy.

SUGGESTIONS FOR FURTHER STUDY

Anthologies

AB, Part 1; BKW, Chap. 7; EP, Chap. 5; F, Part 1: MGAS, Part 6; SA, Part 5; ST, Part 2; TBO, Part 9; TH, Chaps. 23, 24.

Others

Flew, Antony and Alasdair MacIntyre, eds., *New Essays in Philosophical Theology.* New York: Macmillan and Co., 1955.

Hick, John, ed., *The Existence of God.* New York: Macmillan and Co., 1964.

————,*The Philosophy of Religion.* Englewood Cliffs, N.J.: Prentice-Hall, Inc., 1963.

Hume, David, *Dialogues Concerning Natural Religion.* (Various editions and publishers.)

Pike, Nelson, ed., *God and Evil.* Englewood Cliffs, N.J.: Prentice-Hall, Inc., 1964.

MIND
AND IMMORTALITY
III

Will I Survive Death?

The question "Will I survive death?" is one which is probably not new to those beginning their exploration of philosophic problems. At one time or another it seems that almost everyone has pondered the issue, for understandable reasons. The reality of death is with us on every hand. No family or individual is exempt from the ordeal of profound personal loss. News reports keep the fact of death vividly before us with their grim recitation of statistics of highway tragedies and the inevitable fruits of war and violence. It is hardly any wonder, then, that we raise the questions, "Does death end all?" "Does human personality cease to exist when the processes of life are suddenly halted?"

Despite the striking naturalness and significance inherent in the question its answer is far from obvious. In fact, the more we ponder the issue and the more intensive our analysis of it becomes, the more perplexed we are likely to feel. We are fairly clear on what is being asked in the questions, "Will man survive the nuclear age?" and "Will I survive today's exam in Chemistry?" but we rightly boggle at the query "Will I survive death?" The problem is that we are not quite sure what it would be like to "survive the death of our bodies." And I suspect that we are as much or more concerned about the *nature* of a future life as we are about whether or not there will be one.

THE CONCEPT
OF IMMORTALITY

In dealing with any philosophical problem we had best keep clearly in mind the distinction between the *meaning* of a statement and the *truth or falsity* of that assertion. It is especially important that we remember this crucial difference in regard to the problem before us in this chapter. It is one thing to ask, "What does it *mean* to say that we will (or will not) have disembodied experiences?" It is quite another thing to ask whether it is *true* that we will (or will not) have disembodied experiences. Clearly we must determine what a statement means (if anything) before we can go about trying to tell whether it is true or false. What will occupy our immediate attention is an analysis of the phrase "disembodied experiences"; we shall not presume there either are or are not such experiences. Our only concern for the present is that of determining what sort of experiences these could be if in fact we should have them after our bodily death.

It might be objected by some that the phrase "disembodied experience" is a contradiction in terms, since the meaning of the word "experience" is so intimately bound up with the meaning of the words "body" and "bodily." All our experiences are so bound up with bodily function and muscular movement, it is argued, that to say that there are *dis*embodied experiences is as contradictory as claiming that there is "disembodied breathing."

Admittedly, if someone claimed that there could be breathing without a body, he would be uttering something contradictory. The expression "He is breathing" seems to imply "He has a body." The same could be said of a number of other activities such as sense perception. To say that "Sam is having certain sense perceptions" seems to entail that Sam has functioning sense organs, which implies that he has a body. So it does appear that certain kinds of experiences are ruled out as being able to qualify as disembodied experiences. It would be logically impossible to undergo such experiences as breathing and perceiving without a body, and the same could be said of a host of other familiar everyday experiences.

But just because there are *some* experiences which a person could not (logically) have outside the body, it does not follow that we cannot give a meaning to the phrase "disembodied experiences." If there are such experiences, couldn't we think of them as something like the experience we call day-dreaming? The next life could have a dream-like quality to it in that an individual would be aware of memory-images of things he had experienced in his earthly life. Sometimes these memories might come to us involuntarily as they do in a dream, and sometimes our desires and wishes could construct various imaginary situations in roughly the way we do when we engage in day-dreaming, fancying ourselves to be in situations which we "see," so to speak, in "our mind's eye." Admittedly we are not actually doing those things we imagine ourselves to be engaged in, but the images we experience in such activities are oftentimes real enough to make us happy or sad, jovial or angry, depending upon their content.[1]

---

[1] See H. H. Price, "Survival and the Idea of 'Another World,'" *Proceedings of the Society for Psychical Research*, L, Part 182 (January, 1953), 1-25. Reprinted in John Hick, ed., *Classical and Contemporary Readings in Philosophy of Religion* (Englewood Cliffs, N.J.: Prentice-Hall, Inc., 1964), pp. 364-86.

Adjustment to a life which is the joint product of our memory-images, desires and individual character traits might be exceedingly difficult. An existence in which a person could not do most of the things he did in his earthly life might for some people be extremely unpleasant. But what we would *wish* a future life to be like has no bearing upon the question concerning the nature of such a state and whether such a life will in fact be experienced.

A number of fascinating questions arise when we try to construct a concept of personal immortality along the lines we have just suggested. For example, would a life of memory-images and desires leave room for communication with other disembodied persons? What sort of relationships would people have with one another in such a state? Perhaps some sort of telepathy or direct communication with another's experiences would be possible, although such a suggestion is not without its difficulties. Then again, what should we say about those persons who would find the next life extremely undesirable? Would it be possible for a disembodied person to commit suicide? Perhaps one could end his existence completely with a kind of "death-wish" similar to the sort of experience some people have in this life when they reach a point of great dispair and no longer desire to live.

In order to avoid misunderstanding, we point out again that up to this point we have been concerned only with the question of what "disembodied experiences" might be like. Our only interest was to show that at least no logical contradiction is involved in the claim that we shall survive bodily death. Whether *in fact* there are such experiences we must now go on to determine by examining arguments for and against the proposal. What light on this problem can we expect from philosophers? Are there any good reasons to hope for "life beyond the grave" if that is indeed something for which we hope?

There are some philosophers who advance arguments which are intended to show significant differences between what they refer to on the one hand as "physical acts and processes" and, on the other hand, what they refer to as "mental acts and processes." They contend that these fundamental differences point to the conclusion that a human being is not reducible to the bodily processes he undergoes, and that there is an aspect of human personality which is not dependent for its operations on the functioning of bodily processes. These philosophers have been called "dualists" because they view man as composed of two distinct, irreducible parts usually called "body" and "mind" or "body" and "soul." For the dualist, it is quite conceivable that a person could continue to exist beyond his physical death. He would say that the "non-material" aspect or side of human beings could continue to exist apart from the body, and that there are no good reasons to conclude that it will not continue to exist. We shall examine arguments for this position shortly.

On the other side of the dispute are several kinds of "anti-dualists" who argue that the dualists' contentions are fallacious. The anti-dualistic position has been argued by philosophers of varying kinds, and it would be inadvisable to make many generalizations about the nature of their arguments. They are at one, however, in denying that human beings live some sort of queer double-life, one inside their "minds" hidden from public view and another which we can all observe in their bodily movements. Man, in short, is not a compound of two distinct entities called a mind and a body, temporarily harnessed together only to be separated at death. It seems safe to say that it would be quite difficult to hold that a belief in a "next life" is rationally grounded if the anti-dualist is correct. It does not follow, however, that if you are not a dualist in this controversy regarding the nature of man, then you must reject the belief in immortality. You could, for example, be a non-dualist and hold that God will miraculously sustain human personality after death or create some new kind of body for that state. Just what kind of operation this would be is not explained too clearly by those who suggest it.

After we have scrutinized the main arguments in support of dualism and anti-dualism, we shall give some attention to

83

several arguments for the belief in life after death which do not directly utilize the arguments for the dualistic view of man.

PSYCHO-PHYSICAL DUALISM

"Knowing Is a Non-Material Act."

There is an argument for dualism which attempts to argue from the position that knowing something is an act which is not physical in nature but rather is purely a mental act. It proceeds from this analysis of the "act of knowledge" to draw the conclusion that the faculty whereby we acquire knowledge must also be non-material in nature.[2] The argument goes like this:

Suppose we consider a situation in which a claim to know something is made, such as where one might say, "There's an apple on the table." Just what is involved in our knowing that an apple is on the table? How are we able to recognize this state of affairs, assuming for the moment that there really is an apple on the table?

Of course we would say that we see or touch the apple and the table or perhaps both. But regardless of how many different perceptions we get of the situation, we would never be able to *know* there was an apple on the table unless we knew *what* an apple was or what a table was or what is meant for one thing to be *on* some other object. We can identify this situation as an "apple being on the table" only because we recognize enough similarities between these objects before us and similar ones which we have been taught to call "apples" and "tables." In short, we know *what* an apple is or we know the characteristics a thing must have in order to be an apple. Let us call this com-

---

[2] Aristotle, *De Anima*, Book III, Chapter 4. Aquinas, *Summa Theologica*, Part I, Q. 75. Relevant arguments are reprinted in Antony Flew, ed., *Body, Mind and Death* (New York: Crowell-Collier & Macmillan, Inc., 1964), pp. 80-81, 103-104.

plex of characteristics which *all* apples must have in order to be called "apples" a "universal." If we know what an apple is, it is only because we have been able through a number of contacts with various kinds and colors of apples to draw out from those experiences the properties common to all particular instances of that fruit. This process of becoming familiar with the essential nature of things in our experience (i.e., "universals") is a gradual one and ordinarily is one which we are not aware of as it takes place. Nevertheless, our acquisition of knowledge depends upon our being acquainted with a great many "universals" — we can cope with things about us because we know *what* a car is, *what* a tree is, *what* a dog is. Our experience of *individual, particular* cars, trees and dogs would not be knowledge unless we were acquainted with the essential, defining characteristics of these kinds of things.

A question naturally arises concerning the status of these universals which we become aware of through experience with things around us. They seem to be some sort of entity to which we can make meaningful references and which we can store up in our minds for use in recognizing and coping with things around us. Whatever their status may be, it is clear that universals are not material things, that is, objects which take up space and are observable through sense perception. Furthermore, they are not subject to change or destruction as is true of material objects and their parts. Individual *instances* of universals (particular, perceivable things) such as the apples before us on the table do occupy space, are open to sensory observation, and undergo a variety of changes. But universals themselves are non-material entities though apparently manifested or exemplified in individual things and "drawn out" of these objects by the mind. Universals are not perceivable, although by observing a number of individual things of the same type through the senses we acquire our acquaintance with that which is common to a group of similar objects.

Since the nature of what we know is non-material (namely, universals, or the essential characteristics which distinguish one *kind* of thing from another), the *act* whereby we know must be a non-physical one as well. The act of knowing could not be the act of a bodily organ because it is impossible to get into any physical contact with universals. They are not composed of anything material, and consequently we are acquainted with them only by means of a non-material faculty we possess. The power or capacity of intellect whereby we come to know "universals" is purely non-material in nature even though it must be admitted that it depends upon the brain. But this dependence is an *extrinsic* one. That is, the intellect cannot operate without the assistance of the brain and nervous system, but this does not mean that the intellect *is* identical with the brain. The human intellect does not reside in any one part of the body but rather "uses" the brain and the senses to build up its store of universals so it can increase its store of knowledge.

The argument's skeleton has the following form:

1. Knowing something involves being acquainted with "universals."

2. "Universals" are not physical in nature (i.e., they are non-spatial, do not have shape, are not perceivable).

3. Since "universals" are non-physical, the act whereby they are acquired and retained cannot be a physical act.

4. Since the act of knowing is not a physical act, the *faculty* whereby we know things (i.e., the intellect) cannot be physical in nature.

Difficulties with This Argument[3]

(1) The argument hinges upon the use of the expression, "act of knowing." If I know there are apples on the table, does

---

[3] As in the previous chapter, the reader is strongly encouraged to interact critically with the arguments presented. The questions which follow are suggested points of attack and are not intended to be either conclusive refutation of the argument or the only difficulties that could be considered.

this imply that I am *doing* something? It may well be that if I knew such a fact, it would have been necessary for me to have *done* something, namely observed the table and the apples or accepted the word of someone else who observed them. It might also be said that I should be *able to do* or be *prepared to do* certain things like point the situation out to a friend or pick up one of the apples and take a chunk out of it. But am I doing anything like what the argument suggests when I know the apples are on the table? Since each of us knows literally thousands of facts, are we committing thousands of acts simultaneously? Not only do we know a great host of facts, but each of us may lay claim to having abilities to do many different things. But my knowing *how* to do X does not necessarily mean that I am doing X right now, nor does it make much sense to say something like "I am now engaged in the act of knowing how to play golf."

(2) Aren't there sometimes disagreements between people as to what to call a certain thing? Should we call an object which one person can sit on a chair if it has no back? What are the "essential characteristics" of any given object? If we cannot always agree on the answers to such questions, how could we all be "acquainted with" the same "universal"? And if we have differing notions of *what* a thing is, how can we be understood when we use expressions referring to that thing? How could two or more people be said to *know* that there are apples on the table even though they might disagree about the "essential characteristics" of a table or of an apple? Aren't we forced to admit that we can communicate and we can know roughly the same state of affairs as the next person if our circumstances are the same because we know what jobs can be and cannot be done with certain words? Communication then would depend not upon our all being "acquainted with" the same "universals" but upon our being able to do certain things with our words and expressions.

(3) Since the argument admits that the intellect (supposedly a non-material faculty) cannot operate outside its conjunction with the brain and the rest of the body, why should we

expect the intellect to be able to function after the destruction of the body? If the intellect is "intrinsically" non-material, how and why does it *depend* upon the body?

"One Cannot Doubt That He Is a Thinking Being Whereas One Can Doubt That He Is a Material Being."

When philosophers consider which of their group was a "dualist," they all agree that Descartes, the influential seventeenth century thinker deserves the title. And when *philosophers* agree on something, it is truly noteworthy. I shall try to state Descartes's argument in a clear and concise manner so that we can understand and evaluate it:[4]

There is a great difference between the mind and the body; this can be made obvious if we just think along the following lines: I cannot doubt that I am thinking when I am thinking about something. I *can* doubt that what I am thinking *about* exists. I could be mistaken in believing that a book I want is on the table in the next room. I *could* be mistaken about the reality of *anything* outside my own thoughts, for I have been misled by my senses on other occasions. Furthermore, something or someone could conceivably be planting various erroneous ideas in my consciousness. But even if I am being deceived, I am still thinking; thought processes are going on. That I *cannot possibly* doubt.

But the case is totally different concerning physical or material things. I can even doubt whether I *have* a body, because my perceptions of my own body could be erroneous or deceptive. Consequently, I can doubt that while I am thinking any bodily process is going on at all. If my thoughts are really bodily

---

[4] René Descartes, *The Search for Truth*, eds. Haldane and Ross (New York: Dover Publications, Inc.), Vol. I, 319. Also *The Principles*, eds. Haldane and Ross (New York: Dover Publications, Inc.), Vol. I, 221, 244.

processes, electrochemical impulses or something of that nature, then I should be able to doubt the reality of my thoughts as I can my bodily processes. But I can't do this since doubting itself is a form of thinking. Therefore, processes like thoughts and sensations cannot be the same as physical or bodily processes.

Furthermore, my notion or concept of "what I am" does not depend upon any thoughts associated with physical things. My understanding of "what I am" does not depend upon anything I can visualize or picture in my imagination. I can think of what I am without referring to ideas concerning the physical characteristics of taking up space, having a shape, and being perceivable by the senses. I am aware of myself as a "thinking being," that is a mind, a being which thinks, doubts, decides, and imagines various things. It appears obvious, then, that the reason I can get a clear idea of "what I am," apart from any thoughts about material things, is that my mind and its processes are radically different from the body and its processes, if indeed such a thing as my body exists.

In summary, the argument is this:

1. I cannot doubt (without contradicting myself) that I am having mental processes right now.

2. I can doubt (without contradicting myself) that there are processes going on in my brain right now.

3. If mental processes and brain processes are the same, then they should be equally dubitable.

4. But, as premises 1 and 2 state, they are *not* equally dubitable.

5. Therefore, mental processes and brain processes are not the same.

Difficulties with This Argument

(1) Descartes maintains that we may meaningfully doubt whether or not our bodies exist, because our beliefs concerning the body are based upon various kinds of sense perceptions. And

since sense perceptions have led us to make wrong judgments about the way things really are, it is possible that the judgment that our bodies exist is erroneous. Therefore, it makes sense (that is, it is not logically contradictory) to say "I doubt that my body exists." However, in this argument Descartes may be doing some things with the word "doubt" that shouldn't be done. What does it mean to doubt that something is the case? One of the things we ordinarily mean when we use the word is this: it makes sense to say "I doubt P" only if there are some data to which we could conceivably turn in order to resolve our doubt. Descartes's doubt concerning the existence of his body, however, is irresolvable in principle, since he has denied the reliability of the only data which could resolve his doubt, namely data derived through sense perception. Descartes could be charged, therefore, with misusing the word "doubt" as we normally understand it with the result that one of the premises in his argument is without significance.

(2) Can't we carry Descartes's doubt further than he did? If there could be some being, personal or impersonal, which was deceiving him about the existence of his body, couldn't this same source deceive him into believing that his mind is different from his body? Couldn't such a source of deception provide the feeling of certainty regarding the existence of his thoughts just to make him think his body and mind were different? *Why* such a being should do this is beside the point. The point is that it is *possible* (in Descartes's use of the term), and therefore the certainty regarding the fact that he is thinking is thrown open to the same "doubts" as those regarding the reality of the body. If such a thing is "possible" on Descartes's use of terms, then he cannot conclude that the body is different from the mind simply because he can be certain of one and doubtful of the other.

(3) Because we may sensibly doubt that X is occurring but not sensibly doubt that Y is occurring, does it follow that X and Y must be different events? An uninstructed person would

not doubt that there were clouds in the sky as he looks at them, but he might well doubt that what he sees are collections of water vapor. Does this mean that clouds are something different from collections of water vapor suspended in the sky?

(4) Even if we granted everything Descartes is arguing for, namely that thought processes are not bodily processes, would this prove that the thought processes could continue independently of the bodily processes? Couldn't the thought processes be different from bodily processes (processes in the brain) and still be dependent for their existence on their conjunction with the body?

"Mental Processes Are Inherently Private; Physical Processes Are Inherently Public."

This argument,[5] often advanced in favor of dualism, is similar to the previous one in some respects and could be considered to be merely another form of Descartes's position. Whether it is or is not seems unimportant at this point. It at least makes explicit one aspect of Descartes's thinking and so is given separate attention.

We call certain things "mental" (thoughts, desires, emotions, etc.), and we call certain things "physical" (trees, clouds, animals and processes occurring within bodies, etc.). The words "mental" and "physical" are *names*, and names designate, denote, or direct our attention to a certain thing or entity. If I name my dog "Spot," it would be absurd to ask if my dog were really Spot and hence different from my son who is named "Sam." If Sam and Spot were the same beings, we wouldn't have two different names for him. In a similar sense, if the mental and physical were identical, we would not have two different names for the one entity.

---

[5] C. J. Ducasse, "The Case for Dualism," in Sidney Hook, ed., *Dimensions of Mind* (New York: Crowell-Collier & Macmillan, Inc., 1961), pp. 85-90. (Also in anthologies F and TBO.)

The fundamental difference between the "mental" and the "physical" revolves around the way in which the two are known. Mental events and processes are "inherently private," whereas physical phenomena are inherently public, that is, capable of being perceived by anyone who takes the appropriate steps. Mental phenomena are "private" in the sense that only the person having them or experiencing them can know them "directly," that is, without sense perception and without inferring their existence from various pieces of evidence. Such knowledge as we have of our own mental events and states can be gained through "introspection," as it is often called. That I am now thinking or deliberating or feeling pain is known to me in a way which is not available to anyone else.

I can make my mental states *known* to someone else by directly informing him, or he can come to know them by inferring their existence in my consciousness. My behavior after stubbing a toe on a chair will be taken as good evidence by someone observing me that I am in pain. But the mental state itself, my pain, is not felt by another person, and it can become publicly known only if I "publish" it, so to speak. The pain itself is "inherently private."

Physical events and states cannot be known in the same way we know our own mental states. We must receive certain sense perceptions and then draw certain conclusions through a process of reasoning in order to know that which is physical. Even if neurophysiologists at some far distant date could "read our thoughts" by observing some advanced instrument and tell exactly what we were thinking, their knowledge of those states would be different from the kind of knowledge their subjects have of their own mental states. The neurophysiologist relies on "indirect" methods to learn about another's thoughts. Furthermore, even *my* knowledge of the physical processes going on while I think is not received "directly" by me; I must rely upon the sense perceptions and conclusions of the specialist interested in these events in my brain.

The preceding argument may be summarized as follows:

1. I can know that certain mental processes are going on without having to rely upon data received through sense perception. (Such knowledge may be referred to as "immediate" or "direct.")

2. I cannot know that any bodily processes are going on without having to rely upon data received through sense perception. (Such knowledge is called "mediate" or "indirect.")

3. If *A* and *B* are actually the same, then it is impossible that the occurrence of *A* is known without reliance upon sense perception and the occurrence of *B* is known by means of sense perceptions.

4. Let *A* equal "mental processes" and *B* equal "bodily processes."

5. If mental processes and bodily processes are actually the same, then it is impossible that the occurrence of mental processes is known without relying upon sense perception and the occurrence of bodily processes is known by means of sense perceptions.

6. But as Premises 1 and 2 show, mental processes and bodily processes are not known in the same way.

7. Therefore, mental processes and bodily processes are not the same.

Difficulties with This Argument

(1) Can't the same thing have more than one name? My neighbor may call my dog "Sport" while I call him (my dog) "Spot," yet we both are presumably referring to the same animal.

(2) If "mental states" like pain are "inherently private," how can one account for the fact that we interpret certain actions of people to be indicative of their mental states? How could we ever understand another person who said "I am in

pain" if his pain is "inherently private"? How do we know he is referring to an experience at all, let alone the same *type* of experience as I have when I have a toothache?

(3) Is there anything wrong with the statement in this argument, "That I am thinking or deliberating is known to me directly while others must know it indirectly"? Do we ever say, outside of philosophical circles, "I know I am in pain (thinking, deliberating)"? In what circumstances do we say "I know such and such" if not in those situations where some possible evidence would count against our claim to know? But what possible evidence could count against our claim to be in pain? The question of *evidence* for your claim is really out of place, isn't it? You don't *find out* you are in pain or *conclude* on the basis of some pieces of evidence that you are in pain. So why say you *know* you are in pain? What difference is there between saying you *know* you are in pain and saying that you are in pain? What job does the word "know" do in the first statement? If it does not have a use or job, then does it really have any meaning in such a context?

(4) Let's take a close look at this premise in the dualist's argument: "If A and B are identical, then it cannot be that A is known without reference to some sense perception and B is known by means of sense perception." Suppose we let A equal "My present thoughts of Paris" and B equal "The present thoughts of Paris in the tallest man on my block." Now for the sake of argument, let us set aside a previous criticism and admit that it makes sense to say "I know that I am thinking about Paris." Where does this leave the dualist's argument? On his own theory I would know A (that I am thinking of Paris now) without referring to some sense perceptions for such knowledge. Yet in order to know B (the present thoughts of Paris in the tallest man on my block) I should have to resort to a good many perceptions. I would either have to observe the heights of the other men on my block or someone should have to inform me of the facts in this matter. In either case, sense perception on my part is involved. Here is the upshot of this criticism — I *am* the tallest man

on my block and *I* am thinking of Paris right now. My present thoughts of Paris *(A)* and the thoughts of Paris in the tallest man on my block *(B)* are identical; yet that *B* is occurring is known to me in a different way from the way in which I know that *A* is occurring. Consequently, it does *not* follow that if *A* and *B* are identical, then they must be known through the same means. The most crucial premise in the dualist's argument seems to be mistaken, therefore.

"There Is an Aspect of Ourselves Which Remains the Same Through Time, Whereas Our Bodies Undergo Constant Change."

The last argument[6] in this case for dualism attempts to make some philosophical capital out of the alleged fact that we are in one sense the same persons we were a few years, months, and hours ago although during such periods of time the physical changes going on in us have been enormous. It concludes, as we shall see, that the mind or "self" of a person cannot be identical with one's body or any part of the body, particularly the brain. In the course of the argument the notion of "self" plays a crucial role.

It seems clear that we must think of ourselves as relatively permanent beings who continue as we have been regardless of what thoughts we entertain or experiences we have. For one thing, we would not be able to know anything unless we were "continuing agents," that is, unless there were something about us that stayed relatively the same through time. Suppose I know that no one is at home next door. The reasons I know this most likely would be that my neighbor's car is gone, the lights don't come on at night, newspapers pile up on the doorstep, and no one answers the doorbell. When I conclude

---

[6] A. C. Ewing, *The Fundamental Questions of Philosophy* (New York: Crowell-Collier & Macmillan, Inc., 1962), pp. 120-28. (Relevant selection in anthology AB.)

that no one is home, I must be the same person as the one who gathered the bits of evidence and reflected upon them. All cases of knowing involve comparing and connecting data in this way. But it is well known that the body is undergoing change constantly so that from a purely physical point of view we are not the same individuals we were moments ago. Some aspect of ourselves must endure, however, in order to make knowledge possible, and this unchanging part of ourselves may be called "mind" or "self" so as to distinguish it from our bodily processes.

Second, the occurrence of thoughts and decisions implies a thinker and decision-maker which is completely different from these events. How could thoughts which are themselves events *know* anything? Decisions are *made;* they just don't create themselves, and therefore, something must exist to make them which is distinct from what it brings into being.

Third, memory tells me that the person who read a particular book last week is the same person who is writing this now. But my thoughts and experiences which occurred while I read the book last week are over; they belong to the past. However, *I* continue to exist at the present. Therefore, I am more than the mere thoughts and experiences I undergo or have.

There is a difficulty, admittedly, in determining precisely what this "more" is of which I speak. When I reflect on this question I am aware of myself (a) as a being which has these thoughts and feelings, (b) as a being which can *use* various parts of my body,[7] and (c) even as a being which *can be* a number of things in the future. I seem to have a possibility or *capacity* for a wide variety of thoughts and experiences, and if I leave this

---

[7] Plato makes much of the "user-used" distinction in the dialogue *Alcibiades I*. He argues that just as a shoemaker, for example, must be distinguished from the tools he uses in his trade, so the soul must be distinguished from the body because the former uses the latter. The soul uses the parts of the body like the hands and eyes (and even the body as a whole) to accomplish various goals. The selection containing this argument is reprinted in A. Flew, ed., *Body, Mind and Death*, pp. 35-37.

capacity out when I describe what I am, I have omitted an essential item in that description. In short, it seems that we must regard human beings as continuing, relatively permanent agents which cannot be identical with even their own mental acts and states, let alone with their bodies.

Perhaps we should call this enduring agent which *has* various experiences and which uses parts of the body the "pure self" and distinguish it from the "empirical self" which is that aspect of our personalities which is the consequence of our heredity, environment and the experiences we have undergone. The latter may, at least in principle, be completely described and classified by the psychologist, but the "pure self" would be that aspect of ourselves which is inaccessible to investigation by scientific methods and which endures unchanged in spite .of changing conditions in the body, including the most significant bodily change, namely death.[8]

Difficulties with This Argument

(1) What distinguishes one "pure self" from another "pure self"? If my "pure self" is neither affected by nor identical with my experiences or thoughts, how is my "pure self" different from any one else's "pure self"? How are we supposed to know this most important "part" of ourselves?

(2) If the "pure self" is the aspect of man which is non-material because of its supposedly unchanging nature, then this would be the most natural candidate for immortality. If this is so, what kind of existence would such a "being" have after death? If it is supposed to be something different from our powers of memory, feeling, or thought, something above these capacities, just what is it that could continue to exist after death? How can such a dualist even say, "*I* will survive death," when he cannot

---

[8] The notion of the "pure self" will reappear in connection with the problem of free-will, and will be dealt with in greater detail at that time.

tell us what kind of thing he speaks of in this assertion? We know fairly well what we mean by "I am hungry," or "I am unhappy," but how are we to take this new meaning of "I" that is proposed?

(3) If we must presuppose the existence of an unchanging part of man distinct from his brain processes to explain how we can remember the past and draw evidence together so as to arrive at a conclusion, then don't we have to admit that computers have "pure selves" over and above the electrical circuitry and the data composing them? Computers store images and correlate data in order to arrive at conclusions; maybe we should speak to these amazing creatures in personal terms and give them decent burials when they become obsolete.

(4) With regard to the "user-used" distinction mentioned in the argument, several things need attention. First of all, because *A* may be said to use *B* it does not follow that *A* must be mental and *B* must be physical. *A* and *B* may be different organs (or different objects), but both of them may still belong to the same type. For example, the brain may be said to use the heart to get oxygen to its cells. Furthermore, the relationship between a carpenter and his hammer is quite different from that between a carpenter and his hands. A person's hands are rightly considered to be part of himself, whereas a hammer is not. So when a person uses his hands to hold something in place, it is misleading to say that there is (a) the person (the user) and (b) his hands (the used), as though there are two distinct entities involved here.

THE IDENTITY THEORY

Despite their sometimes impressive arguments, dualists have had a difficult time convincing all or even most philosophers that their view of the mind is the correct one. Partly because of difficulties within the dualists' arguments themselves and partly because of great advances in the empirical disciplines of psychology and neurophysiology, some philosophers maintain that mental states and processes are nothing more than very complicated states and processes in the brain. Because they contend that mental processes and brain processes are not two different kinds of events but rather are identical, their view is called the "identity theory." This philosophical theory concerning the mind has had a long history, having been usually advocated by "materialists," those who maintain that everything that exists is some form of matter. However, this view has come into prominence quite recently, and it is its contemporary form which shall receive our attention. The identity theorist[9] argues thus:

Psycho-physical dualism has had an unusually great attraction for many thoughtful people, but it can be shown that no compelling reasons have been given for adopting that position. If the dualists' arguments can be refuted, we have made a strong case for at least the possibility that thoughts and sensations are brain processes. What is being advocated by we identity theorists is that a sensation *is* a brain process in the same sense as lightning *is* a certain kind of electrical charge.

It is obvious that words like "sensation," "thought," and "consciousness" on the one hand, and words like "brain-process" and "physico-chemical event" on the other, do not *mean* the same. That is, the two groups of words are used for different purposes in our language. But just because they are *used* in different ways, it does not follow that they are names for two different things. The expression "the morning star" is used in certain contexts or circumstances, and the expression "the evening star" is used in others, but still they are names for one identical thing. It may well be that someone would know how to use the expression "the morning star" and not know that the

---

[9] J. J. C. Smart, "Sensations and Brain Processes," *Philosophical Review,* LXVIII (1959), 141-56. U. T. Place, "Is Consciousness a Brain-Process?" *British Journal of Psychology,* XLVII (February, 1956), 44-50. Smart's article is reprinted in anthologies EP, MGAS, TBO. Place's article may be found in A. Flew, ed., *Body, Mind and Death,* pp. 276-88 and anthologies AB, F.

evening star was identical with the morning star. The fact that a person knows what thoughts and feelings are, although he might not have the slightest knowledge of neurophysiology and brain-processes does not prove that his mental processes are different from certain processes in his central nervous system.

When the ordinary man reports that something is going on inside him, for example, that he is thinking about something or having a pain, he is not making any judgment as to what *kind* of process this is or in what kind of medium it is taking place. Add to this the fact that an illiterate peasant probably would not know that lightning is a certain kind of electrical discharge caused by ionization of clouds of water vapor. Just because he knows how to recognize lightning and point it out to someone else while at the same time remaining ignorant of electricity, it does not follow that lightning is one thing and electrical discharge caused by ionization, etc., is another thing.

The dualist points out other differences between sensations and brain processes which actually turn out to be merely differences in the ways we use experience-words like "thought" and "feeling" on the one hand and expressions like "brain-processes" on the other. For example, the dualist tells us that we can say that a molecular movement in the brain is in physical space and is fast or slow, but that it would be absurd to say these things of an experience. He also observes that sensations are private, while brain processes are public. It makes sense to say that a number of people could observe A's brain processes but not that this same group could observe A's sensations.

In answer to these objections we may say that so far we have not had any reason to speak of experiences as moving at a certain speed in a certain path or as taking up a certain amount of physical space. If we did have good reasons for speaking this way, we could easily adopt linguistic rules to incorporate such expressions into the language. As a matter of fact, we do speak now of certain experiences *lasting* a certain amount of time and of their being *located* within a certain area. For example, we say, "I have had a pain for the last hour in the small of my back."

100

As for the private-public distinction which is so significant to the dualist, it need only be pointed out that as of now there are no *criteria* for saying, "John is thinking about the party on Saturday night," except John's own reports about what he is thinking. We have adopted a rule of language to the effect that ordinarily whatever John says about the content of his thoughts and sensations is final. After the identity theory has been more widely accepted and ways have been devised for determining by means of instruments what John is thinking, then he won't be the only one who is "directly" aware of his inner experiences.

Difficulties with This Argument

(1) Is not the identity theorist's claim weak when he says that mental processes *may* be brain processes? Does he not base practically his whole case on future findings in the area of neurophysiology, findings which could turn out to cast *doubt* on the identity theory rather than to confirm it?

(2) Presumably not all brain processes are mental processes like thinking, deciding, or feeling. The circulation of blood throughout the brain, for example, does not of itself correspond to some mental act or event. If mental processes are brain processes, *which* processes in the brain belong to the class we speak of as mental? Do the brain processes to which the identity theorist refers, such as perhaps an "S-excitation in the thalamus," refer to anything observable or detectable? Are the expressions referring to brain processes such as "S-excitation in the thalamus" actually left uninterpreted by the identity theorist?

(3) The identity theorist would say that the thoughts corresponding to the statements "All A are B" and "All B are C" are nothing but certain brain processes. And if we conclude, "therefore all A are C," this statement as well corresponds to specific processes in the brain. Yet how can the identity theorist account for the normative or rule-following aspects of such a

course of reasoning? We would say that "All *A* are *C*" is the *correct* statement to make given the other two premises. Must we not conclude that the brain process (or processes) corresponding to the statement "All *A* are *C*" is likewise *correct,* that is, in accord with a rule of reasoning? But what would it mean to say that one event could be more (or less) *logically correct* than some other event? Surely this is a confusion, because the fact that a series of events took place was not logically necessary — that is, there would be no logical contradiction in claiming that a different series of events took place even though it might be factually wrong to do so. In short, since the identity theorist maintains that thoughts are the same as certain events in the brain, he is forced to admit that some events (i.e., brain processes corresponding to conclusions of valid chains of reasoning) are logically correct or valid. What sense does it make to say that a particular occurrence in the world (such as the brain process which happens when a valid conclusion to a deductive argument is drawn) was *logically necessary?* Is it not the case that events take place, but that there is no strict *logical* necessity in their occurring as they do?

A DISPOSITIONAL VIEW OF MIND

Few books in philosophy have created such a stir as Gilbert Ryle's *Concept of Mind.*[10] Philosophers friendly to Ryle's viewpoint and those not so amicable, have regarded the work as a masterpiece of clarity and penetrating philosophical arguments. Perhaps the widespread attention given the book can be further accounted for by the fact that it was the first attempt to attack a large number of problems related to theory of mind employing the methods of so-called "ordinary language" philosophy. The

---

[10] Gilbert Ryle, *The Concept of Mind* (New York: Barnes and Noble, Inc., 1949). Relevant sections reprinted in AB, F, MGAS, ST, TBO.

discussion that follows is by no means intended to be a summary of Ryle's work but rather a statement of the fundamental strands of argument he uses against dualism.

There is one fatal flaw in dualism and especially in Descartes's formulation of that position. It is simply this: if indeed the mind is a special kind of entity or substance in which events take place and certain kinds of acts are performed, and these events and acts are known only to the person in whom they take place, how could we ever come to talk about other people's minds the way we actually do? As a matter of fact, we do know a great deal about other minds. We know how to follow their thoughts, evaluate and appreciate their capacities, teach them how to acquire mental capacities and much more. If the dualistic view were true, we would be utterly unable to do what we do with our mental-conduct concepts. The dualist, in short, proposes that we accept a theory of mind which, if true, would make impossible what we do every day of our lives, namely correctly describe and refer to people's mental qualities.

What *do* we say about minds when we talk about them in non-philosophical discussions? Suppose we say that "Bob knows Russian." Should we think of Bob's knowledge of Russian as some non-material entity or entities existing in a hidden, ghostly way in Bob's "soul" or something of that sort? Should we, as the dualist is prone to do, think of Bob's knowing Russian as a "spiritual" act which his mind is performing behind the scenes, separated from public view? Not at all. Just pay attention to the circumstances in which we make such statements. What do we mean when we say, "Bob knows Russian"? People who have never even heard of the dualistic theory know perfectly well how to use expressions like this in describing a person's mental qualities.

If Bob knows Russian, we would expect him to be able to do certain things in a certain manner. He should be able to pass an exam in the language, converse in Russian, read printed material in Russian, etc. His knowledge of Russian seems to be a number of different capacities which he could exercise with some degree of skill or mastery. From the way we use such expressions as "X knows Y" it would be more correct to call knowledge an ability or capacity, in short, a disposition or dispositions of a certain sort.

It is roughly the same when we say that Bob is intelligent. We are pointing out that he has certain abilities or capacities which are exercised in testable, observable ways. A person's intelligence, therefore, is not an event or a state which is observable *or unobservable* to Bob or anyone. Since skills, abilities or capacities are dispositions, it would be incorrect to say they are the kind of thing which could happen or not happen, be observed or not observed. The *exercises* of these abilities and capacities are the kind of thing that can happen and which can be observed, but the abilities themselves are neither witnessable nor unwitnessable.

If we keep these considerations in mind, then, we can see why it makes no sense to say, "There occur mental processes," and "There occur physical processes." To join or disjoin these two statements makes it look as though mental processes are the types of things which can be compared and related to physical events although the former are purported to happen in a different place, have different effects and can be known in a different way from the latter. Descartes did actually disjoin the two and contrasted mental processes with physical processes. It was then a simple step to go on and speak of the mind as the *place* where mental processes and acts occur, albeit a ghostly, private area not subject to public scrutiny. It is true that doing long division and thinking about Saturday night's date are mental processes, but this does not entitle us to contrast them with physical processes. One's calculating can be done silently or out loud or on paper, but what makes it an act of the intellect is not dependent on its being private or public. What makes it an intellectual act is the manner in which it is done, that is, that certain rules are followed by the person performing the act.

If people's minds were actually what the dualist takes

them to be (non-material places where various kinds of events and acts take place known only to one person, namely the person experiencing them) then we would not be able to make all the testable, factual assertions about them which we make every day. "The mind is not the topic of sets of untestable categorical propositions but the topic of sets of testable hypothetical and semi-hypothetical propositions."[11] For example, to say "Bob decided to take Physics," is not to say something about the inner life of Bob, but to say, "If Bob shops for books, then he'll buy a Physics text," and "If the Physics class meets at 11:00 A.M., then Bob will not take European History which meets at the same time," and so on. We describe the workings of a person's mind, then, by describing certain aspects of his behavior and how he *would* behave *if* he were presented with a given set of circumstances. "To find that most people have minds (though idiots and infants in arms do not) is simply to find that they are able and prone to do certain sorts of things, and this we do by witnessing the sorts of things they do. Indeed we do not merely discover that there are other minds; we discover what specific qualities of intellect and character particular people have."[12]

It is tempting to adopt the dualist's conceptual scheme when we theorize about the mind and talk as though events in the mental world (like thoughts, feelings, and decisions) *cause* events in the physical world, such as the movements of our limbs and other observable states of our bodies. But to theorize in such fashion is to commit a "category mistake," that is, "it represents the facts of mental life as if they belonged to one logical type or category (or range of types or categories), when they actually belong to another."[13] The dualist regards a statement such as "Pete acted as he did because of vanity," as a straightforward, categorical assertion about certain events

[11] Ryle, *The Concept of Mind*, p. 46.
[12] Ryle, *The Concept of Mind*, p. 61.
[13] Ryle, *The Concept of Mind*, p. 16.

occurring in Pete which *caused* his behavior. The dualist construes the word "because" in this context to mean the same thing as it does in the statement "the window was broken because the stone hit it."

Instead of regarding statements about facts of mental life as categorical, causal assertions, we should view them as being hypothetical and lawlike in nature. That is, when it is said that "Pete acted because of vanity," what we mean is that if Pete is given the opportunity or occasion, he will tend to behave in a vain way — he will boast a lot, he will draw attention to himself, etc. To say that he is vain is to indicate the type of situation in which we can expect or predict he will engage in certain kinds of behavior. When we know that a given person is vain, we are in possession of something which might be called an "inference ticket"; "it licenses the inference to the thing's being the case from something else which may or may not be specified in the statement."[14] The primary category mistake which Descartes and other dualists commit, then, is to treat the facts of mental life under the category of cause when, in fact, they should be treated under the category of law; instead of construing statements about the facts of mental life as categorical assertions about occult, privately observable events, one should regard them as hypothetical statements which may justify inferences concerning an individual's publicly observable behavior.

Difficulties with The Argument

(1) Can a dispositional analysis of the human mind adequately explain our ability to acquire, change or eliminate a certain disposition? For example, one might have a tendency to lose one's temper easily, but through various means that same person might acquire a tendency for self-control in the same circumstances which previously made him "blow his top."

---

[14] Ryle, *The Concept of Mind*, p. 127.

Doesn't it seem that we have the ability to control some of our dispositions? If this ability or capacity is a disposition, shouldn't it be considered on a different logical level from all the rest of our dispositions?

(2) Does Ryle's analysis of the concept of mind lean too heavily on the principle that the meaning of a given statement is equivalent to the ways we would verify that statement? Can we adequately explain the meaning of statements about our own and other people's mental states by rephrasing them in terms of hypothetical statements? For example, suppose we say, "Jones believes in the existence of a perfect personal being, i.e., God." What sorts of behavior would we expect Jones to engage in (or be prepared to engage in) in light of his purported belief? Does this statement mean (a) "If Jones is able to attend a place of worship, then he will go," (b) "If Jones is confronted by an atheist, then he will defend the proposition that God exists," and (c) "If Jones considers himself to require divine guidance, then he will pray"? Couldn't Jones have a belief in the existence of God and do *none* of these things? Would we deny that Jones believes in God if he did not do any of these things under any circumstances? We seen to be able to *understand*, however, the statement, "Jones believes in the existence of God," without listing any publicly observable behavior which Jones might or might not engage in. How is this possible if Ryle's analysis of mental states (of which belief is an example) is correct?

(3) It seems obvious that thoughts occur at specific times and that thinking of various kinds takes place without any distinctive accompanying behavior. Ryle admits as much in various parts of *The Concept of Mind*. The question is, *where* do these events take place? If they do not take place in a ghostly, inner world called the mind by the dualist, must they not be processes in the brain? Events or processes must take place somewhere, so is not Ryle compelled to accept the identity theory of mind, which views mental processes as being identical to certain kinds of brain processes?

IMPLICATIONS FOR IMMORTALITY

We began the discussion of opposing theories of mind by pointing out that if a strong case could be made for dualism, then we would have fairly good grounds for holding that the personal survival of death is possible. The dualist would most likely make it stronger than this, contending that the belief in man's immortality would be highly probable for the reason that man is not only material in nature, but also composed in part of that which is not subject to the destructive processes of nature. However, with each of dualistic arguments serious difficulties were suggested which cast considerable doubt upon the dualistic view. Furthermore, even if the dualist could overcome the criticisms leveled at his position and prove that he was correct, it would not necessarily follow that man will survive death. Even if it could be shown that mental processes are different in kind from brain processes, it could still be that the two cannot occur apart from one another. The occurrence of mental processes may very well depend upon the existence of a functioning central nervous system. So even if dualism were proved to be a correct view, the most that could reasonably be concluded regarding the issue of immortality is this: disembodied experiences might indeed be possible, but any claim beyond this would be unwarranted.

As far as the identity theory is concerned, it too has implications for the question of immortality. If this view were the correct theory of mind, then there would be good reason for doubting the possibility of personal survival of death on philosophical grounds. If so-called "mental" processes are nothing over and above certain types of processes in the brain, then when the brain as a functioning organ is destroyed, all experience will cease. It would be just as ridiculous to suggest that brain processes could continue to occur after death as it would be to claim that the liver continues to secrete bile even though that organ has decomposed.

The implications for immortality arising out of Ryle's dispositional analysis of mind are considerably more hazy. At first glance it would look like an open and shut case. We are tempted to say that Ryle's view clearly excludes the possibility of personal survival of death on the grounds that his position argues against thinking of mind as a spiritual entity distinct in nature from the body. Since Ryle attacks Descartes's view of mind, and Descartes's view seems to entail the position that the mind is undestructible, it is easy to see why one would think Ryle's analysis of mind would entail the rejection of immortality.

However, Ryle is silent about the whole question and, I think, for understandable reasons. If he were to deny that there could be any disembodied experiences or the exercises of capacities and dispositions after death, on what grounds would he make such a denial? It seems the only reason he could give for such a position would be that dispositions depend for their existence upon a functioning nervous system. But Ryle would seem to be committed against such a way of talking about dispositions. First, he would probably not want to say that dispositions either *depend* or *do not depend* upon something else, because he has argued that the concept of mind is on a different logical level from that of the body, its processes and movements. No comparison or relation, therefore, between the two seems possible from Ryle's point of view.

It might be that Ryle would pass the question concerning the physical mechanisms involved in dispositions and their exercises along to the neurophysiologist, contending that as a philosopher he is not competent to judge such a matter. The philosopher, he might well say, should confine his work to elucidating *concepts* such as disposition, motive and thought and leave other questions for investigation by the empirical sciences involved.

It is even more probable that Ryle (and a good many other philosophers) would seriously challenge the meaningfulness of the expression "disembodied experiences." What would the exercise of a disposition be if one had no body with which to speak, hear and perform any familiar muscular movements? The whole notion of a "person" who performs actions which are unobservable in principle either to others or to himself strikes some as more than slightly odd.

ARGUMENTS FOR IMMORTALITY BASED ON MAN'S MORAL AND VALUING CAPACITIES

Besides the various arguments for dualism which have been used to bolster belief in immortality, there are those which draw their support from certain aspects of man's capacity for making judgments concerning what is morally right and worthwhile striving for or having. The philosophers using this approach point out that unless human personality continues beyond death, man's highest faculties (the ones which distinguish him from other creatures) are somehow stripped of significance and lasting value. The first argument of this type which we shall consider was advanced by Immanuel Kant, the German genius who lived in the eighteenth century and has influenced the course of Western philosophy ever since. His case goes something like this:[15]

We have an obligation to obey completely or perfectly the moral law, since it would be unreasonable to hold that our moral obligations extend only so far as *partial* obedience to the moral law. Since we have the obligation to obey perfectly the moral law, such obedience must be possible. The principle of "ought implies can" applies here. In other words, if a person has a genuine obligation to do X, then it follows that the carrying out of the obligation must be possible. We would not say, for ex-

---

[15] Immanuel Kant, *Critique of Practical Reason*, Book II, Chapter II, Section V.

ample, that a kleptomaniac has a moral obligation to stop stealing and our reason would be that such a person has no ability to stop stealing. He is inwardly compelled to steal and hence cannot carry out the obligation to stop this type of behavior.

However, no person is capable at any moment of his earthly existence of living in conformity with what the moral law demands. But man's inability in *this* life to live up to his moral obligations perfectly does not release him from those duties. Since a person has certain moral obligations, it must be possible to carry them out, and if that is not possible in *this* life, then there must be *another* life in which perfect moral obedience is possible. Such a state of perfect obedience or complete virtue can be attained only in an endless existence of the personality where progress towards the goal of perfection may take place. Consequently, personality must continue to exist beyond its present life on earth. Unless a person continues to live beyond death, we would have to admit that the moral law commands something which is incapable of being obeyed. But this would violate the principle that "ought implies can" and thereby make a shambles of our moral duties and the meaningfulness of the moral life.

Since the remaining arguments[16] are rather short, we shall present all of them before discussing the difficulties with Kant's argument for immortality. These arguments are mainly based upon the existence of moral and aesthetic capacities in man:

First, man is equipped for much more than a merely earthly environment with its necessities. All of the faculties which distinguish us from other animals are not strictly necessary for the preservation of our lives. The love of beauty and the attempt to know what is morally right, for example, cannot be reduced to the status of being merely tools for success in the struggle for survival. Shouldn't we conclude that since man is outfitted with equipment which exceeds the requirements of

---

[16] These and other arguments for immortality are presented in a short, lucid essay by J. H. Holmes, entitled "Ten Reasons for Believing in Immortality." It is reprinted in anthology EP.

this life, that he was destined for a continued life beyond this one? Just as we infer the length of a ship's voyage by the equipment it possesses (a little boat with neither a source of power nor protection for its passengers would not ordinarily be bound for a transoceanic cruise), so we may infer that man has a longer life than the one upon which he is presently embarked.

Second, there is a lack of proportion between one's personality and his body. As the individual ages, the body begins to slow down, and the processes of decay slowly takes their inevitable toll. But our personality or souls, if you please, continue to grow and mature. Our purposes and our potentialities are as inexhaustible as they were in earlier days. There is, in short, no completion to the life of the personality though there obviously· is an ending for the body. Though not a proof in the strict sense of the term, this fact of disproportion in ourselves "points to" a continuance of the uncompleted life of the personality after death.

Third, consider ourselves as valuing beings. We endow things with value and meaning. We do not find meaning and value just waiting for us in the physical world. Anything that is really worthwhile has that quality because some human being *regards* it as valuable. Without man upon the scene of nature and material things, nothing would be of significance or value. Now, if this view of the origin of values is admitted, how can we sincerely believe that man is subject to the same ultimate fate as that which overtakes every other thing in the world, namely eventual destruction? If nothing has value apart from our endowing things with value, then man must be exceedingly valuable himself. It would be the height of absurdity to think that what is supremely valuable could be completely destroyed as are things with no value in and of themselves. And, furthermore, it would be highly irrational to conclude that what is of supreme value and the source of value (human personality) could be destroyed by those minute specks of matter we call viruses or even by a small puff of air getting into the bloodstream. For if human personality is destroyed along with the body when its death is caused by something like these things, then we would have an arrangement where that which is of no value at all in itself destroys that which is the very source and basis of what is valuable. Surely this would be most absurd. The only way to avoid such a conclusion is to hold that human personality is not destructible but endures despite the death of the body.

Difficulties with These Arguments

(1) Kant's argument faces several crucial problems. First, it is based upon the premise that there are certain acts which everyone ought to refrain from doing and others which they ought to perform. The defense of such a thesis is no small task. However, for the sake of argument let us leave this question until Chapter Five, where we can deal more deeply with Kant's moral theory. Second, what would it be like to engage in moral behavior without a body with which to act? If the future life is to provide us opportunity to progress toward perfection, what would count as an ethical act in such a state? What would count as an *act*? Third, even supposing that the two previous problems can be adequately answered by Kant, yet another remains. If progress toward moral perfection is endless, as Kant insists it must be, then how can he maintain that it is possible to attain? If a person were to progress toward a goal, but such progress were endless, then it would seem that the goal is unattainable. It is doubtful that we should call such endless existence "progress" at all if the goal of this activity (complete holiness) is not possible of attainment by a finite or limited being. However, if the goal of perfect obedience to the moral law is not possible to attain *either* in this life *or* in any other, then on Kant's own principles, we should conclude that we have no obligation to obey perfectly the moral law.

(2) Can we always infer that just because a ship has

equipment suitable for transoceanic voyages, it either has or will make such a journey? Suppose the ship we see in the harbor is used only for sightseeing or entertainment. Whether or not the ship actually uses all its equipment in a distant voyage cannot be determined simply by discovering its capabilities. In like manner, even if human beings have capacities which are not strictly necessary for mere survival on earth, we cannot infer that they will actually make use of these capacities in some other "sea of life" after this one is concluded.

(3) Must we conclude that our capacities for enjoyment of beauty, for being morally aware and for regarding certain objects and experiences as worthwhile are not "equipment for this life"? They may not be abolutely necessary for man's mere survival, but don't animals (which dualists usually regard as unable to survive death) likewise have some capacities which are not necessary for their self-preservation? For example, it is well known that animals have a capacity for play. Having capacities which are not necessary for the mere preservation of life is not a characteristic which distinguishes human beings from other kinds of creatures. Therefore, an argument for man's survival after death based upon a recognition of such capacities would have weight only if the argument were used to prove the continued existence of *all* living things after death.

(4) Is it true that the personality continues to grow with age while one's so-called physical capacities deteriorate? Has the dualist forgotten about senility, increased narrowness of mind, and pettiness that can often develop with advanced age?

(5) Aren't we familiar with cases where that which is of greater value and significance is destroyed by what is of minute value? For example, suppose the life's work of a medical researcher is destroyed in a fire. This would be a case where that which is of lesser value and importance destroys that which is of inestimable significance. So even if it could be shown that the mind and body are different and that the former is of more value than the latter, it would not follow that physical things could not destroy one's mental capacities.

114

CONCLUDING REMARKS

The impression might have been given that the only reason philosophers are interested in topics related to so-called mental activities is that they have bearing on the issue of immortality. While it is true that investigations in philosophy of mind frequently get their impetus from this issue, it is nevertheless not the whole story. We shall see shortly how mental-conduct concepts (as Ryle called them) like choice, desire, intention, and action play a crucial role in problems related to the issue of free will and moral responsibility.

Furthermore, regardless of how we shall ultimately end up (whether continuing to exist after death or some day ceasing to exist entirely), we cannot wholly ignore inquiry into the nature of those capacities and experiences which are distinctively human. In attempting to gain a greater understanding of those features which are characteristic of man, we must explore and elucidate such concepts as perception, feeling, understanding, desire, choice, and knowledge. If these concepts had no bearing upon *any* philosophical problem (which they most emphatically do), they would still be worthwhile pursuing in their own right.

SUGGESTIONS FOR FURTHER STUDY

Anthologies

AB, Part 4; EP, Part 3; F, Part 3; MGAS, pp. 361-420; ST, Chap. 5; TBO, Parts 1 and 2; TH, Chaps. 9 and 10.

Others

Flew, Antony, ed., *Body, Mind and Death.* New York: Macmillan & Company, 1964.

115

Chappell, V. C., ed., *Philosophy of Mind.* Englewood Cliffs, N.J.: Prentice-Hall, Inc., 1962.

Hook, Sidney, ed., *Dimensions of Mind,* pp. 174-280. New York: Crowell-Collier & Macmillan, Inc., 1961.

THE PROBLEM OF FREE WILL AND DETERMINISM

IV

Am I Ever Responsible for My Actions?

A day rarely passes in which we do not make statements blaming or excusing some aspect of either our own or someone else's behavior. We can remember numerous instances where we have either held a person responsible for what he has done in a certain situation or have excused him from responsibility depending upon certain conditions in existence before and during the commission of the act. For example, if we were to learn that Otto Otpelk, whom we know to be a kleptomaniac, has stolen a watch, we would most likely excuse his action (though we might take steps to see that he receives proper psychiatric treatment). We would probably say something like "Poor fellow, he couldn't help it," or "Otpelk can't be held responsible for stealing; he is under a compulsion, you know." On the other hand, suppose your roommate named Richard Rebbor, whom you know quite well has no record of a similar mental disorder, very methodically schemes and steals your prize camera, then tries to shift the blame to someone else. In this case you would most likely say that Rebbor ought to be brought to justice and punished in some way for his act. You would, provided you were assured that he was in control of himself at the time of the act, most likely hold Rebbor morally responsible and feel justified in telling others what a scoundrel he is.

If you were asked to justify the different treatments you accorded Otpelk and Rebbor, you might resort to an explanation along the following lines: "Poor Otpelk *can't help* what he does when he steals. He is *not free* to refrain from stealing. He acts *involuntarily* when it comes to such things. In effect, he is forced to do what he did just as much as if someone had made him steal at the point of a gun. Surely if a person does something not *of his own free will*, it would be grossly unjust to censure him morally for his behavior. To regard Otpelk's stealing of the watch morally reprehensible would be about the same as condemning his dog in moral terms for biting the mailman. Both Otpelk, when he steals, and his dog, when he bites, cannot help what they do, and hence do not act freely.

"Rebbor, on the other hand, acted on his own free will. He knew what he was doing because he schemed for days in order to perpetrate his crime and get away with it. He was not forced at all. At any point he could have chosen to leave the camera alone and try to earn some money in order to buy one of his own. He even admitted later that he just wanted the camera and didn't feel like going to work in order to buy one. This seemed to him like the easiest way of getting what he wanted, as he himself reported."

You may feel fairly secure in the belief that you have judged the acts of Otpelk and Rebbor correctly and fairly, given the set of conditions which prevailed in each case. But suppose after probing deeper into the two cases you find that Otpelk knows he is a kleptomaniac, has been offered free psychiatric treatment and has refused it on numerous occasions. Would you still excuse his stealing after learning this new piece of information? Would you now hold him morally responsible for not accepting psychiatric help when it was offered?

Or suppose we were to learn that during Rebbor's childhood his pleadings for a new camera had been continually refused, and that on one occasion his father took away from him a camera which Rebbor had happened to find. Suppose also that he had sincerely tried to find work for the past two years but had been turned down wherever he went. What would be your attitude then toward his stealing your camera in the light of such facts?

One thing at least seems clear — whether or not we are willing to hold a person responsible for a given act depends upon whether or not the agent could have refrained from performing just that act and done something else instead. If a person could not have behaved in any way other than that in which he did, we find that in the interest of fair play he should not be morally censured for his act. Now the all-important question is (and here the philosophical problem of freedom and responsibility hits us with full force): Can *any* person *ever* do anything other than what he does, given the makeup of his character and the circumstances in which he finds himself? How can we have any assurance that we are not compelled (if not externally, then from within) to perform just those acts which we do? Just as Otpelk, the kleptomaniac, may not know the true source or causes of his stealing, so all of us may be the victims of inner forces and drives of which we may be totally ignorant in spite of a strong feeling or conviction that we do on occasion act without constraint.

Just suppose that after due reflection and investigation we should have to admit that all of our actions are the inevitable results of causes over which we have no control — what would it matter? What implications would such an admission carry with it? It should be easy to see that the consequences for the ethical sphere of life would be considerable. Consideration of the following argument should bring this out:

1. If person *P* was normally obliged to perform act *A* but did *B* instead, then that person must have had the ability to perform act *A*.

2. But no one ever has the ability to do anything other than what he actually does.

3. Therefore, person *P* was not morally obliged to perform act *A* instead of act *B*, which he in fact did.

Premise One states that a necessary condition for a person's being morally obliged to perform a given act is that person's being able to perform that act. "Being able to do *A*" could mean a number of things, of course. Suppose we use an example to explain what could be involved in "being able." You are out for a leisurely drive in your car and come upon an accident victim who is bleeding profusely from his arm. It might be said that you are *able* to render assistance to the unfortunate fellow in one or all of the following senses. (a) You have the *opportunity* to help him: you're in the vicinity. (b) You *know* what would count as assistance in such a case: you know the bleeding must be stopped, and either you know how to stop it yourself or you know how to summon someone who does. (c) You are not prevented from rendering assistance by some compelling factor: you are not paralyzed, no one is physically restraining you from helping, and no compelling psychological drive forces you to flee the scene.

If you have a moral obligation to render assistance to the accident victim, then you would have to be able to do so in these three senses. If you were not in the vicinity, did not comprehend the circumstances in which you found yourself, or were prevented from helping because of some compelling factor, then it would seem grossly unfair, if not meaningless, to assert that you nevertheless had a moral obligation to render assistance to the bleeding victim.

Premise Two is the more crucial of the three premises,

120

since one's acceptance of it as true places him on one side regarding the problem of freedom and responsibility and one's rejection of it on another. Discussion of the reasons given for regarding the premise either as true or as false will constitute the major part of the present chapter, so we shall not go into them at this point. Let us continue with the argument stated above, however, and see what conclusion we are logically compelled to draw if we accept Premises One and Two as true.

It should be recalled that the conclusion of the generalized form of the argument was: "Person *P* was not morally obliged to perform act *A* instead of act *B*, which he in fact did." But let us return to the accident example to make things more clear. Let us regard "act *A*" as "lend assistance to a bleeding accident victim," "act *B*" as "refuse to lend assistance," and let "person *P*" equal "you." Our conclusion now reads: "You were not morally obliged to lend assistance to the bleeding accident victim instead of what you actually did (which, let us suppose, was to refuse to give aid to the person bleeding to death)." What the acceptance of Premises One and Two commits a person to is the position that no one has a moral obligation to do something other than what he does or that no one is morally obliged to refrain from what he is actually doing. For "person *P*" and for "acts *A* and *B*" in our generalized argument, we can substitute *any* person and *any* acts so that there could never be a case in which a person had a moral obligation to do anything other than what he actually did. The position one takes, then, concerning the truth or falsity of the statement that "no one ever has the ability to do anything other than what he does" has some far-reaching implications for the way in which we are to view the moral aspect of human conduct.

A brief look at the three major positions taken on this issue might be in order before we launch into a more full-scale analysis of arguments advanced in support of them.

(1) "HARD" OR EXTREME DETERMINISM. The hard determinist contends that we are *never* responsible for our actions

because there is no such thing as a free choice. All our choices, of which our actions are consequences, happen because of factors over which we have no control. What these controlling factors are vary from person to person, but in each case our choices and ultimately our actions are caused by our character at any given moment, and we did not shape our own characters. We are helpless, therefore, to do anything other than what we actually do regardless of how "free" we might think our choices are. If moral judgments are to be meaningful at all, their sole purpose is that of helping to cause people to act in certain desirable ways.

(2) INDETERMINISM OR LIBERTARIANISM. The indeterminist maintains that it is desirable to retain our notions of moral praise and blame (in short, moral responsibility for certain actions) in order to preserve meaningful distinctions between what is morally right and morally wrong. Part of what is meant by saying that a given act is morally wrong is that the agent deserves moral blame and that the act ought not to have been done. But how can moral obligations and moral praise or blame make any sense if all of a person's actions are caused by factors outside his control? It would be senseless and grossly unfair to hold a person accountable for actions he cannot help committing. If we say "Rebbor ought not to have done X," we imply that he *could* have chosen to do other than X but freely chose to do X anyway. The hard determinist's position makes a mockery of important moral distinctions in life and actually destroys the meaning of ethical categories. The hard determinist, furthermore, reduces man to the level of a complex machine tossed about by blind, irrational forces of fate. In order to preserve man's status as a moral agent we must preserve the notion that a "free act" is one which originates within some part of the agent's personality which is not merely the product of heredity and environment, factors over which he has no control.

(3) "SOFT" OR MODERATE DETERMINISM. The soft determinist attempts to reconcile the two preceding positions concerning moral responsibility. He wants to maintain that our

actions do have causes and are, therefore, determined, but that this does not imply that we are always to be excused for our behavior. In short, the soft determinist maintains that our actions are *caused* but *not compelled*, so that meaningful responsibility may still be preserved. The hard determinist mistakenly concludes that since our acts have causes, we are forced or compelled to act as we do. And such a position, if true, would indeed negate moral responsibility. Actually, to say that *A* causes *B* is merely to say that given a sufficient knowledge of *A* we may accurately predict the occurrence of *B*. The indeterminist's position as well is faulty because of his outright denial of the principle of determinism which states that every event is caused.

ARGUMENTS FOR
HARD OR EXTREME DETERMINISM

"Actions Are the Inevitable Results of One's Character." [1]

In order to understand and explain why things happen as they do, both the scientist and the ordinary man employ what may be called the principle of determinism. This principle states simply that every event is caused. Events do not simply happen for no rhyme or reason, and things do not exist without something's bringing them into existence. Without recourse to such a principle both scientific investigation and our everyday experience would face constant confusion and frustration. For example, if our automobile will not start, we assume immediately that something is causing the malfunction and we seek to find

---

[1] Paul Edwards, "Hard and Soft Determinism," in *Determinism and Freedom in the Age of Modern Science*, ed. Sidney Hook (New York: Crowell-Collier & Macmillan, Inc., 1961), pp. 117-26.

that cause in order to remedy the situation. It doesn't cross our minds for a minute that perhaps there is no cause or reason why it will not start. We constantly make use of the principle that every event is caused, and we find it most useful for discovering and explaining what happens in our world.

But we should not arbitrarily limit the application of this valuable principle. We must carry it with us in seeking to explain events in *all* areas of experience. Not only can we use it to determine why the jalopy won't work, but we can (and do) use it to explain what causes people to act as they do. We should ask what made Otpelk steal the watch or what caused Rebbor to stop looking for a job. People do not ordinarily act capriciously; there are usually motives behind their behavior and various desires which seek fulfillment. We can discover the causes of our decisions and actions just as surely as we can discover causes for events in the non-human realm.

When we investigate the character or the type of person Rebbor is, we can see why he stole the camera. The cause is not obvious at first glance to be sure, but if we delve deeply enough into his past, particularly his childhood, we find certain facts which help explain his present actions. We find, for example, that he had an intense desire to own a camera and that he had always been thwarted by his father in fulfilling that desire. Later in life, when he was presented the opportunity of owning a camera, his desire for it caused him to steal from his roommate.

We may say, then, that motives or desires of various kinds cause our actions in the final analysis. Certainly we may choose or decide upon a certain course of action, but we must always press further in our search for causes. *What caused us to have the desires and motives which are part of our character?* Hereditary and environmental influences make us the kinds of persons we happen to be, so that what we do is traceable to these remote but determining factors.

The crucial point here is that we cannot justly be held accountable for the influences either of our heredity or our

124

environment in shaping our character. We do not choose our own characters with their motives, desires, likes and dislikes. These are what they are because of factors over which we had no control. Since we cannot justly be held accountable for our character (because we had no voice in its shaping), and our decisions proceed from our characters, we cannot be held responsible for the actions which inevitably result from the decisions we make.

"Wait a minute," someone says, "maybe we didn't choose our character in the beginning of its development, but later on in life we surely have the ability to change certain features of our character we no longer deem desirable. By an effort of will we can work toward undoing certain influences of the past. We can even seek assistance from a psychiatrist if that is necessary. Surely, character is a plastic thing and not forever solidified by its past influences."

The hard determinist replies with a question. Where do we get the ability to make changes in our character? Is it conjured up out of mid-air by some magical quality of the mind? If we had the ability to effect changes in our character either on our own or by means of the help of another, then this ability was either with us all the time or somehow acquired.[2] If it was with us all the time, then it too was a product of heredity or environment, and we can neither be praised for having such an ability nor blamed for not having it. If we acquired the inclination and the ability to change our character, it would have to have been because someone we were associated with or something else in our environment produced this factor in us. If we have the ability to change our character, it is because of factors over which we had no control. Some people are just fortunate to have had desirable influences around them, and there are others who are less lucky because they have been surrounded by

---

[2] W. I. Matson, "The Irrelevance of Free Will to Moral Responsibility," *Mind*, LXV (October, 1956), 495.

corrupting influences. People of the latter type are the poor unfortunates who commit socially undesirable acts and populate our penal institutions.

If we recognize the true causes of an individual's actions as being beyond his control, we will be less quick to brand him as "immoral" or "bad" and cease to heap vengeance upon him. Instead of smugly preaching to people and punishing them for their actions, we should seek to arrange conditions and influences which cause people to act as they do in such a way that they will come to desire what is morally right. The only fair place to attach responsibility is to those impersonal factors which mold us into the kinds of persons who sometimes commit acts which are damaging to ourselves and others.

We should still retain our categories of "right," "wrong," "good," and "evil," but we must use them purely for educative purposes. Parents should train their children in such a way that they will feel revulsion towards aggressiveness and selfishness, for example, so that they will be less likely to cultivate these tendencies in their characters. With proper training and the right environment, people could be caused to act in more socially desirable ways. Moral talk, then, could still be retained as a powerful influence in shaping the right kinds of character. The brightest hope for making people truly ethical is to recognize that actions are caused and then discover these causes so as to bring about the desired effects in human behavior.

Difficulties with This Argument

(1) Does it make sense to say that we are not responsible for our characters because we do not choose them? What would it be like to "choose one's character"? Presumably, it would have to be something like "choosing one's motives and desires," since the hard determinist apparently understands the term "character" as encompassing such things as the motives, de-

126

sires, and tendencies of a person. Now the question becomes, "What would it be for a person to *choose* his motives?" It is perfectly proper to say that we *refer to* motives or reasons in justifying or explaining a certain way of behaving, but what does it mean to say that a motive could be "chosen"? How would one go about choosing motives for an action in the first place? If we made a deliberate attempt to choose a motive for a proposed action we would probably end up with a rationalization and not a *reason* for acting at all. Consequently, if it makes no sense to say that one could "choose" his own character (and especially his motives for acting), it likewise makes no sense to say that we did *not* choose our character, as the hard determinist claims.

(2) Aren't we all familiar with actions of our own which have been "out of character" for us? Haven't we at one time or another done that which was purely capricious or whimsical so as to astound not only our friends but perhaps even ourselves with such an unpredictable act? How is this sort of experience to be explained on the hard determinist position?

(3) If the determinist thinks that moral categories should be retained in our lives, what could he mean by saying that a particular act is "bad" or "morally wrong"? Can he consistently say that a wrong act is one which *ought* not to have been done? If it is claimed that X *ought* not to have been done, then must it not also be admitted that X did not *have* to be done?

(4) What is the status of the determinist's key statement, "Every event is caused"? If it is true (as the determinist claims it is), in what way is it true? Is it true analytically, i.e., can its truth be determined merely by examining the meanings of the words "cause" and "event"? This seems very doubtful, because there does not seem to be any logical contradiction involved in saying "Not all events are caused," which there should be if the statement "All events are caused" were analytic.

Perhaps the determinist's principle is synthetic, that is, capable of being confirmed or disproved through sense experience and scientific investigation. Perhaps it is a generalization from experience in the same way as "all crows are black" is. But if it is viewed as a synthetic statement, then the determinist is faced with other difficulties. How can it be claimed that enough events have been examined in order to justify the assertion that *every* event is caused? For every event investigated and shown to be caused, there must be thousands upon thousands which have not been observed and which cannot be observed because of their happening before man appeared on earth and developed sophisticated powers of observation. Then take into account the innumerable events taking place within sub-atomic particles of matter. These are happening with such tremendous frequency and in so many places that to claim that on the basis of the comparatively few events investigated we have a good sample of *all* events seems highly questionable. The statement "Every event is caused" does not seem to be on the same footing, therefore, with the assertion that all crows are black. The number of crows observed is sufficiently high when compared with the total number of crows which exist to justify the claim that all crows are black. But the number of events observed is extremely minute when compared with the total number of events which are occuring. Consequently, general statements about *all* events must be taken with a grain of salt.

In short, if the statement "Every event is caused" is neither analytically nor synthetically true, then in what way can it be true? Perhaps it should be viewed only as a kind of exhortation to scientists which, in effect, says "Keep looking for the causes of events." But, of course, exhortations can be neither true nor false, because they do not assert or claim anything.

(5) There is a question as to what the determinist would regard as counting *against* the statement that "every event is caused." If we were to bring up events which did not appear to be caused or at least whose causes were unknown, the determinist would most likely reply that there *must* be a cause of these events and express faith that someday they will be discovered. Now such defiance of the unknown and faith in the suc-

cess of the scientific method may be admirable. But by refusing to allow any fact to count against the assertion "Every event is caused," the determinist is admitting that his statement is not synthetic or contingent. If a statement is true *no matter what*, then it must be analytic. However, we would not be uttering a self-contradictory statement if we said "Some events are not caused." Since the causal principle "Every event is caused" is neither synthetic nor analytic, what status could it have? About the only thing it could be is something like a useful, working principle, roughly like the exhortation "Keep looking for causes." However, exhortations, though capable of being obeyed or disobeyed, cannot be true or false.

"All of Our Actions Are Caused by the Motive of Self-Interest." [3]

When moralists argue that a person ought to engage in certain sorts of activity or refrain from other kinds of action, they assume that people are morally responsible for their behavior. They say, for example, that if person A sees person B in immediate need of assistance and A refuses to extend some sort of help, A has acted immorally and is morally reprehensible.

But philosophers who argue like this do not realize that individual A *could* not help B unless he deemed it in his (that is, A's) self-interest. Human beings never act except from the motive of self-interest. It is impossible for a person to engage in a particular activity unless he considers the action to be of more benefit to himself than any other open to him at the time. Consequently, no one should be blamed for what he either does or fails to do. The only course open to us would be to convince A that it was in his own interest to help B. If A is convinced of this

---

[3] Baron Holbach, *The System of Nature*, Vol. I, Chaps. XI and XII, trans. H. D. Robinson, first published in 1770. (Relevant selections reprinted in anthologies AB, EP.)

and goes on to help *B*, his act should not be praised as "morally good" or lauded as the act of a morally fine fellow. He would simply be doing what he was determined to do, namely what he took to be in his own best interest or benefit.

Even actions which most people normally consider to be self-sacrificial and humanitarian have the motive of self-interest lurking somewhere in the background. The medical missionary elects to spend the rest of his days caring for the diseased in the leper colony because this gives him satisfaction. He goes to bed at night thoroughly exhausted and closer to an early grave, but he has peace of mind and intense satisfaction knowing that he is accomplishing some good in the world. Perhaps, he thinks, someone might even write a book about his work and bring him fame. Regardless of what motive he claims is behind his activities, he is at his present post because he *wants* to be. He may say he is there because he thinks it is the right thing to do, but he must still *want* to do what he takes to be his moral duty or else he would be doing something else.

People are, then, never really responsible for what they do in the sense that they can justly be punished or reprimanded for their actions. We are moved to act by the powerful motive of self-love or self-advantage, and the only way to get someone to adopt a favorable attitude toward a given line of action is to convince him that it will benefit him more than any other thing he could do in those circumstances. If he does not adopt a more humanitarian point of view, he is not to blame. You, if anyone, are to blame because of your failure to convince him that the action you advocate is in his interest.

Difficulties with This Argument

(1) What is the status of *this* general statement, "every act is caused by the motive of self-interest"? Has the advocate of this statement *examined* a sufficiently large number of actions

and traced them back to their respective origins? How would one go about doing this anyway? Is the statement the result of arbitrarily defining "act" as "whatever is caused by self-interest"? What sort of evidence would the egoist accept as counting against his view? If no fact *could* count against his position, what sort of assertion is the psychological egoist[4] making?

(2) If it is true that one cannot desire anything but self-satisfaction, is the advocate of this argument mistaken, insincere, or just talking loosely when he places his order at the restaurant by saying, "I want a steak, medium rare"? Is he willing to defend the slightly dubious position that a slice of beef is identical to a certain type of mental state, namely pleasurable excitement?

(3) The argument maintains that wanting to do something always implies the presence of the self-interest motive. (Schweitzer wanted to go to Africa; otherwise he wouldn't have gone.) Don't we often say, "I'll do it, but I don't want to"? Is the phrase "wanting to do *X*" exactly equivalent in meaning to "desiring self-satisfaction"? Try to substitute one for the other in statements taken from everyday life. I may want to eat my dinner today, but how can this desire by itself be construed as a *selfish* one? Don't we call some kinds of actions "selfish" and other kinds "unselfish"? If we were to adopt the psychological egoist's suggestion to call everything we do "selfish," how would we mark the difference between actions which we call selfish and those we regard as unselfish?

---

[4] *Psychological* egoism is the view just discussed, namely that as a matter of fact no one ever acts except out of what he takes to be in his own self-interest. This position should be distinguished from *ethical* egoism, which states that a person *ought* always to do what he takes to be in his own self-interest. The latter position purports to tell us how we *should* behave (but perhaps don't), whereas the former view allegedly is informing us about what sort of motives we act from in conducting our lives.

ARGUMENTS FOR INDETERMINISM OR LIBERTARIANISM

"Some Actions Are 'Free'; That Is, They Are Opposed to the Agent's Formed Character."[5]

We must define a "free act" as one which originates solely in that area of human personality which is not the result of hereditary and environmental factors. Any act which happens because of these determining influences within or without the agent cannot be considered to be free. The ordinary man at least believes that there is something for which he is responsible even after allowances are made for his inherited traits and possibly an unwholesome environment. We can hold Rebbor responsible for stealing the camera only if he could have done otherwise. And the statement, "Rebbor could have done otherwise," does *not* mean merely "Richard would have acted otherwise if he had chosen differently or if he had been placed in other circumstances." The question at issue in the problem of free will and moral responsibility is simply this: could Rebbor have *chosen* otherwise than he did? The agent is open to moral blame only if he could have chosen otherwise, and on the determinist's view this is impossible. For the determinist, everything about Rebbor, including the choices he makes are the inevitable products of previous events and conditions. Rebbor's choices are really made *for* him, in the deterministic scheme of things.

Does man, however, possess the kind of freedom that is required in order justly to ascribe moral praise or blame to him? All we need to discover is a small area of human action where

---

[5] C. A. Campbell, *On Selfhood and Godhood* (New York: Crowell-Collier & Macmillan, Inc., 1957), Lecture IX. Also see Campbell's inaugural lecture "Is 'Free Will' a Pseudo-Problem?," *Mind*, LX (1951). (Relevant selections in anthologies AB, EP, F, ST, TBO.)

one is free to choose without the compelling influences from one's formed character's determining his decision. No doubt a large number of our actions are the result of our characters as they happen to be at any given moment. However, when it comes to *deciding whether or not to withhold moral effort* in resisting a strong desire to what is expedient rather than what we believe to be right, we have an act for which the agent is responsible without qualification.

Upon reflection we can see that the essence of the moral decision consists in making up our minds whether we will go along with what our strongest desire at the moment happens to be or whether we will resist it and try to do what we believe is the morally right thing to do. Rebbor's strongest desire was to take the camera; his desire was an expression of his character, a residue of influences from childhood when he was deprived of a camera, and so on. If his act of stealing was a free one, he was quite sure he had the power to exert or withhold moral effort and fight his desire to steal. Perhaps after trying to combat his strongest desire as best he could, he still might have succumbed to it, in which case we might not hold him responsible. But if he decided to go along with the desire to steal the camera without the least resistance, then he is clearly to blame from the moral point of view.

"But," it might be objected, "isn't the decision to oppose some factor of one's character (like a desire to steal) also an expression of one's character? So whether one decides to follow the strongest desire at the moment or to do one's moral duty is determined by one's character which takes the form it does because of extra-personal factors." This objection is mistaken because our character cannot be a factor in determining whether or not we decide to *oppose* our character. When we are confronted with a moral dilemma and we must choose one way or the other, we feel quite sure that we are not compelled to decide as we do. If we choose to do what we take to be morally right, we cannot suppose that this decision, which is directly opposed to

133

our desires (and hence to our character), nevertheless proceeds *out of* our character.

There are other objections raised by determinists against the libertarian but they can be answered satisfactorily. "Indeterminism," they say, "makes it impossible to predict the way people act. Human action is made to appear capricious or without rhyme or reason." But what has just been said should clear away this objection. We correctly predict many human actions. When there is no moral issue before the agent, whatever he decides will be in accord with what he most strongly desires, that is, his formed character at the moment of decision. Only when a *moral* decision is called for is it impossible to predict with much accuracy how a given agent will respond.

The last objection to my view goes like this: "If we can't trace a given act back to the agent's character then we cannot rightly call the act *his*. Consequently, no one could ever be held responsible for his 'free' acts as the indeterminist defines them." However, this objection assumes that a human being is reducible to his character which has been formed by heredity and experience through the years. The libertarian or indeterminist view entails that we must distinguish between what we may call "the nature of the self" and the "character of the self." The "nature of the self" includes, but is not the same as, one's character.[6] It is the creative power we have to fashion and change aspects of our formed character. The "character of the self" which is made up of desires of various sorts is formed by heredity and environment and causes most of our actions from day to day. But when we are faced with a situation where we have to decide between doing (a) what is expedient or what we most strongly *desire* to do and (b) what we believe it is morally right to do, the "nature of the self" decides whether or not to exert or withhold moral

---

[6] This view, sometimes called the "pure ego" or "transcendental ego" doctrine, also plays a part in the case for psycho-physical dualism. The reader may wish to refresh his memory on this score by referring to Chapter Three where it was first discussed.

134

effort against our desires. This decision by the self is a "free" one and one for which the agent is justly open to moral praise or blame.

Difficulties with This Argument

(1) According to the argument, a "free act" is one which is preceded by the decision either to exert or to withhold moral effort against one's strongest desire. ("Shall I challenge this temptation or shall I let it have its own way?") How *much* effort must one exert against a desire in order to say that the agent did all he could but still fell victim to his desires? If Rebbor stole the camera, how can we tell whether or not he is responsible, since we are not told *how* we are to determine whether he made an effort of will "against his strongest desire"? Do we ask him if he tried to fight the desire? Then what do we do if he says, "Yes, but my desire was too much for me. It *made* me do it"?

(2) Don't we know of some people who *desire* to do what is right, who would much rather do what they take to be the morally right thing than what is expedient? Can't a person, therefore, have a strongest desire to do what he believes is his moral duty? If such desires exist in some people, are they a part of their *characters* and, if so, are they traceable to hereditary and environmental factors? If the answer to this is "yes," then when a person *desires* to do what he believes is morally right, we must conclude that any action resulting from that desire is not "free" and, therefore, not morally praiseworthy. This would indeed be an odd state of affairs.

(3) We seem able to predict with a high degree of accuracy how a person will behave when he is confronted with a moral dilemna, contrary to Campbell's claim. If we knew, for example, that a given individual believed that no one ought to break his promises and we know that this person has always kept his word even though it was inconvenient for him to do so, we have good grounds for predicting that, when he makes a promise

in the future, he will keep it. This would seem to indicate that what a person chooses to do in a moral situation is traceable to his "formed" character in which are included the individual's moral beliefs.

(4) What is the nature of that part of the self from which our free decisions are supposed to proceed? By what marks do we recognize it? What is its relation to our "character of the self"? How does one person's "nature of the self" differ from anyone else's "nature of the self"? If a person's "nature of the self" does not differ from anyone else's, why hold a specific individual and not someone else responsible for acts performed by him?

"Some Human Acts Are Unpredictable in Principle."[7]

One of the pillars in the structure of determinism is the contention that if we were able to know everything about a given agent's character (his desires, motives and beliefs, etc.), then we could accurately predict what that person would choose and do in any set of circumstances. This claim can be shown to be wholly mistaken, because what most people mean by a "free choice" is one which nobody could possibly describe to us in advance. The following argument will show why this is so.

Suppose there were a super-psychologist who knew all about me including every detail about my likes, dislikes, desires, and beliefs, as well as how I have acted in the past in every circumstance. (Admittedly such complete knowledge of a person's brain states is not possible in practice as yet, but from the determinist's viewpoint there is nothing in principle to prevent the acquisition of such knowledge and its utilization in pre-

---

[7] D. M. MacKay, "Brain and Will," a paper based on a talk presented on the British Broadcasting Company, published in the *Listener*, May 9, 1957. (Reprinted in anthology EP.) See also J. Canfield, "Determinism, Free Will, and the Ace Predictor," *Mind*, LXX (1961).

dicting the future acts of people.) In spite of such a wealth of knowledge concerning myself, however, he could not describe to me with certainty what I shall do as a result of my free decision. The reason for this is that the super-psychologist could not possibly allow beforehand for the *effects* on me of his telling me about his prediction concerning what my choice will be. He must compute what I will choose to do on the basis of his knowledge of my brain or character (whichever you prefer, it does not matter for the argument) just prior to my choice. But if he tells me of his prediction concerning what I will do, then my brain or character is not the same as it was when he made his computations. A new piece of data has been added to consciousness, namely the information he has given me concerning his prediction as to what I will do at a certain time in the future.

The point is that he will not and cannot know what effects my learning of his prediction will have on my action. If he says, "On the basis of the present state of your brain or character you will do X exactly ten hours from now," I may, when the ten hours are up, do Y for one reason or another, perhaps to display my freedom. If he could know the effects of his telling me that I will do X, then he would still have a problem. He would have to be able to know the effects of his telling me about the effects of his telling me what I will do in ten hours. As we can see, the super-psychologist is caught in an infinite regress of having to know what the effects upon me will be of telling me of the effects of his telling me about the effects of his telling me what I will choose to do at a future time. His difficulty is not a lack of time in which to complete his computations, but rather a logical one which no amount of time and effort could solve.

In other words, in order for the super-psychologist to know that I will do A at time T, he must have already taken into account all conditions causing me to do act A at that future date. But this logically cannot be done — for him to know what I will do he will have had to know what effect there would be upon me if by some means I learned of his computation which he based upon his knowing the state of my brain. But even if he were able to know the effect upon me if I learned of his prediction, he would have the same problem all over again. In order to know that I will do A at time T he would have to be able to know not only the effects upon me if I learned of his prediction, but also the effects upon me if perchance I learned what the original effects upon me would be from being informed of his computations. His problem of computing what I will do will just be placed further and further back without end, since he would be forever chasing the effects of the effects of the effects and so on. Because a super-psychologist could not fulfill the conditions necessary for knowing what a person will do as a result of a free choice, no prediction forthcoming from him can attain certainty. If determinism is a correct view, then such prediction of future actions must be possible at least in principle. But since such knowledge of future actions is not possible even in principle, determinism cannot be a correct view.

It might appear that the super-psychologist could avoid this difficulty by keeping quiet after he computes what I will do at the end of ten hours time. Then he could have certainty regarding his prediction about my future choice. So the determinist, in an attempt to save his position, might contend that all human acts could be predicted with certainty provided that we knew enough about the agents involved and that they were not informed about the results of the computations.

But this way out of the problem does not save the determinist. For if the super-psychologist claims to know with certainty what I will do ten hours from now but that he will be certain *only so long* as he doesn't let me in on his information, we are being asked to adopt an unusual, confused notion of certainty. It's as if a person said, "I'm absolutely certain he will do X, provided specific conditions are fulfilled." When a person says "I know that X will occur," he cannot go on to say "but I could be wrong" without thereby misusing the word "know." If a person *knows* that X will occur, then it is *true* that X will happen; the possibility of something other than X occuring in its place is ruled out. Therefore, to claim certainty for a prediction concerning someone's future acts and at the same time to admit that the certainty is conditional is to misuse the word "certain." Such a prediction would concern only that which *probably* will happen, and so the case is secure against those determinists who claim that, given enough knowledge of a person's character, the latter's future choices could be known before he made them.

Difficulties with This Argument

(1) Aren't all predictions made with some qualifications assumed? We can, for example, predict the future course of a particular planet and be certain of its position at a given time *provided that* the universe stays in existence, provided the planet continues in its usual orbit, etc. Is it any more odd to say that predictions concerning people's actions could be certain provided various conditions are fulfilled, i.e., that the person about whom the prediction is made is not told of it?

(2) If the super-psychologist knew all about the person whose actions he was predicting, would he not know what effects would result from his subject's hearing of his (the super-psychologist's) computations? It seems that a complete knowledge of a person's character and/or brain states would include data concerning the manner in which a person would react when told what he will do at some future time. Such complete knowledge which has been granted the super-psychologist would probably also include data concerning the reaction of the subject to his hearing what the original effects of learning of the prediction would be. If carried far enough, a person just might not be affected at all by his learning what the effects will be of his learning of the effects which his learning of the effects of learning how he will behave in the future. If enough were known concerning the psychological makeup of a person, it could be determined at what point his receiving information about his

future acts would no longer have an effect upon him. Consequently, there would be no reason why knowing what a person will do and telling him of those findings need result in an infinite regress.

Determinism Inevitably Leads to Pessimism.[8]

When faced with the question whether there are any chance occurrences in the world, or whether everything is determined by past conditions, it is tempting to suggest that we consult the facts of science. But facts can tell us only what *has* happened, not what *might* or *might not* have happened. We actually choose to be determinists or indeterminists because we believe one or the other seems more rational, that things make more sense if we accept the one rather than the other. "When we make theories about the world and discuss them with one another, we do so in order to attain a conception of things which shall give us subjective satisfaction."[9] This does not mean that we should believe any proposition whatsoever so long as it makes us feel good; it may be temporarily pleasing to believe, for example, that the world is full of sunshine and goodness, that evil and suffering are merely illusory—but before long, certain stubborn facts will clash with this belief and force us to give it up. The point is that in adopting a philosophical position we should apply the following criterion: accept a proposition as true only if it is useful in helping us cope satisfactorily with our environment and if it satisfies the needs of the whole personality. A true philosophical theory must do more than merely satisfy the requirements of logic and reason; it must also not frustrate the emotive and volitional aspects of human beings. The effects

---

[8] William James, "The Dilemma of Determinism," in *Essays in Pragmatism*, edited by Albury Castell (New York: Hafner Publishing Co., Inc., 1948), pp. 37-64. (Reprinted in anthologies EP, MGAS.)

[9] James, "The Dilemma of Determinism," p. 38.

which adhering to a particular theory have upon our moral and emotional outlook must be taken into account when we frame our philosophical views. The only way, then, of resolving the issue of determinism versus free-will (or indeterminism) is to trace the practical consequences of believing the respective positions in order to determine which one is more subjectively satisfying in the sense we have indicated. What effects would there be on our feelings, our wills, and ultimately our conduct if we adopted either of the two views up for consideration?

The determinist is quick to point out that if we allow a bit of chance into the universe, we thereby admit unintelligibility into things. How could scientific investigation proceed if things do not obey fixed laws and have discoverable reasons for their being the way they are? But in response to the determinist, it should be pointed out that the admission of *some* chance happenings into the world does not turn everything into chaos. Suppose we try to imagine two different universes, both identical in every way except that in Universe *A*, I choose coffee with my meal on a given occasion and in Universe *B*, I take tea as my beverage. Suppose further that I like coffee and tea equally well. How would Universe *A* be any more or less rational because I chose coffee in it rather than tea? It seems preposterous to think that chance occurrences like these could have such far-reaching implications for the intelligibility of the universe as the determinist sometimes seems to think.

Suppose we try to spell out what the determinist's world implies, what it would mean to us in practical terms if we accepted it as a true account of things. A most important consequence is that judgments of regret would have to be viewed differently than they have been. To say that you *regret* a certain thing's having happened is to imply that it *ought* not to have happened. But determinism virtually defines the universe as a place in which what *ought* to be is impossible. If it is true, as the determinist claims, that everything which takes place must necessarily happen as it does, that there was no possibility of anything's turning out differently than it has, then it makes no sense at all to say, "X ought not to have occurred." The latter statement would make sense only if something other than X *could* have happened, and according to the determinist's view that is impossible.

So what of it that we should not say things like "X ought not to have happened"? Just this: part of what we mean when we call something "bad" is that we claim that it ought not to have been. When we regret X, we do so because we believe X to have been bad in some way, and to believe X to be bad is to believe that it ought not to have happened. If the determinist expects us to accept his viewpoint, he must also be ready to give up making judgments of regret and value. But this is asking more than seems practically possible. There are some regrets which are not so easily dismissed. We ordinarily are sorry, for example, when we hear that someone has been murdered or terrorized.

The deterministic view cannot help but lead to pessimism, that is, the attitude which recognizes that try as we may to change things, either evil or error forms a necessary part of the world. Let me explain the dilemma in which the determinist finds himself. If it is incorrect to regret anything (since everything must happen as it does), then acts like murder and treachery are not bad. On the other hand, if it is *correct* to regret that some things happen, then murder and treachery are bad (they ought not to be). Since it is either correct or incorrect to regret some occurrences, either moral evil (like murder and treachery) or erroneous judgments (regretting acts like murder) *have* to take place in our world. No matter which way you turn, the universe must be in a pretty sad state of affairs if it must necessarily include in it either a great number of erroneous judgments (particularly judgments of regret) or a vast number of morally reprehensible acts. Such a conclusion cannot help but produce a thoroughly pessimistic outlook. And the ultimate fruit of pessimism is the destruction of interest and zeal in improving moral conditions around us. Any motivation to improve our own moral natures and strive for a better life is sapped of its strength, since everything has been determined to occur as it does. The only way of avoiding complete pessimism is to maintain that some events which occur do not *have* to take place. Things need not be the way they are, and those acts which are morally bad or ought not to have been performed may meaningfully be regretted only if the deterministic thesis is rejected.

Difficulties with This Argument

(1) What is a "chance" occurrence? Is it an event without a cause altogether, or merely one whose cause has not yet been identified?

(2) If there are occurrences which do not have causes, are a person's "free" acts of this type? If they are, then why should we be held responsible for them? Why hold me rather than some one else responsible for what I do if my acts occurred by chance? Why hold anyone responsible for his actions if they are merely chance or random occurrences?

(3) Couldn't the determinist argue that when he calls X "bad," he means that he would be happier if something other than X had happened, but that he realizes that is impossible? (Things just don't go the way we would like them to go sometimes.) Don't we sometimes call a particular event "bad" and regret its happening, even though we recognize that it was unavoidable? For example, we do meaningfully say that a tragedy such as an earthquake which destroyed hundreds of people was bad, in spite of the fact that there was no way it could have been averted. It looks as if we do make meaningful judgments of regret on occasion, even though we regard what has happened as inevitable.

(4) Is pessimism a necessary result of accepting determinism? Can't the determinist admit that this is a world in which either moral evil or errors in judgment form a necessary part and still try to *reduce* the amounts of evil or error that occurs? Can't

he look upon himself as determined to make such an effort at improving things which he has been caused to regard as needing improvement? The acceptance of determinism does not commit one to fatalism, i.e., the feeling that human actions really count for nothing and that it makes no difference what any of us tries to do.

ARGUMENTS FOR "SOFT" OR MODERATE DETERMINISM

At this point in our discussion, we seem to have reached a stalemate. The position of the hard determinist leads him to say that we can never justly hold anyone responsible for his actions, because what a person does is the inevitable consequence of factors in his character which the agent has no voice in shaping. The indeterminist, trying to salvage moral responsibility from the onslaught of determinism, defines "free" decisions as those which proceed not from one's character but from a different part of "the self." This supposed source of free decisions is shrouded in mystery, difficult to define and subject to no observation. The indeterminist concludes that we may justly be held responsible for acts which are the result of decisions made by this part of the agent. It seems, then, that if the ascription of moral responsibility is to be retained as a genuine, meaningful part of the moral life, we must purchase it at the expense of obscurity and reference to indefinables. This is not a pleasant prospect to most philosophers.

There is another position, usually referred to as "soft" determinism, which proposes to give us the best of both worlds. Not only can we retain the principle of determinism ("Every event is caused"), but we can salvage moral responsibility as well. In fact, not only is the deterministic principle compatible with the ascription of moral praise and blame to people's actions,

144

but that principle is absolutely necessary for the existence of meaningful moral responsibility. "Soft" determinism is proposed then as a reconciling position claiming to cut through once and for all the confusions and obscurities of the positions already covered, by showing that the two traditional combatants need not have been at odds. We shall have to see whether the soft determinist makes a reasonable case for his position.

"An Act Which Is Caused Need Not Be Compelled."[10]

Both the hard determinist and the indeterminist have assumed an erroneous view of the cause-effect relationship. That is, they have a mistaken notion about what is involved when one particular thing or event causes or brings about something else which we call an effect. If, for example, I am told by my dentist that the cause of my toothache is an abscess on one of my molars, how should we understand the relationship or connection my dentist has drawn between my toothache (the effect) and the abscessed molar (the cause)? Some philosophers would say that we must regard the cause as having some sort of "power" or "force" which accounts for its ability to bring about the effect. The connection between a cause and its effect is so intimate, they would argue, that if we could know all about the cause (in this case, the abscess on the molar), we could deduce that it could cause a toothache even if we had never experienced such a thing. Consequently (holders of such a view contend), the abscessed molar necessitates or compels just such an effect as my toothache to occur.

Now such an account of a cause-effect relationship sounds plausible enough until it is analyzed. In the first place, philosophers who hold this view would have us believe that some sort of "power" or "force" lies within the cause which

---

[10] David Hume, *Treatise of Human Nature*, Book II, Part III, Sections I and II. (Selections in anthologies AB, F, SA, ST, TBO.)

explains the production of its particular effect. What sort of entity is this "power"? Can it be observed or detected in some way? What makes it become active when it does? And has anyone ever been able to tell what any particular cause will produce except by observing the effects of similar causes in the past? This whole theory of what it means to say that one thing has caused something else is full of obscurities and unverifiable claims.

A better view of the cause-effect relationship, one based wholly on experience and one which we can understand, would go like this: when we say A caused B ("the abscess on the molar caused my toothache"), what we mean is that on the basis of experience we find that the development of an abscess on a tooth precedes the occurrence of a toothache. The connection between the two is merely that of being associated with one another in a certain way. Dentists have been able to say abscesses cause toothaches because on many occasions in the past a toothache has been preceded by (and accompanied by) an abscessed tooth in their patients. When a particular event A has been found to be followed by another event B and events of the same type as A have been likewise found to be followed by events of the same type as B, then our minds are led to conclude that A *caused B*. This is what is meant when people make causal judgments. There is no need to spin some elaborate, mysterious theory to explain the relationship. All we need to do is describe the way we come to learn that one thing, A, causes another thing, B.

Let us apply what we have just said to the area of human action. The hard determinist mistakenly thinks that when we say that some motive such as greed caused Rebbor to steal the camera, we are saying that the motive of greed *compelled* his action. He thinks that the motive in question had some driving, compelling "force" which inevitably *had* to result in the act which he committed. Consequently, the hard determinist is led to conclude that the action of stealing the camera *had* to take place just as surely as an apple must fall to the ground when dropped. Then he proceeds to ask what the cause of the *motive* behind the act was and continues to think that some cause or causes produced just that motive with equally compelling force. It is no wonder then that the hard determinist looks upon Rebbor, the agent, as the helpless victim of a whole chain of causes and effects inevitably compelling him to think, desire, and act as he did. The hard determinist's conclusion, however, is just as erroneous as the view of causation upon which it is based.

If we adopt the correct view of what it means to say that one particular thing, *A*, caused something else, *B*, we may view the connection between Rebbor's motives and his act of stealing the camera as follows. The motive of greed, let us say, has been found to be regularly associated with acts of stealing. A person doesn't just go around stealing things for no reason at all, unless he happens to be a kleptomaniac. Certain motives are usually found to be present in the characters of people which explain why they act as they do. And the better we know the motives, desires, and dispositions of people, the more accurately we can predict what they would do in any given situation. But to say that certain motives are associated with or accompany certain actions is not to say that the former *compel* the latter.

Here is where the indeterminist jumps into the discussion, greatly agitated by our mention of the predictability of people's actions. "If there are causes of a person's actions," he asks, "and we can predict roughly what a person will do in a given set of circumstances, then how can man be free to act? Surely a free act must be uncaused, one which is unpredictable." But the indeterminist does not realize the consequences of what he is saying. It is commonly admitted (even by the indeterminist) that mentally ill people do not act freely. Yet their actions are usually *less* predictable than those of normal people, because there are no motives or reasons for acting usually associated with their behavior. In short, the actions of severely mentally ill people are uncaused, yet they are not considered free and responsible. If the indeterminist were consistent, he would hold these unfortunate persons *more* responsible for their acts than normal people, since the former's actions are the least caused of anyone's. Not even the indeterminist would find this implication of his view very attractive.

"Two Senses of 'Law' Must Be Distinguished."[11]

"Hard" determinists reach their erroneous conclusion that people are never to be held responsible for their actions not only because of a mistaken notion of causation. They reach it also by failing to distinguish between two kinds of law. They say things like, "Everything obeys the laws of nature," or "Everything is governed by strict, unvarying physical laws." Then they go on to point out how man is a part of nature and must, therefore, be subject to nature's laws. But such talk betrays a radical misunderstanding of two different meanings of the word "law." One kind of law is "prescriptive." An example would be, "All vehicles must stop when the traffic light is red." Such a law prescribes or commands a certain course of action; it states what *ought* to be done in certain contexts, not what in fact *is* done. Another kind of law might be called "descriptive" and is the type which the scientist formulates to describe occurrences and conditions in nature, such as the law of gravity or the laws of planetary motion. The laws formulated by the scientist describe in a general way what actually does happen or what will happen provided certain conditions are fulfilled. The laws of nature do not *prescribe* the action of anything, let alone the actions of men.

The hard determinist talks as though the law of gravity says to the apple on the tree, "Now look here, apple. I command you to fall to the ground when your stem is loosened from the branch. If you don't, I'll make things plenty tough for you." To

---

[11] Moritz Schlick, *Problems of Ethics* (Englewood Cliffs, N.J.: Prentice-Hall, Inc., 1939), Chap. 7. (Selection in anthology EP.)

say "Everything obeys the laws of nature" makes it appear that apples on trees and such things really have a mind to order their behavior and would probably like to do something other than what they do.

The mistake behind the hard determinist's way of thinking is obvious. He has uncritically taken terms which have meaning only in the context of human behavior ("govern," "obey") and applied them to nature at large. He has, in short, made nature some kind of super-sovereign who issues commands which never fail to be obeyed. This is nothing short of full-blown mythology.

Analysis of "Could Have Done Otherwise." [12]

The hard determinist maintains that no one could ever have done other than what he actually did, because no one could have *chosen* to do anything else. The indeterminist, on the other hand, contends that a person could be acting freely only *if* he had been able to make a choice different from the one he actually made on a given occasion. Such an ability to choose otherwise is necessary for moral freedom and responsibility, and we all have a feeling when we are deliberating that we could choose between a number of possible alternatives.

Now just what does the statement "He could have done otherwise" really mean, and what is this "feeling of freedom" the determinist talks about? To answer this, let us get back to our case of Rebbor's stealing the camera. If it is said that "Rebbor could have done otherwise than steal the camera," what is meant is something roughly like this: "If Rebbor had possessed a different character or had been placed in circumstances different from those in which he was, then he would not have stolen the camera." Or it could mean, "Rebbor would have done something

---

[12] Patrick Nowell-Smith, "Free Will and Moral Responsibility," *Mind,* LVII (1948), pp. 45-61. (Reprinted in anthologies EP, ST.) Also, Charles L. Stevenson, *Ethics and Language* (New Haven: Yale University Press, 1944), pp. 298-318.

besides steal the camera if he had desired or chosen to do so."
If we take the original statement to mean this, then all of us on
certain occasions could have done something other than what we
actually did. When I miss an easy two-foot putt, I rightly say that
I could have made it, because in the past I have sunk putts of
equal length under conditions similar to those at present. What I
mean by saying "I could have made that putt" is, "I would have
holed that putt if I had used the same form and judgment that I
did on those two-footers I made in the past."

At this point the hard determinist presses us with the
question, "But could Rebbor have *desired* anything other than
what he did, given the constitution of his character?" However,
this question does not make sense. The words "could" and
"could have" make sense when applied to the area of *actions*,
but not when they are applied to speech about the springs or
sources of action.[13] In other words, "could" and "could have"
have meaning when employed in statements like "I could have
done a lot better on the exam had I studied more" or "He could
be the starting quarterback on the team if he would apply himself." "Could" is a "power-word" which is learned from and has
its ordinary, intended use in contexts where something is said
about a person's observable behavior. To take "could" out of this
context and ask "Could Rebbor have *desired* differently?" is to
violate the standard meaning of the term. It is, in short, to ask
something without meaning.

In regard to the "feeling of freedom" which exists when
we are deliberating what to do, several things need to be said.
First, the consciousness of freedom is only the conviction that
one is acting because of one's own desires. It never extends to
the point where we feel we could have willed something else,
but only that we could have acted differently if we had willed
differently. Second, the reason we might think that we act free

---

[13] John Hospers, "What Means this Freedom?" in Sidney
Hook, ed., *Determinism and Freedom in the Age of Modern Science*
(New York: Crowell-Collier & Macmillan, Inc., 1961), pp. 139-42. (Re-
printed in anthology TBO.)

from causes is that our attention during deliberation is turned to the future and not to the past.[14] We are trying to decide what to do and attempting to determine the consequences of various alternatives. We do not stop to consider the various sources of causation from the past which lead us to choose the alternative upon which we finally settle.

Difficulties with This Argument[15]

(1) If, as the soft determinist maintains, motives and desires *cause* some actions in the same sense as one billiard ball *causes* another to move when it is hit by the first ball, then how can actions caused by motives and desires be anything but inevitable? Given the properties of the two billiard balls and further conditions concerning the surface of the table and the motion of the first ball, we find it hard to explain why the second ball moved in a certain direction without saying something like "the first ball *forced* the second one to move." Admittedly no logical contradiction would be involved, if we were to say that the second ball stayed where it was when the two balls hit. Yet more seems to be involved in the causal situation than merely the movement of one ball *followed by* movement in another. It seems perfectly natural to say that the first ball moved in such a way that the second ball was *forced* to move as it did; it was not *physically* possible for it to move in any other direction. Now if motives *cause* some actions (i.e., free actions) as the soft determinist maintains, aren't we also committed to saying that motives *force* us to do those acts in such a way that it is physically (but not logically) impossible to do anything other than what we do? If we view the relation between motives and free acts as causal in nature, than it seems that we are compelled to act

---

[14] Brand Blanshard, "The Case for Determinism," in Sidney Hook, ed., *Determinism and Freedom in the Age of Modern Science,* p. 22.

[15] Several criticisms of the hard determinist's position apply equally to the arguments of the soft determinist. See especially difficulties on pages 127-29.

151

when we have a motive just as much as we are when we are compelled to act under the influence of a drug. The particular motive we have or the particular drug we have taken makes it physically impossible to do anything other than what we do.

(2) If the deterministic thesis "Every event is caused" is correct, then what comfort is there in the soft determinist's contention that the statement "A could have acted otherwise" means "A *would* have acted differently if he had chosen otherwise or had possessed a different character"? If the determinist is correct, a person's choices are, so to speak, made *for* him or determined by factors outside his control, and there is no possibility of a person's having a character different from the one he actually has. If, as the determinist maintains, we are caused to act as we do because of factors in our characters, and these in turn are the products of forces which shaped us into what we are, then why call any of our acts "free" or of the sort for which we may be justly held accountable?

(3) The soft determinist maintains that an uncaused action is one which is done without a motive and hence should be regarded as "unfree." And, he contends, no one should be held responsible for his unfree acts. But, suppose a person were to throw a brick through a store window and then claimed that he did it for no reason; he "just wanted" to break a window. We would rightly hold such a person responsible for the act simply because *he did it*. We would not have to be assured that he had a motive for the act, nor would we require that such an action be shown to be *characteristic* behavior on his part in order for us to blame him for what he did.

Conditions of Moral Responsibility[16]

Suppose we agree with the soft determinist in his contention that both the hard determinist and the indeterminist are

---

[16] Hospers, "What Means this Freedom?" *Determinism and Freedom in the Age of Modern Science*, pp. 126-42.

fouled up on this question of free will and responsibility. In opposition to the hard determinist, who claims we can never justly be held responsible for any action, the soft determinist wants to hold that we *are* justly held accountable for many of the things we do. But we are not responsible for them because of the reason the indeterminist gives. We are justly held responsible for certain actions, says the soft determinist, not because they are uncaused, but precisely because they are *caused*, because they result from our motives, desires, and decisions.

(1) The first condition for ascribing praise or blame for a particular act is that it be *the consequence of the agent's own desires and decisions*. The bank teller who hands over the cash at the point of a gun cannot be held responsible for losing money for his employer, because he was forced to do what he did. True, the teller might have decided to disobey the gunman, but no one would seriously hold that there is any genuine alternative in such a situation. The kleptomaniac, as well, is not responsible for his acts of stealing, because ordinarily such a person desires *not* to steal and does not *decide* to take things from other people at all. Such acts are the result of inner compulsion and no one should be held morally responsible for their commission.

Ironically, if we were to adopt the indeterminist's position that uncaused acts are the only ones for which we can be held responsible, we would end up without a sensible concept of moral responsibility at all. An uncaused act would hardly be one for which you could justly hold a particular person responsible. If Rebbor's act of stealing the camera were uncaused, why blame Rebbor for it? Why single *him* out for punishment if the act just happened to take place without a cause?

(2) The second condition for ascribing moral responsibility (and it is closely related to the first) is this: the agent in question must have been *capable of having his course of action affected by certain kinds of rational considerations*. That is, the degree to which an agent is responsible for committing a given act is directly proportionate to the degree that he is capable of being affected by reasoning. If the agent is convinced by another

person's argument or his own independent reasoning that a certain proposed action is morally wrong, and that it will have wholly undesirable consequences both for himself and for others, but nevertheless goes ahead and commits the act, then there is good reason to conclude that the agent acted not freely but compulsively. Sometimes the situation will yield an even more clear-cut conclusion, as in those cases where a person commits a certain act while in a state of intense rage or jealousy. An individual in such an emotional state usually is not affected by someone's presenting reasons to him as to why he should not commit the act he has either threatened to perform or could be expected to perform in such a condition.

Voluntary actions are caused by characteristics that may be strengthened or inhibited by the promise of rewards or the threat of punishment. For example, suppose Rebbor knows the probable consequences of his stealing the camera. Suppose further that he is convinced either through someone else's persuasion or through his own reasoning that he will be caught and jailed, that he will lose his reputation and good standing in society and in everything else that really matters to him. If, after being convinced by a number of reasons that he ought not to steal the camera, he still goes through with the act, then his behavior would indicate he was acting under some inner compulsion and stands in need of treatment, not moral censure.

Of course, there are degrees of responsibility, and just how responsible someone is is not always easy to determine. But these are the two conditions which we do in fact take note of in affixing moral praise or blame to actions. We must, of course, always temper our moral praise and blame with facts regarding the causes of human behavior as they are discovered by the behavioral sciences. At our present stage of knowledge our concepts of moral responsibility still have applicability, and there is considerable difference between a compulsive action and one which is voluntary. Nothing would be accomplished if we began to consider all actions as compelled, since we would

154

soon discover great differences among people with regard to the degree of their compulsiveness. We should still require terms like "voluntary" and "free" to mark off those actions which were least compelled and most susceptible of praise or blame.

REASONS FOR ACTIONS
AND CAUSES OF ACTIONS

In approaching a philosophical problem a person may take one of three fundamental stances.

1. He may completely *ignore* the problem;

2. He may attempt to *solve* the problem by proposing a solution to it; or

3. He may *dissolve* the problem.

When the last approach is attempted, the philosopher tries to show that the problem under review arises from mistaken assumptions on the part of those who pose the issue. The dissolution of a philosophical problem amounts to a questioning of the question, so to speak. This way of looking at the free-will problem has become increasingly popular with some philosophers in recent years. It has been argued that the question, "What causes human action?" is misleading because it contains the partially concealed assumption that human actions may properly be spoken of as "caused" or "uncaused." The question contains an assumption in roughly the same way as "Have you stopped beating your wife?" does.

Philosophers were led to ask, "What causes human actions?" or "Are human actions caused or uncaused?" because they uncritically assumed that the actions of people were events of the same type as the movements of billiard balls and other phenomena studied by the physicist. They assumed that since

155

every event has a cause, and human actions are events, human actions must have causes like everything else. Then the problem became one of locating and identifying these causes. The most qualified candidate was "acts of will"—or "volitions," as they came to be called. The usual account of these alleged mental acts goes something like this: "The cause of my arm's rising is contraction in certain muscles in my arm, and the cause of the muscle movement is a volition on my part. I bring about an act of will, and the movement takes place. The volitions are like thrusts or releases of energy in the physical world except that they occur in my mind when I so desire."

Now the stage has been set for the combatants in the free-will dispute. The dispute begins between the determinist and the indeterminist when a most natural question is asked— "What causes my volition or acts of will?" Surely we cannot cut short the search for the causes of action and say that acts of will simply begin without a previous cause. The determinist keeps pressing the search and concludes that our volitions are caused by factors like heredity and environment, while the indeterminist claims that somehow acts of volition (or those mental "thrusts" which translate intentions into bodily acts) are created out of nothing by the "will."

This interminable philosophical fix could have been avoided had the parties involved stopped to analyze the question they were trying to answer. They should have realized that it is wrong even to ask whether human actions are caused or un-caused, because human actions are not events on a par with those phenomena described and explained by reference to the causal laws of mechanics. This can be proved best by showing that there are no such acts as volitions as they have been tradi-tionally conceived. They enjoy a purely mythical station postu-lated out of necessity to preserve a mistaken view of human behavior. If this contention can be backed up with good reasons, then we will have to look for a way of explaining human behavior which does not resort to causal explanations.

Arguments Against the Existence of Volitions[17]

(1) The nature of alleged acts of volition has not been explained. Theorists who hold that such acts occur and cause human actions cannot say how many volitions have been performed in any given time, how long they lasted, or whether they were easy or difficult to perform.

(2) The connection between these alleged volitions and bodily movements is mysterious. Just how do volitions get translated into actions?

(3) The theory concerning volitions states that some other mental happenings are caused by volitions, such as when a person wills to think about a particular problem puzzling him. But what causes volitions? If, in order for a given act to be voluntary, it must be caused by an act of volition, what causes the act of volition? It would be quite arbitrary to halt the search for causes after "discovering" volitions, and if we keep on pressing the causal hypothesis that every event has a cause, we will have to have a cause for the cause of the cause of an act of will *ad infinitum.*

(4) The theory that volitions cause actions could not allow that volitions ever fail to bring about an action. If once "weakness of will" were admitted to be possible, then further acts of some sort would have to be postulated to explain how volitions are sometimes successful (that is, they result in the action willed by the agent). But it is perfectly clear to everyone that we sometimes don't do what we have wanted to do. What are these mental acts which must take place in order to make volitions successful on those occasions when they are?

The preceding difficulties point up how extremely difficult it is to explain the occurrence of human actions by employing the theory concerning "acts of volition." Philosophers

---

[17] Ryle, *The Concept of Mind*, pp. 62-69. (Relevant section reprinted in MGAS.)

who have resorted to such a model of explanation have these troubles only because they uncritically assumed that the question, "What causes human action?" is perfectly appropriate and makes just as much sense as does the query, "What makes a metal rod expand when placed in fire?"

Explaining Human Behavior[18]

We surely must admit a difference between a voluntary act and one which is involuntary. But the distinction cannot be that voluntary ones are caused by volitions whereas involuntary acts are not. When my arm rises due to a muscle spasm, for example, we should not consider this an *action* of mine at all. It is something which happens to me rather than something I *do*. But when I raise my arm to signal or wave to someone, I am performing an act. When my arm goes up because of a spasm in my muscles, we are right to search for a *cause* of the happening. But when I raise my arm because I want to signal or wave, the search for a *cause* of the act is out of place. To explain why I raised my arm, I would give a *reason or motive* for my act. I would say, for example, that I wanted to signal the driver behind me that I was preparing to make a right turn, and this would explain why I raised my arm.

There is a large difference between giving a motive or reason for an action and trying to state its cause. Motives are not the right sort of things to be causes, because they are not events or happenings. Something can be classified as a cause only if it is an event or group of events. If I say I had a particular motive or reason for what I did, I am not saying that my motive took place or occurred at all. Motives are neither acts nor occurrences and, therefore, cannot be regarded as *causes* of anything.

Another argument can be used to show how utterly

---

[18] A. I. Melden, *Free Action* (London: Routledge and Kegan Paul, 1961), Chaps. 5, 7, and 14; pp. 43-55, 199-215.

different motives and causes really are. Suppose the engine in my car is misfiring, and I discover that a fouled spark plug is at fault. We would say that the fouled spark plug was the cause, and the misfiring engine was the effect. Now notice that we can explain perfectly well what a fouled spark plug is without mentioning the misfiring engine in my car. And we can understand what a misfiring engine is in general without referring to a fouled-up spark plug. In a case where a causal connection has been discovered, what we call the cause is comprehensible apart from any reference as to *what* it is the cause of. The connection between a cause and its effect, we might say, is empirical —that is, discoverable through experience.

Now notice how different the situation is when we examine a case in which some motive or desire is referred to as the explanation for some particular action. If the relationship between motives and actions were a causal one, then we should be able to elucidate the concept of motive (and desire and intention as well) without any reference to action of any sort. But this cannot be done, for a motive is understandable only as a motive to *do* something or to be *prepared* to do something. There can be no understanding of the concept of motive without reference to the concept of action. The meaning of one is bound up with the meaning of the other, and consequently the relationship between motives and actions cannot be a causal one. It is not at all like the relationship between a fouled spark plug and a misfiring engine, both of which are quite understandable apart from one another.

Philosophers have so often assumed that the actions of human beings could be explained by using the same categories as were employed to explain the movements of bodies. Just because mechanistic, causal explanations worked in the nonhuman realm, they uncritically thought that the same principles could be applied everywhere. Both the determinist and the indeterminist agree that the question, "What causes human actions?" was a meaningful and properly-put question. But there seem to be good reasons for believing that the question is based on a failure to distinguish reasons from causes, and that the tangles involved in the free-will problem are, in part, the consequences of this important oversight.

SUGGESTIONS FOR FURTHER STUDY

Anthologies

AB, Part 3; EP, Part 1; F, Parts 4 and 5; MGAS, pp. 422-462; SA, pp. 129-183; ST, Chap. 9; TBO, Parts 3 and 4; TH, Chap. 11.

Others

Berofsky, Bernard, ed., *Free Will and Determinism*. New York: Harper and Row, 1966.

Hook, Sidney, ed., *Determinism and Freedom in the Age of Modern Science*. New York: Collier Books, 1961.

Morgenbesser, Sidney and James Walsh, eds., *Free Will*. Englewood Cliffs, N.J.: Prentice-Hall, Inc., 1962.

Pears, D. F., ed., *Freedom and Will*. London: Macmillan & Company, 1963.

THE PROBLEM
OF MORALITY

V

Can I Know What Is Morally Right?

At first glance it may seem easy to dispose of the question we have proposed in the present chapter. One might be inclined to say, "Of course I know what is morally right. When I was a child I learned the difference between right and wrong. Among other things, it is wrong to kill, to steal, and to tell lies. It is right to help others in need, obey society's laws, and tell the truth. Everyone knows that, so what is there to discuss? The only problem that needs solving is how to persuade people to live up to these rules of conduct." It would be nice if problems of morality were really this simple.

There are a number of reasons why the search for correct moral rules is necessary, that is, why one should engage in a systematic, disciplined study of ethics. These reasons should convince us that the approach stated above is not only an oversimplification, but that it actually can be a serious obstacle to mature ethical thought and action.

(1) Many people seem to have a narrow, childish concept of morality. Their moral rules can be adequately represented by a small list of traditional do's and don'ts: don't steal, don't lie, don't kill, pay your taxes, obey the law, and so on.[1] Such an approach to morality has usually been instilled at an early age, and it is often uncritically accepted and assumed to be perfectly consistent and applicable. Everyone knows what stealing is, we are told—it is taking someone else's property without their permission. The bankrobber and the shoplifter are highly immoral people because they steal things. But what about the student who cheats in his school work? How about the lengths to which we go to keep from paying our fair share of income tax? Aren't these stealing? And then what shall we say of the person who, in order to get a promotion in his business or profession, circulates rumors reflecting upon the character and competence of his competitors, each of whom he knows to be better qualified than he for the job? Is not such action an attempt to steal what rightfully belongs to someone else?

The basic defect with the morality that is reducible to a few traditional rules is that it applies to only a small number of real-life situations. This "childhood morality" is deceptive because it tends to make us think that if we have not, for example, taken some physical object from another person, we have not stolen and have therefore not broken any moral rule. It fosters the double standard which tends to flourish in many sectors of our society. We would be horrified if a certain political candidate deliberately murdered his opponent. Yet that same candidate, by using the most vicious and slanderous means, could destroy

---

[1] This simplistic approach could be called the "vice squad" concept of morality. Those who adopt it find it easy to conclude that anyone who stays out of trouble with the law (especially the "morals" squad) and normally obeys certain other traditional rules *must* be a moral person.

his opponent's character and reputation, and we would not only consider such behavior by our public officials acceptable, but even come, as we have in fact done, to accept it as normal. Undoubtedly, the prevalence of the double standard in our personal lives, in business, and in the affairs of government, is due in great measure to a failure to develop our moral rules beyond the childhood stage.

2) We are prone first to decide what we *want* to do and then to concoct reasons (any reasons whatever) for doing it. This is the process called rationalization. The employee who pilfers tools and material from his employer can rationalize his behavior quite easily. "The boss is a millionaire; he won't miss the trifles I take home with me from time to time. Besides, I'm not paid enough for my work. I can consider these things I take as salary." And so it goes. We all rationalize our behavior when we think it is necessary to ease our consciences or to save face with others. The philosophical study of ethics will not necessarily make us ethical creatures or keep us from rationalizing certain features of our behavior, but it should help us acquire some criteria to determine what counts as a *good* reason for choosing a certain course of action and better enable us to recognize mere rationalization when we see it. The study of ethics, in short, should help make us more perceptive concerning the difference between rational and irrational ways of behaving and of justifying that behavior.

3) Most moral rules cannot be taken at face value; they require amplification and explanation. The terms composing them must be defined so as to spell out what sorts of actions are and are not covered by them. We must somehow decide what exceptions (if any) may be taken to the rules which we have adopted and spell out clearly the grounds for those exceptions. For example, suppose we consider the traditional moral rule, "Do not kill." Usually people who would hold this rule would also allow exceptions to it. Killing in self-defense, a policeman's killing another person in the performance of his duty, and taking

the life of an enemy in a time of war (at least *some* wars) would probably be regarded as justifiable by most people. The moral rule would be better stated if it were to read, "Do not murder (and murder is defined as unjustified killing)." Now the crucial question is how we are to tell what killing is *justified?* Has this rule concerning the act of murder really told us anything? It presupposes that we already know what counts as an unjustified act of killing, when the major task of ethical enquiry is to *determine* what sorts of acts are right (or justifiable) and which are not.

Another kind of statement looks like a helpful, defensible moral rule until it is exposed through analysis. We are told, "You ought always to do your duty" or "you ought always to do what is right." This is little more than a truism, hardly enlightening or helpful. For the question that is of concern to the morally conscientious person is: what *is* my moral duty? What *is* morally right? If someone were perplexed by a moral dilemma and asked us for advice as to what he should do, he would think he had surely come to the wrong place if we were to tell him, "Oh, you ought to do what is your duty or what is the right thing."

(4) There is a further reason why we need a philosophy of morals (that is, a theoretical enquiry into the meanings of ethical terms and the means of formulating correct moral principles). Quite often there are cases in which several moral rules seem to conflict, and a decision has to be made concerning which rule will be followed and which one does not apply. Suppose you were an aide to Senator Clodd and you had knowledge of certain "irregularities" in the ways your employer had acquired a rather hefty bank account. As his confidant, you have access to papers and records incriminating this "public servant" in illegal activities. What ought you to do in such a situation? Should you (a) expose the illegal enterprises of Senator Clodd and thereby obey the moral rule which states that one should do what he can to expose and prevent unethical acts of those in a position of public trust, or (b) keep quiet about what is going on because your exposure of Senator Clodd would necessitate removal of

documents which are his own private property? After all, removing such material from the Senator's office in order to have reproductions made of them seems like a case of betraying a confidence at the very least, and could also be rightly viewed as stealing.

Let us suppose another moral dilemma in which any of us might find ourselves at one time or another. Suppose your best friend and his mother have been involved in an auto accident. Your friend has been killed, but his mother has survived the mishap; she is in critical condition and does not know the fate of her son whom she loved very much. Suppose she calls for you in order to find out how her son came through the crash. What should you do? Should you (a) tell her the truth or (b) make up some story to the effect that her son is alive and well. By doing (a) you would be obeying the moral injunction, "Always tell the truth," but you would be causing great unhappiness for another person, since to receive such tragic information could impair the recovery of your dead friend's mother. On the other hand, if you concoct some story to tell her, you would be breaking the moral rule "Always tell the truth" so that you could keep the rule which reads "Do not cause another person unhappiness or pain." What ought a person to do in such a situation? Which of the two principles should be followed and on what grounds?

Somewhere the thoughtful person must decide as to which of the so-called traditional moral rules he will adopt and live by when they are in conflict. It is always possible simply to flip a coin to decide between alternative courses of action, but this is not a very satisfactory way of ordering one's life. It could hardly be called *ordering* one's life at all, but rather having one's conduct determined for him by factors of chance. There seems to be in most people the desire to feel that *they* are making their own decisions, and that no one or nothing can strip them of this privilege. If we desire the opportunity to make our own decisions, then it would seem to follow that we should want to act in the most rational way, doing what can be defended with the best

165

reasons. The individual who is not concerned with such matters as reasonable behavior might just as well decide what he will do by the flip of a coin. We have a term for such an attitude, however—it is called "irrationality."

THE CHALLENGE OF THE RELATIVIST

As we begin our search for correct moral rules, we are almost bewildered at the great number from which to choose. Almost every moral principle imaginable has been or is now being applied in some corner of the world, with the result that some of the most peculiar practices are regarded as morally binding upon people. Some people are particularly impressed by the diverse number of moral codes which are used to guide human conduct in various cultures in the world, and conclude that such diversity shows clearly that no one set of moral rules or single moral rule can be universally correct. Neither is one moral standard better or worse than any other, since there is no independent criterion to which we can appeal in judging their relative merits. People who adopt a position like this have been called "cultural relativists."

Argument for Cultural Relativism[2]

When we study societies different from our own, we can see how many different moral codes there are and how the principles of conduct in one society may be turned upside down in another. The Eskimos think it is right to take one's aging parents out into the frozen wastelands and leave them to die, rather then to keep them in the village. The Spartans taught

---

[2] W. G. Summer, *Folkways* (Boston: Ginn and Company, 1907), Chaps. 1, 2, 5, 11. Ruth Benedict, "Anthropology and the Abnormal," reprinted in anthologies MGAS and AB.

their youth that it was wrong to get *caught* stealing but not that it was wrong to *steal*. The Dobu tribe in New Guinea believe that stealing someone else's vegetables is more honorable than growing one's own. Now don't get me wrong: I'm not advocating that we in this society adopt these principles. For our society, stealing *is* wrong. But for some other societies, stealing *is* right. There is no way to compare the two ethical beliefs against a common standard. What "right" and "wrong" mean is determined by the particular society of which you are a member. Consequently, there can be no "correct" set of moral rules if by "correct" we mean "what everyone ought to acknowledge as universally valid and applicable."

Difficulties with This Argument

(1) What is a society? Is it a group with certain common interests? If so, don't we belong to many groups? From which one should we derive our moral code? Even if these problems could be overcome by the advocate of relativism, how is he to know which (if any) of the moral rules he has derived from the "group" he has consulted *applies* to the various situations one finds himself in in daily life?

(2) How many in the group we select must agree to adopt a certain moral rule before it is right? Is a majority in *any* group always right? If a majority of a group one day says, "A is right," and the next day it declares, "A is wrong," can they both *be* correct judgments as the relativist seems to suggest?

(3) Does the relativist reason correctly when he says, "There are diverse moral codes in existence; therefore, no one moral code is correct"? Could it not be that one of the existing moral codes is the correct one, but that holders of the others have failed to discover this for one reason or another? Perhaps we might discover that all cultures agree in certain fundamental moral precepts, but that they differ in the methods they use to apply these tenets.

167

Argument for Emotivism

In all fairness, we should explain that the emotivist would be quite unhappy with us for making him share the company of the relativist. The relativist maintains that society A's moral code is right or correct, and society B's moral principles are also correct, even though they might appear to contradict one another. The emotivist on the other hand, argues that it is a mistake to call *any* moral judgment either true or false. Moral judgments, he claims, are merely expressions of feeling. The emotivist has been asked to share quarters with the cultural relativist at this point because they both reject the notion that there is any one moral rule or set of rules which is correct and which, therefore, everyone ought to adopt.

The emotivist's argument[3] runs as follows: we should start by noting what kind of statements can be either true or false, and then it will be easier to see why we must conclude that ethical utterances like "Stealing is wrong" cannot be either true or false.

Again, we must keep clearly in mind the distinction between analytic and synthetic (or empirical) statements. Should an utterance like "Stealing is wrong" be regarded as analytic? The answer is obviously no. The word "stealing" does not mean "wrong"; it cannot be determined merely by analyzing the meaning of these two terms that the sentence "stealing is wrong" is either true or false. Furthermore, you would not be uttering a logical contradiction if you said, "Stealing is not wrong." So, ethical utterances do not belong to the analytic camp.

How about considering them to be synthetic or empirical statements? If you think they are of this type, then you should be prepared to specify some possible sense perceptions that a

---

[3] A. J. Ayer, *Language, Truth and Logic* (New York: Dover Publications, Inc., 1936), Chap. 6. (Reprinted in anthologies AB, EP, MGAS, ST.) C. L. Stevenson, *Ethics and Language* (New Haven: Yale University Press, 1944), pp. 1-111. (Selection in anthology TBO.)

person could have which would help settle the question concerning the truth or falsity of utterances like "Stealing is wrong." You *could* point out various perceptual procedures for determining whether the assertion "This society *holds* that stealing is wrong" is either true or false, but that is another matter. It seems abundantly clear that no perceptual evidence of any sort could help us determine whether or not the moral utterance "stealing is wrong" is true or false.

We must conclude that the moral judgment "Stealing is wrong" is not a factual statement at all and is incapable of being either true or false. When people make such utterances, they are not asserting facts, but are *expressing their feelings* of disapproval with stealing. "Stealing is wrong" functions roughly like the expression, "Stealing—ugh. I hate it!" Just as a moan, which is ordinarily taken as an expression of pain, cannot be true or false (though it could be sincere or insincere), so the utterance "Stealing is wrong," which expresses a different kind of feeling, cannot be either true or false. A moan does not *assert* anything, and neither does an ethical judgment.

The person making the utterance "Stealing is wrong" is not only expressing his disapproval of stealing but also ordinarily attempting to influence the conduct of others by arousing similar feelings of disgust at this kind of action. Ethical utterances, therefore, may be viewed as having the force of a command. For when we say to someone, "Stealing is morally wrong," we are indirectly telling him not to steal. The use of ethical judgments in helping bring about actions which we deem desirable on the part of others has been grossly overlooked by moral philosophers.

Because moral judgments have the dual function of expressing our own feelings of approval and disapproval with certain types of action and of influencing the conduct of others by arousing similar feelings in them, such utterances can be neither true nor false. They are not factual statements at all, because they do not assert anything about a state of affairs which could be verifiable through observational means. Strictly speaking, there can be no such things as "ethical facts."

Difficulties with This Argument

(1) If all true or false statements are capable of classification as either "analytic" or "synthetic," in which camp do the statements contained in this theory itself belong? What would happen to the emotivist's theory if his own statements were shown to be neither analytic nor synthetic?

(2) If I said "Stealing is wrong" without feeling, would my utterance be without any meaning whatsoever? Suppose I make this ethical utterance without desiring to arouse feelings of any sort in another person. Wouldn't my utterance be understood by those who hear it, and if so, how can the emotivist account for this?

(3) Suppose an animal were caught in a trap and suffered many hours of excruciating pain before being released by a passerby. For the emotivist, the animal's suffering was not bad in itself but only so if someone came to disapprove of such treatment of animals. If no person learned of the creature's pain, then nothing bad would have occurred, from the emotivist's standpoint. Would we not want to say that any unnecessary pain which a sentient being undergoes is bad, whether or not anyone eventually learns about its occurrence and disapproves of it?

(4) If I say "Stealing is wrong," and someone else says "Stealing is not wrong," aren't we in a genuine disagreement? Don't our utterances contradict one another? Could mere expressions of feeling be said to contradict one another? If I say that I like chocolate, and my friend says he hates it, any argument that I might advance to show him he is "wrong" would be absurd. Argument is out of place in such matters. But when we disagree on a moral issue, we can sensibly marshal arguments of one sort or another to support our respective positions, thereby

showing that ethical disputes are not merely disagreements concerning what one happens to like or dislike.

(5) In his account of the functions of moral utterances, the emotivist seems to have fastened his attention to their expressive and evaluative jobs and overlooked another important feature in their makeup. When we say, for example, that Schweitzer was a morally better man than Hitler, we are not saying merely, "Yay for Schweitzer!" and "Boo, hiss for Hitler!" We are saying something *about* these two men and their actions; we are in a way *describing* them. To say "X is a morally good man" is to say at least "X does not inflict unnecessary pain, sorrow, and death on millions of people." It is also to say that "X is sensitive to the needs of others and treats them humanely." Something like this is what the phrase "morally good person" means when it is used to characterize someone's character.

(6) If the emotivist is right, it would be contradictory to say something like "That's the right thing to do, but I don't approve of it," or "I know it's wrong to do X, but I like doing X." Surely there have been times in everyone's life (even the emotivist's) when a course of action was believed to be morally wrong, but nevertheless was approved of and performed by the same person who regarded it as wrong. Yet this can be done without any apparent logical contradictions taking place.

WHAT IS MORALLY RIGHT
IS DISCOVERABLE THROUGH
MORAL INTUITION

The advocates of the positions we shall deal with in the remainder of this chapter argue in one way or another that there are certain types of action which are right and others which are wrong, whether anyone recognizes it or not. What is morally right is not, they contend, dependent upon anyone's feelings, customs or special circumstances. There are certain moral rules which everyone *ought* to adopt, regardless of what their present moral beliefs and principles happen to be. Each of these views, then, may be regarded as at least an indirect response to the challenge of the relativist.

The view we shall examine first is usually referred to as "ethical intuitionism." The advocates of this position (and they include in their number some very able thinkers)[4] contend that neither knowledge about the world or of ourselves, nor the reasoning of the best minds, could ever help us determine what our moral duties are. They maintain that knowledge of facts and the employment of argument are neither necessary for, nor capable of discovering, one single moral obligation. Rather, we arrive at our knowledge of right and wrong through something they call "moral intuition" (not to be confused with "woman's intuition," that most reliable and honorable among human faculties). The intuitionist would defend his case in the following manner:

Philosophers who theorize about morality make a fundamental and glaring mistake if they believe that from the examination of various facts they can validly conclude what we morally ought to do. For example, we may have good factual grounds for the statement, "He will cause a great deal of unhappiness if he steals the old woman's life savings," but we have no logical justification for concluding, "therefore, he *ought not* to steal her money." According to the rules of right reasoning which we learn in logic, such an argument is fallacious. It would be a proper argument only if one included the additional premise, "Causing unhappiness is morally wrong (ought not to be done)." But how do we go about proving this last statement? If we try to defend it by saying, "No one wants to be made unhappy," we are stating

[4] G. E. Moore, *Principia Ethica* (London: Cambridge University Press, 1903), Chaps. 1 and 5. (Selection in anthologies EP, MGAS, TBO.) W. D. Ross, *The Right and the Good* (London: Clarendon Press, 1930), Chaps. 1 and 2. (Selections in anthologies AB, MGAS.)

172

what might be another fact, which again makes it improper to conclude "therefore, one ought not to cause unhappiness for another."

In other words, the following argument is not valid:

1. Victims of theft are caused unhappiness.

2. Mrs. Frugal would be a victim of theft if someone stole her life savings.

3. Therefore, one ought not to steal her savings.

Premises 1 and 2 are possibly true factual statements — we will not debate that here. But in neither premise does the word "ought" appear; neither statement refers to any moral obligation which someone might be under. The conclusion (Statement 3), however, does contain the word "ought" and is an assertion that someone has a certain moral obligation based upon the two preceding premises both of which, we repeat, are factual in nature. This line of reasoning, wherever it occurs, is fallacious because it purports to derive from the premises more than they contain. One cannot derive by a process of reasoning the truth of an "ought" statement (or a statement prescribing some norm for action) from an "is" statement (or an assertion describing some factual state of affairs). No list of factual statements however long can serve as adequate logical grounds for a conclusion of a normative nature.

One way to frame a valid argument which contains a normative conclusion would be as follows:

1. One ought not to cause another unhappiness.

2. Stealing Mrs. Frugal's savings would cause her unhappiness.

3. Therefore, one ought not to steal her savings.

From a strictly logical point of view the argument is valid because the term "ought" (in other arguments some other moral term such as "wrong" might be used) occurs in at least one of the premises. Consequently, it is logically permissable for it to be used in the conclusion of the argument. However, we must not regard this conclusion as true unless we have some way of determining whether Premises 1 and 2 are true. And although the second premise is in all likelihood true, we have a more difficult time with the first. If we attempted to show that it is true by a chain of reasoning which is composed only of factual assertions, then we would be guilty of going from "is" statements to an "ought" statement. We would be trapped in the same logical fallacy as we have just pointed out.

The only way out of such a difficulty is not to abandon the use of normative statements (assertions prescribing how people ought or ought not to act), but to admit that the truth of such statements cannot be proved by any line of reasoning whatsoever. It must be acknowledged that the truth of certain normative statements is simply self-evident. The truth of the statement, "Promises ought to be kept," for example, is self-evident. That is, any person who truly desires to know his moral duties and who has reached sufficient mental and moral maturity[5] can simply "see" immediately that this statement is true. The statement, "Promises ought to be kept," neither requires nor is capable of proof, for it is known to be true in the same way as the statements, "the whole is greater than any of its parts" and "Hugo is either in Houston or not" are known to be true. Our faculty of moral intuition is not identical to some mysterious hunch, but is of the same type as the faculty we have for arriving at the truth of certain axioms in mathematics and logic. What is true but incapable of being proved either deductively or through scientific and perceptual procedures must be self-evident.

The faculty of moral intuition may be less fully developed in one person than in another, however. It can be dis-

---

[5] Ross, *The Right and the Good*, p. 41. "We have no more direct way of access to the facts about rightness and goodness and about what things are right and good, than by thinking about them; the moral convictions of *thoughtful and well-educated people* are the data of ethics. . . . The verdicts of the moral consciousness of the *best* people are the foundation on which he (the moral theorist) must build." (Italics mine.)

torted (or even destroyed) through lack of exercise or through mistraining, so that some individuals may be "morally blind" or lacking in "moral perception." In fact, we often use such phrases when we describe certain individuals, such as the Nazis who calmly practiced the grossest butchery during the last World War.

It is suggested by some that even though we cannot prove the truth of normative statements by appealing to factual statements, we can still *define* ethical terms like "right" and "good." For example, may we not say that good is definable as "that which is pleasurable" and then define "right" actions as those which tend to bring about pleasure? This will not work either. This approach, as well as the other one, commits what may be called the "naturalistic fallacy." This is the mistake of trying to define good in terms of something other than good itself. In our example above, the meaning of "good" is taken to be equivalent in meaning to that of the word "pleasure." An ethical term is purported to be definable by using a nonethical term (or terms)—a mistake made by a good many moral philosophers.

The fact of the matter is that the word "good" and the word "pleasure" stand for two completely different objects. They cannot, therefore, be equivalent in meaning. The word "good" stands for a non-natural property, and the word "pleasure" (as do words like "red" and "yellow") stands for a natural property. Natural properties are those which can be perceived through the five senses, and non-natural properties are those which can be discovered neither through sense perception nor by employing more sophisticated, scientific means of detection.

It is ludicrous to say that "good" can be defined in terms of any other property. It would be like trying to define "red" in terms of "yellow." Each of these color words stands for an object which is completely distinct in character from the other. Good is a non-natural property in that you cannot perceive it through the senses as you can the color red; it is also a "simple" property (that is, it cannot be analyzed or broken down into smaller parts). Things which are composed of parts, of course, can be analyzed and are, therefore, capable of definition. But

175

when we consider the property good, we can see that it is indefinable in the sense that it cannot be broken down into smaller parts. Good is simply good and nothing else. It is not pleasure or happiness or anything else you can think of. It is no more definable than is, for example, the color yellow. True, you can point out things which are yellow, but yellow itself cannot be defined. In the same way you may point out things which *are* good, as in the statements "There is a good person," and "This is a good thing you are doing." But good itself is not capable of definition or analysis.

Once we acknowledge that it is logically incorrect to argue for the truth of normative statements by appealing to factual statements, and that it is impossible to define good, what grounds have we for saying that we can know what is morally right? The ordinary man claims to know that it is right to keep one's promises and help those in distress, but how can such claims be backed up? The only possible way to know what is morally right is through a direct intuitive grasp similar to the way in which we apprehend the basic propositions of mathematics and logic.

Difficulties with This Argument

(1) Whose moral intuition can we trust? Who are the people who have a "well-developed moral sensitivity"? How do we tell who are the "best" people, so that we may use their convictions as the foundation for our ethical theory? Can the moral intuition of these people ever be mistaken (even granting that we know how to identify them)? If so, how are we to tell when they have failed to apprehend a moral truth? It is tempting to draw an analogy between a person who is color-blind and one who seemingly is "blind" to the moral aspect of life. We have *tests* for determining whether or not a person is color-blind, but by what means are we to detect "moral blindness"?

(2) Can there be genuine moral disputes if the intui-

176

tionist's theory is correct? If there can be, how are we to resolve ethical disagreement, since it is claimed that no argument can prove the truth of any moral judgment? Isn't the intuitionist committed to saying that all moral disputes result from either insincerity or an inability to "perceive" what is right by one of the parties in the dispute?

(3) What justification is there for talking about the terms "good" and "right" as though they stood for or named some sort of property? Perhaps those who hold this theory have assumed that if one person says "X is right" and another says "X is not right," their utterances could not be contradictory unless "right" were regarded as a property. This view, then, *seems* to preserve our ordinary belief that there can be genuine contradictions in the realm of moral discourse. However, all that is needed for there to be a contradiction between the utterances of two parties engaged in a moral dispute is that the *reasons* each of them gives for his respective position be different. If we were to ask those in the dispute whether or not X is right, we would not be asking them about the property "rightness," but rather what reasons (if any) there are for doing X as opposed to not doing it.

(4) The so-called fallacy of arguing from purely factual premises to a normative conclusion deserves some critical scrutiny. There do seem to be occasions in everyday life when we draw a normative conclusion based on factual premises and regard such a procedure as perfectly reasonable and proper. For example, suppose all of the following statements are true: (a) I need a dependable, economical automobile. (b) Honest John's Auto Sales, which has a spotless reputation in the car business, is offering to sell a certain car at a price 50% less than his competitors. (c) Honest John guarantees in writing that the car will give at least 20 miles per gallon, and he also has an unusually generous service warranty. In the light of these facts, it would seem perfectly reasonable for me to conclude: (d) I ought at least to go down and look over the car. If I did *not* draw this conclusion could I not rightly be called unreasonable or irrational? Yet the conclusion (Statement d), although non-moral

in nature, is a *normative* one, and the grounds for it are taken by me to be factual and only factual statements.

AN ACT IS RIGHT IF ONE COULD WILL ACTS LIKE IT TO BE PERFORMED BY EVERYONE

Most of us would like to think that we are rational beings and that we are ordering our lives in the most reasonable way. After all, Aristotle has told us that man is a "rational animal," and one would think that most people are interested in being true to their status as human beings. So when someone claims that we should choose our moral rules only after checking them out at the bar of reason, he seems to be pointing us in the right direction. What better way is there to avoid the influence of our vacillating feelings and prejudices which so often lead us into unethical and even self-destructive action? Immanuel Kant proposed that we base our ethical judgments upon the dictates of reason so that we would have a way of knowing our moral duties which is reliable and binding upon everyone. He continually pointed out that moral *rules* could not be based upon the individual's feelings and desires, because these are subject to great and violent change depending upon the circumstances at any given moment. Rules cannot originate in our whims and fancies; genuine moral rules cannot apply one moment and then be lifted the next as we please. They simply cannot bear such treatment and remain rules.

Kant's argument continues as follows: there are two kinds of principles or rules which we can use to guide our conduct. On the one hand, there are what may be called "hypothetical principles." Examples of this sort might be, "If you want to be well-liked, then repay your debts," or "If you want to be a success in business, then be honest in your dealings with others." These are called hypothetical principles because

THE PROBLEM OF MORALITY

there is a condition stated in each of them. *If* you want to be well-liked by others, then (so the principle states), you ought to repay your debts. The statement seems to suggest that if you don't want to be well-liked, then you are under no obligation to pay back what you owe. The obligation to repay debts, if such a principle is adopted, is conditional upon your desire to be well thought of. What happens if one day you don't really *care* what others think of you? What if every time you start to repay a debt you tell yourself that other people's opinions of you don't really matter? Doesn't the obligation to repay your debt disintegrate if it is tied to your likes and dislikes of the moment? To adopt hypothetical principles as moral rules of conduct would be to destroy the whole notion of moral *law* and with it the whole of moral obligation.

The other kind of principle we must consider is a "categorical" principle. Examples of this might be, "Repay your debts," or "Be honest in your dealings with others." There are no conditions stated in these principles. They simply say, "Do such and such, with no 'ifs,' 'ands,' or 'buts' about it." It is the sort of command which an Army drill sergeant would be prone to give. "Repay your debts whether you like it or not and whether it is convenient or inconvenient." Categorical principles have the force of commands or imperatives, and if there are any universally valid moral rules, they must take this form. What we need to do now is to determine what specific categorical imperative or imperatives they are, and to spell out how a person can arrive at them.

In reality there is only one categorical imperative: "Act only on that maxim whereby thou canst at the same time will that it should become a universal law."[6] That is, I should adopt and

---

[6] Immanuel Kant, *Fundamental Principles of the Metaphysics of Morals* (New York: Library of Liberal Arts, 1949), p. 38. (Selections in anthologies AB, BKW, MGAS, SA, ST, TBO.) Kant maintained that the categorical imperative could also be formulated as follows: "So act as to treat humanity, whether in thine own person or in that of any other, in every case as an end withal, never as means only." (p. 46). His arguments for this principle are found in Section II of the same work.

act upon a given rule of conduct, only if I can will that this rule or maxim be given the status of a law which is binding upon any person who finds himself in a situation similar to the one in which I find myself. If I cannot "universalize" a proposed course of action in the way just cited, then I know that I would be acting in obedience to a rule of conduct which is not in accord with moral law, and my action would therefore be immoral.

But what is meant by saying that a person must be *able to will* that a particular rule of conduct be made into a universal law? In one sense of the word "can," we can will that almost any rule be universally adopted: we are capable of *desiring* that a certain rule have this status and then *saying* "I want this rule to be a universal law." However, being *physically* or *practically* able to will something is not the same as being able to will something with *logical consistency.*

Some maxims cannot even be *thought of* as universal laws; if they were adopted by everyone, these rules of conduct would destroy themselves by being internally contradictory. There are other maxims which would not cancel themselves out if elevated to the status of universal laws but which are, nevertheless, unacceptable as moral rules. By our very act of *willing* that these maxims become universal laws, we would be contradicting other acts of will which we are compelled to make merely because we have certain basic needs and desires as human beings. Any given maxim, therefore, must satisfy two conditions in order to be suitable as a correct moral principle: (1) the maxim must be of such a nature that it can be *conceived* as a universal law — it must be capable of being understood and obeyed by everyone; (2) the maxim must be capable of being *willed* to become a universal law without such an act of will contradicting other acts of will we necessarily must make in the course of life.

Let us consider a maxim which fails to pass the first test of consistency. Suppose we wanted to know if the following rule or maxim could be made into a universal law: "Make promises you don't intend to keep when this would be to your advantage."

If this rule were adopted by everyone, then, on those occasions when a person made a promise, no one would believe him. Everyone would know that a person making a promise would be obliged to go back on his word if he so desired. In such a situation, no one could "make a promise" as this act is presently understood, since, in order for a promise to be made, at least the *possibility* of its being believed must exist. But there would be no such possibility if there were a law which obliged everyone to make deceitful promises when it was considered advantageous. The maxim "Make deceitful promises when you consider it to your advantage" could not be obeyed if it became a universal law, since the very act of promise-making would be stripped of meaning. The words "I promise" would be just so many empty symbols. "The promise itself would become impossible, as well as the end that one had in view in it, since no one would consider that anything was promised to him, but would ridicule all such statements as vain pretences."[7] Consequently, the maxim "Make deceitful promises when you consider it to your advantage" does not qualify as a moral rule; it is inconsistent in the sense that it would necessarily destroy itself as soon as it attained the status of a universal law.

As we have already mentioned, some maxims may pass the first test for consistency but nevertheless be unsuitable as universal laws. Their elevation to the status of universal laws would involve our *wills* in a contradiction; that is, the very act of willing that certain maxims become universal laws would involve contradicting other acts of will we necessarily must make as human beings. Suppose a person is at such a point of despair that he regards his life as not worth living and proposes to act on the maxim "End your life if by such an act you can rid yourself of an intolerable existence." The very act of willing that such a maxim be a universal law conflicts with or contradicts a principle within us which impels us to extend and enhance our lives.

---

[7] *Kant's Critique of Practical Reason and Other Works on the Theory of Ethics,* trans. T. K. Abbott (London: Longmans, Green, & Company, Ltd., 1909), p. 40.

This inherent, natural principle could be called the principle of self-love or self-interest; its presence compels us to will those acts which will preserve and improve our lives. We would contradict ourselves, therefore, if we willed that a particular maxim such as the one we are considering be made into a universal law. By this act of will we would be contradicting those acts of will which we must make in order to obey the natural law of self-love, or the law of self-preservation which all men have within them.

The same line of reasoning can be used to show that the maxim "Refuse aid to those in need of it," cannot be made into a universal law. A person might contemplate acting on such a maxim, if he himself were not in need of any sort of assistance at the moment. He might find it more convenient for himself to adopt such a maxim as a rule of conduct than if he were to act benevolently to those in need of his help. But an individual ought not to act on the maxim "Refuse aid to those in need," if by such an act of willing he contradicts other acts of will which he must necessarily make, simply because he has certain needs and desires as a human being. Regardless of how wealthy or self-sufficient a person might be at the moment, there will be occasions in his life when he will be in need of something which can only be given to him by others. It might be the need for love and sympathy or perhaps even for medical aid of various sorts. As a result of these needs, a person will necessarily desire or *will* that someone help him in his distress.

But suppose a person has willed that the maxim "Refuse aid to those in need" be made into a universal law, that is, be adopted by everyone as a correct moral rule. If this maxim became a universal law, it would be in effect at all times and apply to everyone without exception. It would be in effect, therefore, on those occasions when a person, because of some need, willed that he be *given* aid, not *refused* it. Willing that the maxim "Refuse aid to those in need" be made into a universal law would involve a person in *contradicting his will;* on one occasion he would be willing that *no one* should ever be given aid, and then, at another time, he would be willing that *someone* (namely, himself) *should* be given aid when it is desired. It is, therefore, impossible to will that the maxim "Refuse aid to those in need" be made into a universal law, since one would thereby create a contradiction within his own will. One is morally obliged, therefore, to refrain from acting in obedience to this maxim and to act instead in accordance with the principle, "Extend aid to those in need."

In summary, it has been shown that by employing these tests derived solely from reason, we can arrive at a knowledge of what is morally right and wrong. And since a given act is morally right only because it is in accord with a principle which has passed certain rational tests and not because performing the act in question will make things turn out better for us, it is clear what the motive for a moral act should be. We ought to perform our moral duties simply because they are our duties and for no other reason. The truly moral man acts out of pure respect for the moral law whatever it happens to command and regardless of what he believes is "in it for him."

To adopt a certain course of action because we think it will produce good consequences such as happiness or well-being could lead to all sorts of immoral practices. The moral man does not calculate whether a given act will enhance his own well-being, but performs his moral duties because they are the right things to do. This is the one characteristic which distinguishes him from the prudent schemer who adopts only those rules of conduct which he believes will advance his own interests, even at the expense of others.

Difficulties with This Argument

(1) Kant's contention that you ought never to make a deceitful promise or tell any sort of lie for that matter seems questionable. Suppose a man, obviously enraged and carrying a

loaded gun in his hand, appears at my door. He asks me if that "dirty so-and-so Westphal" is at home so he can fill him full of lead. Now according to Kant, I should not lie to the man; I should acknowledge that I'm the man he's looking for. However, Kant also maintained that a person has the principle of self-love or self-regard within him, which impels him to preserve and improve his life. If I told the truth to my would-be killer, I would be disobeying the implanted principle of self-love, and, if I choose to take due regard for my own life, it may necessitate telling a lie. Admittedly, I could refuse to answer the fellow or try to talk him out of it, but suppose he pressed me for a yes or no answer to the question "Are you Westphal?" Either silence or an attempt to dodge the question on my part would most likely be taken as an affirmative answer. There seem to be some situations, therefore, in which telling the truth would necessitate our disobeying some other principle which Kant takes to be a universal rule. Wouldn't Kant be forced to admit that by obeying one moral law we would thereby have to disobey another equally binding law? Such an admission seems to undermine his view of the moral life and its duties, but it nevertheless seems to be an inescapable conclusion.

(2) It seems possible to will that certain maxims which pass the tests Kant laid down become universal laws, but which nevertheless would strike us (and even Kant himself) as unacceptable from the moral point of view. Suppose you were a slave-owner and you proposed to act on the following maxim: "Slave-owners who were born on April 13, 1932, are over six feet tall, weigh over 200 pounds, and speak English may torture their slaves whenever they please." Such a maxim would not be internally contradictory or destroy itself if universalized, and you need not involve your will in a contradiction if you willed it to be adopted by everyone. The chances of your ever being a slave are extremely slim, and it is even more unlikely that you would ever be a slave owned by someone who answers to the description specified in the above maxim. You would not, therefore, ever be in a situation where you would will *not* to be tortured

by a slave-owner of the above type. Willing that the maxim "Slave-owners who were born on April 13, 1932, are over six feet tall, weigh over 200 pounds, and speak English may torture their slaves whenever they please" be adopted by all involves no contradiction in your will, so there could be no objection to this maxim being a moral law. Yet there is every indication that Kant would regard this rule of action as morally incorrect; consequently, the criteria suggested by Kant whereby we are to determine our moral duties must be inadequate.

(3) Does it seem correct to say that if a person comes to the aid of another solely because he has great affection and regard for the well-being of others, then his action is without moral value? If an individual fights injustice because he hates it and desires more just arrangements in society, it would seem that his actions have moral value even though they proceed from his feelings of indignation and his desire for improvements in social conditions and not out of "pure respect for the moral law."

(4) Kant at times makes reference to principles of conduct which he regards as implanted in us "by nature." He argues, we recall, that we have a natural principle within us impelling us to self-improvement and self-preservation and that, therefore, we have no moral right to act on a rule of conduct which permits suicide. We should, however, be wary of such appeals to "laws of nature" when they are construed as prescribing certain types of conduct. The scientist formulates laws of nature to serve as general descriptions of what happens in the world which then form the foundation for the explanation and predictions of other phenomena. But to view these laws of nature as commands is surely to invite confusion. Just because human beings seek to preserve their lives, it does not follow that they are under any obligation to do so. Even if some of these so-called "implanted natural principles" could be discovered, there would be no justification for concluding that they ought to be obeyed. There is some difficulty even in making sense of the expression "obeying a law of nature," since such laws are best viewed as descriptive rather than normative in character.

AN ACT IS RIGHT
IF IT TENDS TO PRODUCE
PLEASURE OR HAPPINESS

Some philosophers, while still acknowledging the great contributions of Kant to the study of ethical theory, have contended that his approach leaves much to be desired. It is argued that the process of arriving at a knowledge of what is morally right must involve some calculation concerning the *consequences* of our actions. Kant's own second consistency test looks very much like asking the question, "What will happen to *me* in the future if everyone adopts the rule of conduct in question? Wouldn't it be foolish of me to wish a certain rule to be adopted by everyone when there is a good chance it will turn out to my disadvantage in the future?" A strong case could be made for the position that even Kant did not succeed in dismissing as irrelevant the probable *consequences* which a certain rule's adoption would have for one's own well-being.

Utilitarians[8] are one group of philosophers who emphasize that the consequences of any given act determine whether that act is morally right or wrong. The motive or intention behind an action may be of the most commendable sort; the agent may be acting with the firm conviction that he is doing what is right, and still be doing the morally wrong thing. Philosophers who maintain that actions are morally right or wrong depending upon the consequences produced differ on what sort of consequences a given act must produce if it is properly to be regarded as moral. The utilitarian position is that actions which tend to produce happiness (or, the presence of pleasure and the absence of pain) are right, and those which tend to result in the opposite of these are wrong. We now take up their arguments for this contention.

---

[8] John Stuart Mill, *Utilitarianism*, 1863. (Selections in anthologies BKW, SA, ST, TBO.) Jeremy Bentham, *An Introduction to the Principles of Morals and Legislation*, 1789.

The crucial concept in this theory is that of happiness or pleasure, and it is one which is quite familiar to all of us. Yet we find it hard to define the word "pleasure" except by mentioning various examples of what people generally consider to be pleasurable or enjoyable experiences. It's the type of feeling you have when you are eating your favorite dish, reading an exciting book, or having fun at a party. This is about as far as a definition of pleasure can go, and probably no more is required to let people know what you are talking about when you use the word "pleasure." The difficulty lies not so much in defining "pleasure," but in trying to show what *kind* of pleasure or enjoyment must be produced by morally right acts. Surely we would not say that torturing another person because it gave us enjoyment would be a morally right act. However, aren't we forced to conclude that according to our utilitarian theory almost any sort of behavior *could* be justified so long as pleasure is produced by it? But this is not the case, for we must distinguish between various grades or kinds of pleasure. For human beings, some pleasures are superior to others, and it is these which we should aim to bring about by our actions if at all possible. The inferior type of pleasures are still valuable simply because they are pleasures, but they should be sacrificed in favor of the "higher" ones if both cannot be brought about in a given instance.

But which pleasures are superior and which are inferior? How do we tell one type from the other ? Who is to say that his pleasures are better than someone else's and therefore deserve to be promoted? The only test to rely upon here is that of experience—but not just anyone's experience. We ought to ask those people who have had a reasonably thorough acquaintance with *all* kinds of pleasure which ones they find most desirable. People who have had wide experience in various kinds of enjoyment will generally agree that if they *had* to choose between a life in which only the pleasures of intellectual and aesthetic activity were possible and an existence in which the only pleasures available were those of a physical or sensual nature, they would prefer the former. Happily, in this present life both sorts of pleasure are open to us. We may enjoy the pleasures which result from using our intellects in thinking and reading, we can be pleasantly excited by objects of beauty, and most of us are fortunate enough to experience the joys of friendship and love. But along with these superior or higher pleasures we also rightly enjoy those pleasures which are more closely associated with the body—satisfaction of our desires for food, physical recreation, and sexual activity.

Human beings require higher forms of pleasure because they have the higher faculties of intellect, imagination and feeling. No human being who really thought it through would trade places with one of the lower animals, whose whole existence appears to be a constant round of fulfilling a few basic bodily drives. "It is better to be a human being dissatisfied than a pig satisfied; better to be Socrates dissatisfied than a fool satisfied."[9]

This may answer the question as to *what* pleasures ought to be promoted by our actions, but another difficulty arises. *Whose* pleasures should be advanced? We should think that the individual who takes pleasure in seeing others suffer or the person who steals a stereo set in order to enjoy the beauties of Mozart surely should be thwarted. Any act which contributed to pleasure in these two circumstances could hardly be called morally right. How do we decide *whose* happiness ought to be promoted and how one ought to go about attaining pleasurable experiences?

First of all, we ought to do that act which would produce the greatest amount of happiness or pleasure among those acts open to us. It will help if we remember that no one individual's happiness is any more valuable than the next person's—each person counts for one and no more. It is rather like the "one man,

---

[9] Mill, *Utilitarianism* (New York: Liberal Arts Press, 1957), p. 14.

one vote" principle applied to morals. Considered strictly by itself, the happiness or well-being of A is no more or no less valuable than the happiness of B or C or anyone else. But if A desires his happiness *at the expense* of the happiness of others, or if A's notion of what will make him happy undermines or destroys the happiness or pleasure of others, then it is clear that we ought not to promote A's happiness. More happiness and less pain will result if we refuse to promote A's interest and take positive steps to block them, than if we had otherwise allowed him freedom of action to pursue his goals. Happiness or pleasure of any sort is of itself valuable and the only thing inherently worth having, but on occasion some people's pleasures must be sacrificed in order to bring about the greatest amount of good (happiness) in the world.

Furthermore, it is often the case that some of our own short-range pleasures must be sacrificed in the interest of more lasting well-being in the future. For example, it may be that you receive great pleasure from eating particularly rich and highly caloric desserts. Without a doubt, you would receive pleasure from having a second or third piece of your favorite pie with your meal, but there is a good chance that you would be forfeiting future happiness if you were to indulge at the moment. With the additional portions of tasty food come the inevitable increases in weight, causing an additional strain on your vital organs which might contribute to a painful illness and an early death. So in order to maximize the *total* amount of pleasure you can experience, some pleasures simply have to be forgone. These sacrificed, momentary pleasures are not evil in themselves, of course, but it would be wrong to indulge in them because of their potential for leading to bad consequences in the long run.

What proof can be given for saying that the only thing worth having or striving for, the only good in itself, is pleasure and that, consequently, a right act is one which promotes the greatest amount of it? If the kind of proof we are looking for is of the sort we get in mathematics and logic, then there can be no proof of this principle of utility. How would you go about constructing a proof for the proposition, "Pleasure is the only good worth having or striving for"? We would all admit that health is good or worth having, yet how would we go about proving it? There are a good many beliefs we can't prove in the strict sense of that term but which we nevertheless regard as acceptable on intellectual grounds. The principle of utility can be "proved" to be true only in the sense that arguments for it can be advanced which are capable of convincing the intellect. Beyond that we cannot go.

What are these considerations which may be used to back up the principle of utility? The only way of showing that something is desirable is to point out that it is desired. The only way of proving that a particular thing is visible is by pointing out that someone is seeing it. We do, in fact, all desire happiness of one sort or another, and we search for it in a variety of places with diverse methods. We may assume that the presence of pleasure and the absence of pain are desirable, therefore, in and of themselves.

Since utilitarianism is a doctrine which has been greatly misunderstood and maligned, some of the more usual objections to it should not go unchallenged. The first objection goes like this: "It is impossible to attain happiness in this life. There are so many things which can quickly destroy our enjoyments — sickness, harmful actions of other people, the ravages of nature, and finally, death, always waiting in the wings, ready to enter at any moment. How could life be happy under these conditions? The utilitarian is asking us to do the impossible when he says that we ought to act so as to promote the greatest amount of happiness." But this objection seems to assume that the type of happiness we desire is that of continual exultation and exhilarating rapture. *This* truly is impossible, but a life relatively free from prolonged periods of pain and made up of many and various pleasures is within man's grasp. By continually trying to improve man's living conditions and, above all, by cultivating his mind and feelings, a growing number of people can enjoy a relatively good or pleasurable life.

When a person is unable to find enjoyment in life, the usual cause is selfishness. The person who cares little or nothing about the interests of others and desires happiness only for himself is likely to find his existence a lonely and miserable one. Part of the happy life, then, is actively to seek to promote the interests of others. The next most important reason for unhappiness (after the needs of the body have been taken care of) is the lack of a cultivated mind. By this I mean a mind that has been initiated into a knowledge of the workings of nature, the wonders of art, and the ways in which sensitive and creative persons have expressed themselves in literature, history, and philosophy. A person capable of enjoying the pleasures these activities afford has an excellent opportunity to live the good life. Most of the things which cause unhappiness and pain in the world would be less effective if human beings would take the proper steps to subdue them. The principal method of making the good life available to the greatest number is to prepare people for it through a liberal education. Along with this should come the application of scientific knowledge to the elimination of ignorance, poverty, and disease.

Another objection to utilitarianism is this: "The principle that we ought to do what we can to promote happiness, including our own, is simply another way of advocating that we do what is expedient. The utilitarian seems to be saying that if by stealing, for example, a person can make either himself or others happier than they would otherwise be, then he ought to steal. Or suppose that I make a promise to a dying friend to the effect that I will do certain things to assist his family after he is gone. Then I find that it will involve great inconvenience or sacrifice on my part to keep my word. Suppose further that my friend's family is generally an ungrateful, indulgent lot who would only squander my aid anyway. According to utilitarianism, I need have no qualms about breaking my promise if more happiness will result from breaking it than would result from keeping it. This is mere expediency and highly immoral."

This objection fails to take account of the fact that *all* of the consequences of a given act must be considered and not just the ones close at hand. What will be the lasting results upon the moral character of the individual who breaks a promise whenever he thinks it convenient to do so? "The cultivation in ourselves of a sensitive feeling on the subject of veracity is one of the most useful and the enfeeblement of that feeling one of the most hurtful things to which our conduct can be instrumental."[10] We must remember that what we do may not only affect other people, but can also affect ourselves. If we break a promise on one occasion for no reason other than expediency, it becomes much easier for us to break promises *all* the time. Such a tendency on the part of the moral agent could cause unhappiness to many people, and if enough people practiced such behavior, a great deal of unhappiness would result. Society would no longer be based on laws and mutual trust, but the "law of the jungle" would reign with all of its insecurity and violence.

In short, the consequences of a *single act* of stealing in a particular instance may be beneficial not only to the agent involved but also to a number of people. But an intelligent moral agent can see that he ought not to perform an act if it belongs to a *class* of actions whose results would be harmful if *generally* practiced. If people stole when they felt like it or thought it expedient, all sorts of unhappiness would result. Taking exceptions to moral rules which have been adopted at large because of their beneficial consequences for mankind is a very serious matter and ordinarily is unethical.

There are cases, however, in which exceptions may be taken to a moral rule like "Do not lie." If a man comes to my house with gun in hand and angrily asks when my "dirty so-and-

---

[10] Mill, *Utilitarianism*, p. 29.

so" neighbor will be home, I have no moral obligation to tell the truth. We would say that my obligation is to lie to the would-be murderer if that will save my neighbor's life. Saving a life rates higher than telling the truth if veracity on a given occasion would most likely contribute to someone's death.

It is part of the task of ethics to define the limits to the exceptions that may rightly be taken to accepted moral rules like "Do not lie," "Do not steal," "Do not kill." The definition of such limitations must always, however, be made in the light of the principle of utility. The test must always be, "What would be the most likely consequences for human happiness if a certain exception is included in a given moral rule (e.g., 'Do not tell lies, except in order to save a human life')?"

This leads us to a consideration of the last objection to utilitarianism. "There is not enough time to calculate the consequences of a given course of action. By the time we try to weigh the possible results of each alternative action open to us, disaster may have struck." Such an objection assumes that we approach each situation in life starting from scratch. The fact of the matter is that we have centuries of human experience upon which to rely. There is no such thing as absolute certainty concerning the consequences of a given course of action. But we know that almost all of the time certain consequences can be expected to result from certain courses of action. We know, for example, that if a person tells a lie, he often must tell another lie to cover up the first and another after that. The final consequences of the original lie can often be exposure, embarrassment, and a damaged reputation as well as great harm to those who have relied upon our veracity.

Our actions have important consequences regarding the development of moral character, and these cannot be overemphasized. With every commission of an act which promotes happiness in ourselves and others, one's character becomes more sensitive to the rightful place of moral considerations in daily life. And each time one commits an act which cannot be justified by the principle of utility, it becomes just a little easier to ignore the legitimate interests of others and compromise our standards in other moral situations.

We can know, then, something of the short and long range consequences of different kinds of action if we will take the time and effort to learn from the lessons of past experience. If we are to have a relatively objective moral code, then knowledge gained from experience must provide us with the data upon which to build. Any other approach to morality leaves too much room for personal feelings and biases to distort one's judgments.

Difficulties with This Argument

(1) Suppose we all agree after taking account of the consequences of wars that they are evil. In spite of the fact that a few good things have resulted from war, we conclude that generally speaking, more unhappiness than happiness can be traced to it. In the light of man's experience with the consequences of war, what sort of moral rule should we formulate to guide action preventing it? Suppose we can show that the principle "do not engage in any action which will be likely to cause another physical harm" would, if generally adopted, lead to more happiness than unhappiness. If everyone (including one's potential enemies) followed this principle, then wars would cease and with them all the suffering and sorrow which they cause. But what do we do if another nation (or individual) decides to break this moral rule? Are we justified in breaking it too just because someone else violates it first? Are we forced to place a qualifying phrase in the rule so that it will read, "Do not engage in any action which will likely cause another physical harm except in self-defense"? But what counts as "self-defense" both for an individual and for a nation?

(2) Aren't there many occasions in which it is difficult if not downright impossible to judge the probable consequences of a given act? Suppose you hear a call for help from someone

drowning. You realize you are only a fair swimmer, and the fellow in trouble is about a half mile out in deep water. No one else is around; there is no boat or raft available. The question running through your mind would probably be, what will happen if I try to save him? Can I make it out there and then pull him to safety? Perhaps there will be *two* drowning victims, and what will that prove? What about my family and those who depend upon me for their well-being? Suppose further that you are a brilliant scientist engaged in a research project whose findings could ultimately save thousands of lives and relieve the suffering of many more thousands? Can the utilitarian view or *any* ethical theory help you arrive at your moral duty in such a situation?

(3) Suppose two different acts, A and B, were to have identical consequences; would we say that the two actions must both be right or both be wrong as the utilitarian seems forced to admit? Suppose you happen to have a boat handy, and you row out to the fellow drowning. You manage to get him to the edge of the boat, but he slips out of your hand, only to go under and drown. Suppose, however, the victim were to drown under quite different circumstances. When you get him up to the side of the boat, you recognize him as your most bitter enemy, one who is competing with you for a particular position you prize very much. After you look around to see that no one is watching, you push the unfortunate fellow under and hold him there until he drowns. The consequences of both acts were identical—the individual in the water drowned. Suppose further that there would be no effect upon your character from pushing the fellow under, because you had access to a drug which would erase all memories of the event from your mind. Wouldn't we all admit that the two acts were not equally moral, that an unsuccessful attempt to save the life of another could still be morally commendable, whereas deliberately taking someone's life is morally wrong? How could the utilitarian agree with this conclusion and remain true to his theory?

(4) From the fact (if it is a fact) that everyone desires

only pleasure or happiness does it follow that only pleasure *ought* to be desired? And when Mill says that a certain thing is desirable because someone actually desires it, just as a particular thing is visible because it is in fact seen, doesn't his analogy break down? Apparently he wants to say that the only reason that can be given for a thing's being *worthy* of being desired is that it actually is desired. But in order to maintain the parallel with the word "visible," the only thing he seems entitled to say is that one can prove that something is *capable* of being desired only by showing that someone desires it.

WHY BE MORAL?

We may disagree on some of the details of morality, but suppose we agree that certain fundamental principles like "Do what you can to help another in distress," and "Promote the interests of others as well as your own," are good moral rules. The question may still be asked, however, "*Why* should I do what is right? Maybe it is more ethical to promote the happiness of others than to cause them pain and hardship. But suppose on a particular occasion I don't want to do what is right. Why ought I always to do what is moral?" Such a question has not gone unanswered and we shall now deal with some proposed solutions.

"You Ought to Be Moral Because It Is in Your Own Interest."

You ought to adopt the moral point of view in your life because it pays to do so. You will be a happier, more satisfied person if you cultivate and exercise the moral side of your personality than if you disregard the interests of others and adopt a purely selfish, self-centered attitude. No one respects and admires the person who thinks only of himself and who expects others to live by certain established moral rules, but acts as though he is some sort of privileged character. If you get the reputation of being a person who does not keep his word, who is indifferent to the interests of others and who may even do them harm if it will benefit you, people will avoid your company, they will be suspicious of your every move, and more than likely no one will care what happens to you when *you* are in need of their aid. The most happy people are those who do not deliberately seek only their own happiness, but who actively promote the well-being of others. This attitude might be called "disinterested altruism" because it advocates that we do good to others not *in order that* we ourselves will be happy. Rather, the moral man is happy as a result of his adopting the moral point of view.

> The unselfish man (i.e., the moral man) is he who finds satisfaction in the happiness of other people, and sorrow in their sorrow. The selfish man is he who does not make the happiness of others his end at all, because he receives no satisfaction from it.[11]

However, some philosophers have thought that this approach makes the moral man's happiness too dependent on outward circumstances. It is so easy to conclude that if others do *not* respect you for being moral, and you do *not* get much happiness from seeing others happy, then you are not obliged to do what is right. Plato,[12] for example, argued that the moral man (or the "just" man, as he put it) is happy regardless of the reaction of others to him. His happiness or satisfaction depends only upon an inner state of mind which is characterized by peace and harmony. Aren't we all familiar with cases in which a person has done the morally right thing only to be rewarded with persecution for his stand?

Plato maintained that the just man is the individual who

---

[11] W. T. Stace, *The Concept of Morals* (New York: Macmillan & Co., 1937), p. 279.

[12] Plato, *Republic*, Book I.

has attained self-control, who is able to maintain a check on his desires or passions. Unless a person takes a firm hand with his unruly passions by means of reason, all sorts of self-destructive things will happen. The emotions know no limit but simply clamor for satisfaction without any realization of the ultimate consequences to the agent if he allows them to have their own way. For example, we all know what the eventual outcome would be for us if our desire for tobacco were allowed to exert its influence unchecked. Excessive cigarette smoking has been shown to be damaging to health and capable of contributing to an early death.

The just or moral man allows each of his desires to be satisfied just so far as such satisfaction will contribute to his overall well-being and harmony. We may look at the moral man, then, as the only person who is truly *free*, because he is not under the control of his desires (which for Plato are the inferior aspects of the personality). But by exerting his will in accordance with the dictates of reason, the just man *rules himself* and is not tossed about by the unthinking demands of his emotions. The just man is happy because he has learned how to harmonize the conflicts between his reason and his passions and can, therefore, attain peace and harmony no matter what his outward conditions of life may be.

What should be said of the view that it is in one's own interest to be moral? While it may be true that some moral persons are happy, a man *could* be moral in his dealings with others and be unpopular because of it; it is also obvious that the moral man is not necessarily free from intense physical pain. A person who is in virtually constant pain would have a very difficult time being happy regardless of how moral he is. However, it may be contended that all *immoral* men are unhappy, and this proposition seems to be at least closer to the truth. The criminal, the inhumane dictator, and the scheming, self-centered egoist must each contend with various sorts of anxieties, fears, unsatisfied desires, and untamed aggressions which rob him of peace of mind and self-respect. The blatantly immoral way of life is probably not worth the cost to the individual if he must regard every man as a potential enemy to be conquered by one means or another.

However, we need to be wary of most generalizations, and the one which states that all immoral men are unhappy is no exception. It may be true that the *extremely* immoral man (the practitioner of brutality, murder and aggression) cannot be happy, but what about the person who is less *obviously* immoral? There are many people who simply mind their own business and do what they can to further their own interests while at the same time being completely indifferent to the needs of others. They try not to violate the law openly, and if they do something unethical, they take every precaution to ensure that no one learns about it. It would be quite difficult to show how the person who practices his immorality "discreetly" must necessarily be less happy than the moral man.

"You Ought to Be Moral Because God Commands It."

According to this answer to the question, "Why be moral?" the rewards for being moral and the punishments for being immoral originate with God, the perfect personal being who commands certain acts to be done and others to be avoided. Not even the immoral act committed in secret will go unnoticed, and the moral act which may cause the agent great personal unhappiness in this life shall someday reap its due reward.

Undoubtedly, there are many people whose behavior is actually motivated by the threat of punishment and the promise of reward from God, which they believe will be meted out *perhaps* in this life but surely in the life to come. But it is doubtful if such considerations are good reasons for being moral. Obviously, for those who do not believe in a perfect personal being, this reason for acting morally is completely without value. However, let us suppose there is a God who is the source of certain commands concerning what is right and wrong. Would we then have good reasons for being moral? Some philosophers[13] have thought not, for the following reasons:

Either God has a good reason for what he commands, or he doesn't. If he does *not*, then his commands are merely arbitrary fiats, and our only reason for obeying them would be fear of punishment. Just *why* should we obey a person who issues commands for no good reason and who demands our obedience merely because we believe he has the power to punish us? We could rightly doubt whether such a being is *worthy* of our obedience, for he may be merely a very powerful person and not morally good at all.

However, if God *does* have a good reason (or reasons) for what he commands us to do, then our obligation to do what is right depends on these reasons and not on God's commanding us to do it. If a particular act is a right one, and God commands it simply because it is right, then our obligation to do it is logically independent of his commanding the act to be done. We would be obliged to be moral, then, whether God existed or not and whether God commanded it or not.

"But," it may be objected, "we ought to do what is moral not from the fear of punishment or the prospect of divine reward, but because of love and devotion to God." The problem with this response is that it presupposes that one loves and is devoted to a God who is *worthy* of such an attitude. It assumes that God has the best moral qualities and that we should love him because of these qualities. But if this is the basis of the reason for our being moral, then the real answer to our question should read: "We ought to be moral because we love God; he is worthy of such devotion because he is good and desires the happiness or well-being of man." Again, the ground of our obligation to be moral would seem to be independent of our belief that there is a good God who is worthy of our devotion and

---

[13] A. C. Ewing, *The Definition of the Good* (New York: Crowell-Collier & Macmillan, Inc., 1947), pp. 106-109.

who commands that we adopt the moral point of view. In any event, such a reason as "God commands us to be moral" can have an effect only upon those who believe that (a) such a being exists, (b) such a being is morally good, and (c) such a being has revealed to man in some way what is morally right. Some serious difficulties in maintaining at least the first of these propositions have been discussed in Chapter One, and the truth of the other two statements is equally difficult to substantiate.[14]

"You Ought to Be Moral Because It Is in Everyone's Interest."

If we are going to give an adequate answer to the question, "Why be moral?" we must remind ourselves why moral rules exist at all. The major purpose in having established, known rules of conduct which are to be followed by everyone is to solve conflicts of interest. Moral rules play a major role in harmonizing and adjudicating those conflicts which necessarily arise between individuals in a society. If everyone were to adopt the policy of following his own self-interest exclusively, then most likely no one's interests would end up being satisfied. We would have what Hobbes called "a state of nature" in which no one would be free from fear, insecurity, and violence. The people with the most power to enforce their wills would have their self-interest fulfilled, but only for a brief time. Before long

---

[14] W. R. Dennes, "Preface to an Empiricist Philosophy of Religion," in *College of the Pacific Publications in Philosophy*, III, (1934). Reprinted in part in *Problems of Ethics*, ed. by Dewey, Gramlich and Loftsgordon (New York: Crowell-Collier & Macmillan, Inc., 1961), pp. 98-101. Dennes, on page 99 of the latter volume, raises the problem concerning the criteria for determining what the commands of God actually are. "How are we to determine which of the various commands, offered to us by diverse religions as having divine origin and authority, are actually what their sponsors say they are? . . . Unless we know what is right by some mark other than that a god (or even all the gods) commands it, we shall be unable to distinguish the commands of gods from the commands of imposters."

another individual or group of individuals would get what *they* wanted—at the expense of everyone, if need be.

In order to prevent such an unhappy, insecure state of existence, we adopt certain moral rules which everyone is expected to be able to learn and obey. "The answer to our question, 'why should we be moral?' is therefore as follows. We should be moral because being moral is following rules designed to overrule reasons of self-interest whenever it is in the interest of everyone alike that such rules should be generally followed."[15]

Obviously, all of a person's interests cannot be satisfied if he is to remain a member of society. Some of them must be overruled by moral considerations which should be regarded as superior to considerations of self-interest. One may consider it to be in his interest to break a promise merely because it calls for some sacrifice on his part to keep it, but for the good of everyone *alike,* the moral point of view ought to have precedence over the standpoint of self-interest.

Unless the moral point of view is generally adopted and practiced, the interests of everyone alike will be threatened, since the only alternative to having human conduct subject to certain moral rules is to maintain one's existence by the principle that "might makes right." The adoption of moral rules to guide human conduct is definitely superior to resorting to the "law of the jungle," in that the former arrangement provides the best opportunity for benefitting everyone alike and not simply those individuals with the most physical, political, or economic power.

"You Ought to Be Moral Simply Because It Is Right."

There are still those who will not be put off. They are not satisfied with anything we have said up to now and continue

---

[15] Kurt Baier, *The Moral Point of View* (New York: Random House, Inc., 1965), p. 155. (Selections in anthologies AB, TBO.)

to ask, "Why ought I to follow moral rules on a given occasion if I find it in my interest to disregard them?" It is clear that what they seek are reasons *based* on self-interest for deciding to act *against* their own self-interest. But this is to ask for something which logically cannot be given.

In order to show how odd the question, "Why be moral?" really is, suppose we imagine the following conversation taking place:

A: I ought to go help Jones with his algebra.

B: Why?

A: Because I promised him I would.

B: But ought you really to go?

A: Yes, I ought to do whatever I promise someone.

B: But why should you keep promises?

A: Because *anyone* ought to do whatever he promises *anyone* else he will do.

B: Why?

Notice that *B* in the conversation is trying to press his questions further than they can go. "Beyond this point, however, the question cannot arise: there is no more general 'reason' to be given beyond one which relates the action to an accepted social practice."[16]

---

[16] Stephen Toulmin, *An Examination of the Place of Reason in Ethics* (Cambridge: Cambridge University Press, 1953), p. 146. One might rightly question whether or not a particular accepted social practice is a *moral* one, whether or not it is morally right to continue a certain kind of conduct which is acceptable in a given society or culture. This is where the going in ethics gets particularly tough, for we seem called upon to provide some independent standard which can be used to judge various kinds of actions as morally right or wrong. We have noticed in this chapter some of the difficulties philosophers have run into in their attempts to defend various versions of such an objective, independent criterion.

The question "Why be moral?" does not make sense within the discipline of ethics. The question suggests that perhaps we *ought* to do something other than what is moral or right. But what *ought* we to do if it is not what is right? When we have justified a particular action by giving *moral* reasons why it should be done, we have given the very best reasons that we can possibly come up with. It seems like a contradiction in terms even to suggest that we ought to do something other than the morally right thing, and therefore the question "Why be moral?" sounds almost as odd as the query, "Why is a circle a circle?"

SUGGESTIONS FOR FURTHER STUDY

Anthologies

AB, Part 2; BKW, Chap. 2; EP, Part 4; F, Part 6; MGAS, Part 5; SA, Part 6; ST, Chap. 10; TBO, Part 5; TH, Chaps. 19 and 20.

Others

Hospers, John, *Human Conduct, An Introduction to the Problems of Ethics,* esp. Chaps. 1, 5, 6, 7 and 11. New York: Harcourt, Brace and World, 1961.

Oldenquist, Andrew, ed., *Readings in Moral Philosophy.* Boston: Houghton Mifflin Co., 1965.

Taylor, Paul W., *The Moral Judgment, Readings in Contemporary Meta-Ethics.* Englewood Cliffs, N.J.: Prentice-Hall, Inc., 1963.

THE PROBLEM
OF KNOWLEDGE
VI

When Can I Say That I Know?

We should remind ourselves again that when doing philosophy we should be as clear as possible concerning the issue at hand before we begin advancing some particular point of view. We must clear up any doubts as to what is being asked if confusion is to be avoided. When we raise the question, "When can I say that I know?" one answer might be, "whenever you please: no one is stopping you." But our question is concerned with something less trivial than this. What we are asking in this chapter is, "When am I *justified* in making a claim to know something?" Our enquiry is obviously not about the political right to free speech but about the *logical* right to make a claim to knowledge.

We may say that a person is justified in making a claim to know some particular state of affairs if he has *good reasons* for the claim. But what will count as a good reason for one type of knowledge claim will not be an acceptable justification for a different kind of claim to know. For example, we would give quite different sorts of reasons for the truth of the statement,[1] "Rain is falling in Rio," than we would if we tried to substantiate the claim that every cube has twelve edges of equal length. And if we wished to back up the claim that the universe came into existence because of a "big bang" billions of years ago, we would produce reasons which are distinct in type from the first two kinds. Furthermore, we would be confronted with yet another sort of reason should we ask a friend how he knows that we are in a sour mood. To give a fairly complete answer to the question, "When can I say that I know?" we would have to examine various kinds of statements making some claim to knowledge, and see what we actually accept as good reasons for each type of claim. Unfortunately, the scope of the present chapter will not permit such a comprehensive treatment. But at least we can get the investigation under way by focusing our attention on the first two types of knowledge-claims we have just mentioned.

NECESSARY AND CONTINGENT TRUTHS

We might regard the two statements "Rain is falling in Rio" and "Every cube has 12 edges of equal length" as representatives for two very large classes of statements with which we

---

[1] The word "statement" has been used throughout the book synonymously with the expression "indicative sentence," and we shall continue the practice in the following discussion. Some philosophers prefer to keep the two quite distinct, maintaining that a statement is an assertion or claim made by means of a sentence which may be spoken or written in English, French, German, or some other language. In this view, statements are what is asserted, while sentences are those devices by means of which the asserting is done. See J. L. Austin, *Philosophical Papers* (London: Oxford University Press, 1961), pp. 85-89, especially.

are all acquainted. The statement "Rain is falling in Rio" belongs to the same class as ones like "Jones is wearing a blue suit," "Paris is the capital of France," and "The book you want is on the second shelf from the bottom."

The assertion, "Every cube has twelve edges of equal length," belongs to the family of statements which also has as members the following: "A gander is a male goose," "$8 \times 7 = 56$," and "Either Hugo is here, or he is not." What we shall do now is to show what family resemblances these two groups of statements have, and we shall do this by regarding "Rain is falling in Rio" and "Every cube has twelve edges of equal length" as representatives of their respective families.

"Rain is falling in Rio."	*"Every cube has twelve edges of equal length."*
1. Contingent	1. Necessary
2. *A posteriori*, or empirical	2. *A priori*, or logical
3. Synthetic	3. Analytic

What is meant by each of the terms in these two lists? What characteristics of these two sample statements are being marked out by these words?

First, the statement "Rain is falling in Rio" is called contingent because its truth is dependent upon certain conditions being present in the publicly observable world. Its truth is *contingent* or dependent upon its being the case that rain is falling in Rio at the present time, and also upon the condition that there really is a place which is referred to by the name "Rio." However, things are quite different with the statement "Every cube has twelve edges of equal length." The truth of this assertion is not dependent upon certain events taking place in the observable world. If anything is a cube, then it *must necessarily* have twelve edges of equal length, regardless of whether or not there is such a thing as a cube in existence. It is *always* the case that cubes have twelve edges of equal length, and consequently, statements of this type are called "necessary."[2]

Secondly, the statement about rain's falling in Rio could be regarded as making a claim such that it must be judged true or false *a posteriori*. That is, the truth of the assertion can be arrived at only after appropriate steps have been taken to verify it and such verification involves someone's actually perceiving the rain falling in Rio. It is not possible to determine whether the claim is true or false simply by examining the meaning of the words in the statement; rather, some observations are required in order to know what weather conditions prevail in Rio at the present moment. But since, as we have already seen, the statement "Every cube has twelve edges of equal length" is necessarily true, we need not wait until certain observational procedures on someone's part have been made in order to know it is true. All we need to do is to know the meanings of the terms employed in the assertion in order to determine whether it is true or false. We can, in short, know that our statement about cubes is true *prior* to having any particular sense perceptions, and consequently, the truth of the assertion "Every cube has twelve edges of equal length" may be said to be known *a priori*.[3]

If someone were to challenge our claim that rain is falling in Rio, we would defend ourselves by pointing out that we just heard it reported on the radio or saw it on a live television broadcast. If you happened to be in Rio at the time, you would perhaps justify your assertion by saying that you were feeling the rain hit you or seeing the rain drops at first hand. But if we were

---

[2] More precisely, the statement "Every cube has twelve edges of equal length" is necessarily *true*. There are statements which are necessarily *false*, such as "Every cube has twenty edges of equal length."

[3] Because knowing that a particular *a priori* statement is true or false requires only that a person knows how certain words are *defined*, statements of this type are sometimes called "logical." *A posteriori* assertions (since they require some experience to determine whether they are true or false) often go by the name of "empirical."

challenged to defend our statement about cubes, we would simply point out that that is the way the word "cube" is *defined*. And if we were asked to prove that it was true by pointing out from what perceptions we derived its truth, we would know that our challenger did not understand the meaning of what we said.

Some philosophers like to mark the distinction between these two kinds of statements by using the terms "synthetic" and "analytic." The statement "Rain is falling in Rio" would be considered synthetic, and the statement about cubes would fall in the "analytic" camp. In calling a particular statement "synthetic," philosophers are not implying that there is anything phony or bogus about the assertion. They are simply pointing out that statements like "Rain is falling in Rio" can be denied without landing oneself in a contradiction. Certainly a person would not be uttering a contradiction if he said "Rain is not falling in Rio," even though he could be factually mistaken in saying this.

Look what happens when we try to deny the analytic statement "Every cube has twelve edges of equal length." If we were to say "Every cube does *not* have twelve edges of equal length," we would land ourselves in a self-contradiction. In making such an assertion we would show that we did not understand what a cube was or what the word "cube" meant. A cube must necessarily have twelve edges of equal length because this is part of the definition of such a solid. The same sort of self-contradiction would result if we denied the statement, "All uncles are males." If we were to say "Some uncles are not males," our statement would be a dead giveaway that we did not understand the terms involved in our statement. We would be caught in a self-contradiction; consequently we can see that the statement "All uncles are males" is analytic.

The self-contradiction involved in denying that every cube has twelve edges of equal length may be easier to see if we state it like this. "Every cube (i.e., a regular solid having twelve edges of equal length) does not have twelve edges of equal

209

length." A contradiction results because what is asserted in the subject is denied in the predicate. It's like offering a gift with one hand and taking it back with the other. Applying the same technique to the statement "Rain is falling in Rio," we can see that no contradiction results if we deny or negate it. "Rain (i.e., water falling in drops condensed from vapor in the atmosphere) is not falling in Rio." Admittedly, people might wonder about you if you happened to say this while walking the streets of Rio during a blinding rainstorm. But at least you would have the comfort of knowing you weren't stating a *logical* contradiction.[4]

Claims are often made concerning matters whose verification has not yet been possible in practice. For example, no one has yet had the sense perceptions necessary to determine whether the statement "There is life on Mars" is true or false. Yet there is good reason for considering this assertion synthetic or empirical in nature. It is possible to specify at least in a general way what would count as evidence for or against the proposition even if that evidence is not yet available. This statement could in principle be verified even if the actual means for such verification are yet to be developed.

---

[4] Now that you know the difference between *a priori* statements on the one hand and synthetic statements on the other, you should be introduced to a problem which has bothered more than a few philosophers. The question is: Are there any synthetic *a priori* statements? That is, are there any statements whose denial would not involve a self-contradiction but which are known to be true prior to or apart from experience or sensory observation? Kant maintained that there were some true synthetic *a priori* statements, one of which is "Every event has a cause." It was argued that to say "Some events are not caused" is not self-contradictory (and hence this statement is synthetic). But the truth of the statement is known prior to or apart from sensory experience and therefore must be *a priori* in nature. If you are inclined to saying that there *are* some true synthetic *a priori* statements, you would be siding with rationalists in the dispute concerning the nature and origin of knowledge. Should you deny that there are any true synthetic *a priori* statements, you would be lining up with the empiricists. A discussion of these two approaches to the problem of knowledge is the next order of business.

Suppose, however, that someone were to say "There are creatures on Mars whose nature and presence eludes any means of detection that we have now or ever will have." This utterance is not at all like the genuine synthetic or empirical assertion concerning life on Mars. Here we have a claim which is not even verifiable in principle, and although it looks like a genuine assertion about a factual state of affairs, it is in the final analysis "empirically empty." If someone claims that such-and-such is the case but at the same time denies us any means of checking his assertion, then we may be assured that whatever else he might be doing with his utterance, he has asserted nothing empirically significant.

Before we move on, we had better give our old friends "the borderline cases" their due. There are some statements which are not clearly members of either the analytic or the synthetic camp. First, a number of borderline-case examples take the form of "all A's are B" such as "all crows are black." Should this assertion be taken as a generalization based upon experience (and hence synthetic), or should its user be regarded as stating a necessary condition for a thing's being called a crow? If it is intended as the latter, it would be classified as an analytic statement; to say "That bird is a crow but it is not black" would be contradictory.

Second, consider the statement "I exist" made by Hugo Hunt. When *he* says "I exist," it seems he is saying something analytically true since, if Hugo were to say "I don't exist," he would be contradicting himself in some sense of that term. However, if someone other than Hugo were to say "Hugo Hunt exists," he would clearly be making a synthetic and contingent assertion.

Third, some first-person psychological statements have a peculiar logic to them. If I were to say "There is a sharp pain in my elbow," there is no way I could be wrong in what I say, provided I am sincere and I know how the words composing my statement are ordinarily used by people who speak English.

Nothing could count as evidence for or against my assertion as far as I am concerned. Yet, for other people my assertion about the pain in my elbow must be treated as an item of evidence to be taken account of, when they decide if what I say is true or false. *They* must find out about my pain, but it doesn't even make sense to say that *I* find out about my pain. Here is a case, then, of a statement which is synthetic and contingent for some people but not for me. We might want to say that it is analytic, but even then we would have to add "but analytic only for me."

Fourth, there is a great host of statements which we find difficult to place in either the analytic or the synthetic camp, but which we would still like to classify as statements and hence capable of being true or false. I refer to what might be called "philosophical statements," such as "there are correct moral rules which everyone ought to adopt" and "mental processes are identical to certain processes in the brain." These assertions resemble synthetic statements more than they do those of the analytic variety, since we could say "mental processes are not identical to brain processes," for example, without thereby stating a contradiction. Yet when we try to determine if philosophical assertions are true or false, the usual procedures for verifying synthetic statements do not help. We would use various perceptual tests to tell if rain is falling in Rio, but such tests fail us when we try to determine if there are any correct moral rules which all people should adopt.

Some philosophers have rid themselves of the problems concerning the classification of philosophical statements by placing them outside the category of genuine statements altogether; they regard them neither as analytic nor as synthetic and therefore as being incapable of being true or false. But this ploy is not without its problems. Since these philosophers take the statement "All genuine statements are either analytic or synthetic" to be true, in what camp do they place the aforementioned assertion? Is *it* not a *philosophical* statement and therefore incapable of being true or false according to their own view?

There has been an understandable tendency on the part of some philosophers (Plato and Descartes being the most noteworthy among them) to regard necessarily true statements as vastly superior when compared with contingent or empirical statements. It is tempting to rate them higher because they are true all of the time under all conditions; one need not rummage about in the grubby world of perceivable things to arrive at their truth. Philosophers so impressed with the iron-clad certainty of necessarily true statements have usually been called rationalists. They have been so enamored with the *a priori* that only necessarily true statements or ones which cannot be doubted or shown to be false deserve the title of "knowledge" in their eyes. They have, in short, made an ideal out of certainty and refuse to speak of the data derived through the senses by that title at all.

Contingent statements, even if true in a loose sense of the term, are completely dependent upon certain conditions being the case in the physical world. But we all know that conditions in nature are constantly changing: by the time we make the assertion "Rain is falling in Rio," it may already have stopped raining there. Contingent, synthetic statements may be true one moment and false the next. Then consider, so the rationalist argues, how misleading and inaccurate the data are which we receive through our senses. What appears green to one person may appear blue to another individual, and what on one occasion may seem square in shape may appear rectangular on another. We are all familiar with those cases where we are sure that we have seen or heard some particular thing, only to find out that our eyes or ears have played a trick on us.

The rationalist wants none of the inconclusiveness and guesswork associated with the so-called "knowledge" derived through the senses and reported in contingent or synthetic statements. "Give me the old, reliable, rational and indubitable necessary truths," he says, and for this reason the program of the rationalist could be called "the quest for the unquestionable." It is undoubtedly *psychologically* reassuring to believe that you

213

have hit upon some statement which cannot even be sensibly doubted, let alone proved to be wrong. But it is just as much *philosophically* comforting to think that one has formulated a philosophical position on a certain question which is invulnerable to criticism. This has been the essence of the philosophic dream for centuries, at least for those philosophers who believe their major task is to come up with knowledge that goes beyond the realm of the senses and of scientific discovery.

For a great many other philosophers (usually called empiricists) this dream, admirable and desirable as it may be, is little more than that. The members of this group may differ on a number of issues in philosophy, but they all agree in this: knowledge is ultimately derived through sense experience. It may be true (as the rationalist is so quick to point out) that our judgments based on sense perception are not infallible. We sometimes experience illusions, and on occasions we must "take back" a statement we have made about something in the observable world. But why are we not entitled to say we *know* something unless we are absolutely certain of it, without any possible doubt surrounding it? The empiricist contends that even though we must sometimes qualify our claims to knowledge with phrases like "on the basis of the evidence available . . ." or *"probably* such and such is the case," we need not look down our philosophical noses on such claims.

The empiricist just as much as the rationalist would *like* to be certain when he makes a claim to know something. But we must not go looking for absolute certainty where it cannot be found. The empiricist would admit that some of our statements are necessarily true, but they are so, he contends, because of the way we *define* words. In the realm of mathematics, for example, we can attain certainty because there we start with various axioms (or definitions) and merely work out their logical implications and relationships in various ways. Mathematical symbols have certain stipulated meanings, and propositions made up of these symbols, like "$8 \times 7 = 56$," are true simply because the set of definitions which we adopt makes them true. But, the empiricist is quick to add, the areas where we can attain certainty without any possibility of being wrong are restricted to mathematics and logic. To make an *ideal* out of the *indubitable* and define knowledge in terms of it is an arbitrary move on the part of the rationalist.

These, in a very brief and general way, are the main lines of the dispute between the empiricist and the rationalist. We should not think that *all* rationalists and *all* empiricists agree among themselves on the major issues in philosophy, however. Perhaps it would be better to refer to the account just given as rationalist and empiricist *tendencies* toward the problem of knowledge in order to prevent misunderstanding on this score.

In the section which follows we shall examine the approach of a representative rationalist, René Descartes, whose argument for mind-body dualism we have already discussed in a previous chapter. Our purpose in returning to his thought at this point is to show how a typical rationalist carries on his "quest for the unquestionable." We shall see how each step in his search for certainty is made and why he takes the approach he does. As usual, at the end of the argument some crucial criticisms will be suggested for your consideration.

THE RATIONALIST'S APPROACH: "THE QUEST FOR THE UNQUESTIONABLE."

Descartes, like other rationalists, maintained that genuinely true statements must be those upon which we can rely completely.[5] We may rightly claim that we have *knowledge*

---

[5] René Descartes, *Meditations*, first published in 1641. *Discourse on Method*, first published in 1637. Both works are available in a number of editions by various publishers. (Selections reprinted in anthologies AB, BKW, EP, F, MGAS, SA, ST.)

in a given matter only if it would be meaningless to doubt whether or not what we claimed was the case. Any statement whatever which is based upon data we derive from the senses is open to doubt. We could always be mistaken in anything we say about the world around us. Therefore, we must look for genuine knowledge somewhere other than in the realm of sense experience. Descartes's problem (and that of every rationalist) is to find some starting point in the quest for the unquestionable which is in no way whatsoever influenced by what he has experienced. If the point of destination (the attainment of absolute certainty) is to be reached, then one must start in the right direction. The following is an account of how one rationalist started and conducted his "quest for the unquestionable."

We are surrounded by conflicting opinions and beliefs as to what is true and false. One authority claims one thing, and another—equally renowned—says just the opposite. If we choose to find something out for ourselves and think for ourselves, we don't know where to start. The senses *appear* to be our most reliable guides, but how do we know when to trust them and when to discount their testimony? If we believed everything we see or hear, we should have to believe that sticks bend when submerged in water, or that green rats exist if we think we see them run across the room. Even if our senses were reliable 99% of the time, we could not know on which particular occasions they were leading us astray.

Furthermore, how do we know that what we perceive really exists outside our minds? Perhaps all of our perceptions are actually no more caused by real physical objects than are the "things" we experience in our dreams. Also, just suppose that something or someone like a very powerful, malicious being exists and places ideas in our minds just to deceive us. Be careful not to misunderstand here—I am just *supposing* this. No one knows whether or not there is such a being, but as long as its existence is a possibility, we have no justification for accepting any data derived from the senses as true. The only safe approach is to withhold judgment on everything until it has been proved to be true. The only reasonable thing to do is to adopt consistently an attitude of doubt toward everything we have hitherto accepted as true concerning the world around us and even about ourselves.

In fact, by doubting every last thing we are meaningfully *able* to doubt, we shall ensure an absolutely correct starting point in our search for knowledge. Then when we come across a statement which is impossible to doubt no matter how hard we try, we can be sure that we have a true statement. By employing this method of doubt, we can slowly but *surely* proceed to extend the list of statements which are true and build the structure of knowledge. We must be very careful, however, that every statement we accept as true passes the test. If we allow a statement to pass through which is not indubitable even if it is extremely *likely* to be true, we might have allowed a bit of falsehood to influence our conclusions. To be on the safe side, every statement, every step on the way to certainty must itself be absolutely certain — that is, beyond doubt.

Are there any statements which pass the test of indubitability? Fortunately for us there are. Let us assume the very worst, namely that there actually is a great deceiver like the one just mentioned who can exert some power over my mind. Suppose he (or it) is constantly leading me into error. There is still at least one thing about which he could not possibly deceive me — that I exist. For even if he is deceiving me all of the time, I must necessarily be existing all the time he is deceiving me. We may say that even though all my thoughts might be mistaken, I am still thinking; and that I find impossible to doubt. As long as I am thinking, I must be existing, so the statement "I think, therefore I am" must be necessarily true. It *cannot* be false even if it should be the case that some malicious being is producing my ideas in me. Since we do not know that such a being does *not* exist, we must regard its existence as an open possibility; but in any case we are now justified in taking our first steps in knowledge — "I think, therefore I am."

But where do we go from here? Do other persons exist? What about my other ideas? Is it not still possible that all of my other ideas are erroneous, and if they are, what has been gained by this first step? As long as it is still possible that a malicious, deceiving being exists which produces my thoughts, no further progress in knowledge is possible. How can we know for certain that no such being exists — or if he does exist, that his influence over me is extremely limited? We must be absolutely certain that if a source of deceptive thoughts exists, its existence could have no lasting effect on our ability to acquire knowledge. But how can we attain absolute assurance on this score so that genuine knowledge can be rendered possible for man to attain? The only way to discount the damaging effect of such a devilish being is to prove beyond a doubt that there is an all-powerful, all-good personal being who is able to put the clamps on any evil being which might possibly deceive us. In short, we must prove that God exists, and we must do this without relying on any of the so-called facts we supposedly get from sense experience. We must prove it by the use of reason alone, employing the method we used to prove our own existence. Let us number each of the steps in the proof and proceed in the same manner as we would if we were proving a conclusion in geometry.

(1) I am certain that I have ideas, one of which is the concept of a perfect personal being. Admittedly, this proves nothing yet about the actual *existence* of such a being. But that the idea is with me I cannot doubt.[6]

(2) This idea of a perfect personal being had to have a cause. It is an effect, and I know that every effect must have a cause; something cannot come from nothing.[7] This is a principle

---

[6] The "I" speaking in this argument is Descartes; since he maintained that the search for knowledge was an individual enterprise, it seemed especially appropriate to use the first person pronoun in presenting his position.

[7] Let us call this "causal principle I."

which it is impossible to doubt, and I call it, therefore, a "clear and distinct idea."

(3) The cause of my concept of a perfect personal being could not be myself, my parents, nature, or anything which has limitations. But how do I know that the source of my idea of God can be none of these? Another principle I cannot doubt is the one which may be stated as follows:[8] "The cause of a particular effect must be at least as great (in a qualitative sense) as the effect which it brings into being." If this principle were not true, and an effect *were* greater than its cause, we would be left without an adequate explanation as to how any particular effect came into existence. The principle stated above, then, is undoubtedly true and, like the principle in our second step, is a clear and distinct (or "self-evident") truth.

(4) Since my idea of God is an idea of a *perfect* being (of a being without any limitations), the cause of this idea must be a perfect being—that is, one without limitations. The self-evident principle in Step 3 permits us to draw this inference. If my idea of a perfect personal being were caused by anything or anybody other than the perfect personal being himself, then the absolutely true principle explained in Step 3 would be violated. The cause of the idea of perfection must be as perfect as the idea itself; therefore, the cause of my ideas must be a perfect being. Only a being which actually exists outside someone's mind could produce effects, so the perfect personal being really exists beyond any doubt.

(5) The perfect personal being (God) also is the only possible cause of my own existence. How can we know this? Well, the only thing I am certain of concerning myself at this point in the argument is that I am a thinking being. I can doubt that I have a body but not that I have a mind. A mind could not be brought into existence by anything which has so many limita-

---

[8] Let us call this "causal principle II."

tions as matter does, because of the principle spelled out in Step 3. Another mind with unlimited power and knowledge would be required for the job. Only God, a perfect personal being, would be capable of such a task. God might have used my parents to produce my body (if I have one), but they could not have created my mind. Neither could blind, unthinking matter have produced purely on its own the first human mind which came into being. The cause of the existence of mind must be as great in a qualitative sense as mind itself, and surely properties in matter are more limited, and, hence, less perfect than those possessed by a mind. Consequently, the human mind could be caused only by another mind capable of such a feat, namely the perfect personal being.

(6) Since God created me with my various faculties, among which is a strong inclination to believe my senses, I have the very best reasons for now believing what my senses present to me. Since God is a being without limitations, he must be all-good as well as all-powerful. He would not create me with faculties which were not usually trustworthy. And if there is a malicious, deceiving being who is trying to mislead me, an all-powerful and perfectly moral being like God would not let me fall under the spell of such a creature. Those errors which I do fall into from time to time are my own fault, not God's. I make mistakes because I jump to conclusions without first using my reason to make certain that what I claim to know is beyond doubt.

Before we suggest some difficulties with Descartes's argument, we must draw attention to some special features in the rationalist's *modus operandi*. First of all, notice that the method of argument is deductive. That is, be begins with what he takes to be a true statement, namely that he exists. Then he points out another statement which he likewise regards as true, namely that he has an idea of a perfect personal being. He then draws the conclusion that this idea has a cause. His grounds for saying this is another statement he takes to be certain, namely that every effect has a cause. Each step is like a link in a chain which is held together by the rules of valid reasoning. He places two allegedly true statements together and draws out of them another true statement. He then uses the "truth" he has derived in this way as logical grounds for concluding something further. As long as he does not break any rules of correct reasoning nor incorporate into his proof any false statements, Descartes is on safe logical ground.[9]

Second, at no point does the argument appeal to any so-called "fact" gained through sense experience. In order to be successful from Descartes's standpoint, the proof must put aside such data because of its doubtful or uncertain status. At least this was Descartes's intent; there is some question whether he was completely able to disregard in his reasoning all data derived from sense perception.[10]

Third, Descartes holds the doctrine of "innate ideas"

---

[9] In order to understand the logical form or structure in Descartes' argument better, we might symbolize it as follows:

I = I have the *idea* of a perfect personal being.
C = My idea of a perfect personal being was *caused*.
A = The cause of my idea of a perfect person being must be *adequate* to account for its existence in my mind.
$-L$ = The cause of my idea of God is a being who does not have any *limitations*.

Steps in the proof:	*Justification for each step:*
1. If I, then C	Causal principle I.
2. I	Report of something he is certain exists in his mind.
3. C	Inference from putting Steps 1 and 2 together.
4. If C then A	Causal principle II.
5. If A then $-L$	Causal principle II.
6. If C then $-L$	Inference from putting Steps 4 and 5 together; (like saying that if all C's are A's, and all A's are $-L$'s, then all C's are $-L$'s).
7. $-L$	Inference from putting Steps 3 and 6 together.

[10] For Descartes' views on the nature of perception see especially *Meditations* II and VI.

as other rationalists do. The idea of a perfect personal being, according to Descartes, is present in the mind from the very beginning of its existence, having been put there by God himself. The concepts relating to cause and effect relationships, which play such a crucial role in the course of his argument, are also taken by Descartes to be part of the original furniture of the mind. As the argument tries to prove, the idea of God had always to have been present in the mind, because no other explanation can account for its existence except God's having placed it there. Rationalists in general are fond of pointing out that we have certain concepts whose existence cannot be adequately accounted for by any other hypothesis except that of the "innate idea" theory.

Difficulties with This Argument

(1) Is it possible to have an intelligible concept of a perfect personal being? (The difficulties with this notion have been covered in Chapter Two, and it is not necessary to repeat them here. It might be well to consult the discussion there again if you need to refresh your mind on this point.)

(2) Suppose we press the method of doubt which Descartes used to the point beyond which he himself took it. When he says he cannot doubt the truth of the statement "I think, therefore I am," is he not assuming that he *remembers* what each of the words in this statement mean? Memory has deceived him in the past, so how does he know it is not leading him astray here? The method of doubting everything unless and until certainty is attained, rather than being a fruitful means of building a body of true propositions actually leaves us with nothing we can rightly claim as knowledge. A consistent application of the method of doubt can end only in complete scepticism — that is, a belief that knowledge of any sort is impossible to attain. Descartes's method then does not serve his purpose in philosophy, but rather undermines it.

(3) Does it make any sense to say "a cause must be as

great as its effect"? If we are not clear as to what this expression means, how can we regard the statement which contains it as being true? We cannot even begin to treat a statement as true or false until we know what it means. And if this proposition is obscure (not "clear and distinct"), it is difficult to see how it can be used as a major step in Descartes's argument—since he demands such clarity and distinctness in a proposition in order for it to be true.

(4) If there are some ideas or concepts which are innate, as Descartes claims, how is it that we were not always conscious of them even when we were children? If the "innate idea" theory were correct, it should make sense to say of a child one year old, "Johnny has ideas concerning God, the principles of causation, and certain laws of reasoning." But what would such an assertion mean when in fact Johnny does not have even a rudimentary grasp of language? Wouldn't it be something of a joke to claim that he *understands* these concepts? If so, then it does not make much sense to say that he *has* ideas in his mind. Of course, Descartes would deny that an infant *actually* has these ideas in the sense that he could be aware of them and reflect upon them. He would say that they are just "potentially" present in the mind, until a person matures intellectually. But this explanation of the status of these ideas is even more obscure; just what is it for an idea to be "potentially" present?

(5) Descartes has been charged with arguing in a circle, that is, using in the premises of his argument the very statement he is attempting to prove. Until he has shown that an absolutely perfect being exists who can guarantee the reliability of his faculties for knowledge, how can he rely upon these faculties in constructing such a proof? If he consistently applies his method of doubt to *all* propositions on the grounds that an evil being could be deceiving him concerning their truth, then the rules of deductive reasoning he uses in his argument and the causal principles upon which he relies so heavily should not be regarded as true. In short, Descartes is caught in a dilemma: he cannot prove that God exists unless he already knows that a

number of other statements are true, but he can't know that these other statements are true unless he has already proved that God exists.

THE EMPIRICIST'S APPROACH: "THE EMPHASIS UPON EXPERIENCE"

Rationalism has fallen upon bad times. There have been periods in the history of philosophy when it was the height of respectability to be known as a rationalist. But certain developments have led to the undoing of rationalism, particularly in the twentieth century. First of all, it would reach the point of preposterousness to suggest to contemporary man that no knowledge worthy of the name comes through the senses. We have been experiencing a "fact explosion" of mammoth proportions in recent decades, and—what is more troubling for the rationalist—the scientist has been performing some pretty remarkable feats by using these "second-rate" facts. The amazing accuracy and precision of scientific prediction is beyond dispute nowadays, and anyone's suggestion that the scientist is trafficking in "mere opinion" or "guesswork" because his statements lack absolute certainty would not be taken too seriously.

The second factor which has helped puncture the rationalist's approach to knowledge is the development of various non-Euclidean geometries and diverse mathematical systems. The rationalist always pointed to the absolute certainty of mathematical statements as evidence for his belief that the principles involved in this area were innate or unlearned. He elevated them to a place of near reverence so that they virtually became a model for any kind of truth. He made an *ideal* out of mathematical certainty and believed that *all* knowledge worthy of the title must be comprised only of necessary truths.

It has become quite apparent that we can, if we so

choose, start with almost any mathematical axioms and develop a system in which, for example, 2 plus 2 need not equal 4. The necessary, non-empirical status of mathematics is still acknowledged by many philosophers, but the reason for this is not that we are born with *the* principles of mathematics already in our minds. The truth in this area is completely dependent upon the definitions of the symbols we have accepted and upon the axioms from which we start. But it is pointed out by the empiricist that *which* axioms and *which* definitions we choose to employ is up to us. In short, the principles of mathematics which we use are what they are not because they are part of the original furniture of our minds, but because they have been *defined* that way. There is no longer any need to invoke the doctrine of innate ideas (which has theoretical difficulties of its own) to explain why we can make various statements which are necessarily true or *a priori*.[11]

In spite of this requiem for the rationalist we should not think that everything is clear sailing for his opponent, the empiricist. If you are inclined to side with the empiricist on the question of how we ultimately get our knowledge, you should be prepared for some philosophical trials and tribulations. If you maintain that all of our knowledge is derived from sense experience or sense perception, you should be prepared to face several embarrassing problems. In fact, much of philosophical activity in the twentieth century could be called "the case of the embarrassed empiricist." The two problems which have caused empiricists an unusually large amount of trouble have been referred to as the "problem of induction" and "the problem of perception." We shall devote the remainder of this chapter to a discussion of these two issues and try to point out why their existence is somewhat embarrassing to the philosopher who argues that all knowledge is ultimately derived from sense experience.

---

[11] For further treatment of the *a priori* by an empiricist, see A. J. Ayer, *Language, Truth and Logic* (New York: Dover Publications, Inc., 1946), pp. 71-87. (Selections in anthologies AB, EP, F.)

The Problem of Induction.

THE NATURE OF INDUCTION. If there is a problem about induction, we had better first get some idea of what constitutes the process of induction. It might be easiest to understand all this if we use an example which involves a very simple case of inductive reasoning. We reason inductively virtually every day of our lives, and the same sort of reasoning is employed by the scientist as he attempts to acquire knowledge in his particular field of facts. Suppose you claim that it is going to rain very shortly, and I ask you why you think so. You would most likely mention such things as the presence of dark clouds overhead, the flashes of lightning, and the sound of thunder nearby. You would perhaps also remind me that the weather bureau predicted rain for today. But I might press you further and ask you to explain why all of the facts you just mentioned lead you to conclude that rain is near. Most likely you would then say something like this: "Well, in the past whenever these conditions were present, we almost always got rain. And the weather bureau has a pretty good record in predicting such things."

Your conclusion that rain will most likely fall quite soon is based upon your observations of a number of occasions in the past which resemble the circumstances prevailing now. When conditions like the present ones existed in the past, we usually got rain. Because roughly the same conditions are present now, we can expect the same type of thing to happen. On the basis of your observations in the past, you have arrived at what may be called an "inductive generalization": "Whenever conditions C_1, C_2 and C_3 are present, we may rightly expect (or predict) result R." Whenever there are dark clouds overhead, there is lightning and thunder, and the weather bureau predicts rain, then we may justifiably expect (or predict) that shortly rain will occur.

In your arriving at the inductive generalization concerning the conditions prior to the occurrence of rain, and in your conclusion that rain is about to fall, you would be making use of what some philosophers refer to as the "principle of induction." Bertrand Russell, for example, states the principle as follows:

> When a thing of certain sort A has been found to be associated with a thing of a certain sort B, and has never been found dissociated from a thing of the sort B, the greater the number of cases in which A and B have been associated, the greater is the probability that they will be associated in a fresh case in which one of them is known to be present.[12]

David Hume stated the same principle in slightly different language. "Instances of which we have had no experience, must resemble those of which we have had experience . . . the course of nature continues always uniformly the same."[13] Applied to our expectation or prediction that it will rain shortly, we could say that instances of which we have no experience (the future course of the weather) must resemble those of which we have had experience (past occasions when conditions like those present prevailed), and that the course of nature continues always uniformly the same. The laws of nature which account for rain falling are still in operation, which is to say that we may continue to use them in explaining why things occur as they do.

One additional feature of the conclusion concerning the rain should be noted before we explain why there seems to be a problem connected with induction. Conclusions based on inductive reasoning do not attain absolute certainty. We would very wisely qualify our conclusion that it will rain by use of the phrases, "most likely," or "it is highly probable that." After all, it could very well be that the clouds overhead will pass by and drop their moisture somewhere else. And we all know that weather reports are sometimes mistaken. Even if it has rained

---

[12] Bertrand Russell, *Problems of Philosophy* (New York: Oxford University Press, 1912), p. 66. (Relevant selections in AB, EP, MGAS.)

[13] David Hume, *Enquiry Concerning Human Understanding*, Bk. I, Part III, Section VI, p. 89. (Relevant selections in AB, EP, TBO.)

when these. conditions were present in the past, perhaps this will be the first time when it fails to rain in spite of all the signs. So to play it safe, we should realize that there is an element of uncertainty surrounding any conclusion based upon inductive reasoning. This, of course, does not ordinarily discourage us from making such inferences and relying upon them in everyday life.

CAN THE PRINCIPLE OF INDUCTION BE JUSTIFIED? The empiricist, then, would point with pride to the process of induction and the principle upon which it is based, because by utilizing it we can get to know some general facts about the world and the way things may be expected to be in the future. By means of induction we can compare and relate experiences in the past with those of the present, and thereby increase our store of knowledge.

But an embarrassment arises for the empiricist when he is asked to *justify* his use of the principle of induction. If this principle constitutes an important part of the very foundation of knowledge, we would expect it to have nothing but the very best reasons for its adoption. But we are disappointed when we find that the principle of induction itself not only has not been proved to be true, but that it is incapable of proof. The very principle upon which knowledge is founded is devoid of any proof. We cannot appeal to anything from *past* experience to show that the principle of induction will hold in the future. All that one has a right to claim is that "the course of nature *has* continued always the same," not that "the course of nature *continues* always the same." The *future* course of things could be radically different from the past, regardless of how uniform they might have appeared to us before.

What a sorry state for the empiricist this seems to be. For if no justification for the principle of induction is possible, our only course seems to be that of *assuming* it to be true or merely having *faith* that it is true. But what happens then to the empiricist's position that all of our knowledge is ultimately derived from sense perception? It appears that he is obliged to add an embarrassing qualification to his original statement— "All knowledge is derived from sense perception and is based upon a principle which must be taken on faith alone." Can this be the sorry fate of the hard-headed, "just-the-facts-and-nothing-but-the-facts" approach of the empiricist?

"Not so fast there," someone might say, "let's not give up the ship so soon. We can know that the future will resemble the past because times which were once 'future times,' so to speak, have become part of the past, and we have found that these futures resemble the past. Every day we are experiencing more 'future times' becoming part of the past, and the resemblance between what we *once* called the future and what we now call the past is still there. Isn't that good evidence for saying that the future will be like the past? And aren't we justified therefore in using the principle of induction which presupposes this resemblance?"

This seems like a plausible response, but it assumes the very point at issue. We can only say that future times we have already *experienced* are like the past because they are really part of the past which we can know. The future which is *really* the future is yet to be, and consequently is incapable of being experienced now. No amount of resemblance between various events in the past can be evidence for the claim that the past resembles the future. You cannot compare A and B if you don't know what B is. You cannot say A (the past) resembles B (the future) unless you have somehow attained the knack of experiencing the future before it occurs in order to make the comparison.

Consequently, we are left with the not too desirable option of either accepting the principle of induction on its own ground or giving up any hope of finding a rational justification for our expectations and predictions regarding the future. Undoubtedly, we will all keep using the principle of induction in our daily lives, and the scientist as well will rely upon it in his work. It is not being suggested that we discard it from use, but rather that there is no way of proving that the principle is true.

ATTEMPTS TO "DISSOLVE" THE PROBLEM OF INDUC-TION. Some recent philosophers have chided Russell and Hume for having gotten upset over nothing when they raised the "problem of induction." [14] All of their difficulties are traceable to several simple but crucial mistakes. For example, once you start with the assumption that the boundary between the past and the future is fixed, you are headed straight for the tangles involved in this problem. Russell, we remember, argues that just because all that is now part of the past was once the future and we are able to see that the principle of induction has held in the past, we still have no rational grounds whatsoever for concluding that "future futures will resemble past futures." [15] Had Russell remembered that the boundary between the area of the past and that of the future is moving so that we *are* actually experiencing more of the future every day, he would not have said something so paradoxical. With the passing of each moment of time, the boundary between past and future moves ahead, so to speak, so that what we have experienced up to now can be rightly used as evidence for what to expect tomorrow and the next day. When tomorrow gets here, we can see whether or not it resembles the past, and if it does, our expectations concerning the future not yet experienced are better grounded.

One of the main reasons why Russell and other sceptics cast doubt on the principle of induction is that they fail to distinguish two senses of the word "future." In one sense of the term (we may call it "future-1") it means a time when events and things may sometime occur or exist as the line of the present continues to progress. If someone said in the year 1954 that

---

[14] F. L. Will, "Will the Future Be Like the Past?" *Mind*, LVI (1947). (Reprinted in anthologies EP, MGAS.) P. Edwards, "Bertrand Russell's Doubt about Induction," *Mind*, LVIII (1949), reprinted in A. Flew, ed., *Essays in Logic and Language*, First Series (Oxford: Black-well, 1951).

[15] Bertrand Russell, *Problems of Philosophy*, p. 65.

things would continue in roughly the same way in 1955, he would be referring to the future in the sense just delineated. However, one may use the term "future" in another sense (we may call it "future-2") so as to refer to a time which is always beyond the present and which never comes and cannot logically come. This is the sense of the term which Russell is using when he raises doubt concerning induction. For in Russell's view, the future never gets here, and we never *could* experience the future because once it is experienced, it is transformed into part of the past. Russell's approach resembles that of the self-styled prophet who says that next year the world will come to an end. Then when the next year has ended without the cataclysmic event's having taken place, the prophet gets off the hook by replying, "But you must not have heard me. I didn't say *this* year the world will end. I explicitly predicted that *next* year it will occur." The point is that our prophetic friend is misusing the word "next" in such a way that his "prediction" can neither be confirmed nor denied. Russell is doing much the same thing with the term "future." He is using the word so that he is forced to say that the future never comes, is never experienced, and is, therefore, unknown and unknowable in any sense whatever. For him, the future must necessarily remain completely and irremediably beyond our knowledge.

If the term "future" is interpreted in the sense of "future-1," then there are many beliefs concerning the future which are being confirmed by countless instances every day of our lives. Suppose a person said in 1954 that 1955 would be like the past in certain specific ways. He would be claiming that the future (in the sense of future-1) would resemble the past. And when 1955 rolled around, the claim that it would be like 1954 could be confirmed or disproved by comparing events which took place in those two years. Empirical evidence for the claim concerning the future (at least for 1955) would be quite relevant; no sceptical doubt need arise when predictions concerning the future (in the sense of future-1) are made. Admittedly, no one can produce evidence for the statement that at a certain time which never comes (nor could come) certain events will take place which resemble those of the past. But "no scepticism is entailed by this admission so long as it is made with the understanding that there is evidence about the other kind of future, the time that will come and in which events do occur." [16]

One final word might help dissolve this "problem." What do we mean in our language when we refer to a certain person as "rational"? Certainly part of what we mean is that such a person uses past experience to influence his beliefs and expectations about the future.[17] If a person disregards what has happened in the past as though it were of no account in determining what *will* happen, we would think such behavior "irrational." "So to ask whether it is reasonable to place reliance on inductive procedures is like asking whether it is reasonable to proportion the degree of one's convictions to the strength of the evidence. Doing this is what 'being reasonable' *means* in such a context."[18] What Russell and Hume are really asking for, then, when they raise the problem of induction, is a reason or justification for being rational instead of irrational. They seem to be asking us to justify a principle the adherence to which determines in great measure the degree of rationality in a person's thought and action. But this is to ask for the logically impossible, since it cannot be shown that it is reasonable to do X if doing X is what is meant by the expression "being reasonable." One might just as well ask "Is the standard yard at the Bureau of Weights and Measures *really* a yard?" or "Is the law legal?"

---

[16] F. L. Will, "Will the Future Be Like the Past?" Mandelbaum, Gramlich, Anderson and Schneewind, eds., *Philosophic Problems*, p. 144.

[17] Antony Flew, *Hume's Philosophy of Belief* (New York: Humanities Press, 1961), Chap. IV. (Selection in EP.)

[18] P. F. Strawson, *Introduction to Logical Theory* (London: Methuen and Company, 1952), Chap. 9. (Reprinted in AB.)

The Problem of Perception.

Since the empiricist claims that all of our knowledge is derived through sense perception, it is necessary for him to expend a good amount of effort trying to explain what is involved in this process. Part of his problem is to determine whether there are any good reasons for believing that physical objects *exist* at all. The problem of perception then may be stated as follows. "What do we perceive? Do material things exist outside our minds, or are there only various perceptions which occur in our minds?" Like the problem of induction, this question puts the empiricist in an embarrassing position. Unless he can come up with some good reasons for believing that there are things which exist independently of our experience of them, he seems forced to admit a somewhat paradoxical conclusion. What we call knowledge would have to be regarded as *knowledge merely of the contents of our own minds.* In fact, if the empiricist intends to remain true to his doctrine that all knowledge must be derived through sense perception, he may have to admit that he does not know whether there *are* any minds other than his own.[19]

It might seem odd to someone approaching philosophy for the first time that anyone could seriously bother himself over an issue like this. What could be more obvious than the fact that things like trees, automobiles and chairs exist? Who could be so silly as to believe that these sorts of things are "all in our minds"? If we can be sure of anything, it is that there is a world "out there" which we can see, hear, touch, smell, and taste. But before we dismiss the problem of perception in so curt a manner, perhaps we should hear a little more. Perhaps what

---

[19] Bertrand Russell, *Human Knowledge* (New York: Allen and Unwin, 1948), p. 193. "We cannot enter into the minds of others to observe the thoughts and emotions which we infer from their behavior." (Since we touched upon the "other minds" perplexity in Chapter One, we shall not pursue it further at this point.)

appears so obviously true at first is not so upon more careful consideration. There have been a number of keen philosophical minds who have challenged the easy assumption that what we perceive are most certainly physical objects outside the mind. One of the most provocative and incisive among this group was George Berkeley, a bishop in the Anglican church who published his famous *Treatise Concerning the Principles of Knowledge* in 1710. Let us carefully follow the good bishop's arguments and then ask ourselves whether we are still so sure that there are material things which exist independently of anyone's experience of them.

MATERIAL THINGS ARE ONLY GROUPS OF IDEAS IN SOMEONE'S MIND.[20] It should be obvious to anyone that what constitutes our knowledge are ideas of various sorts. We have, for example, imaginary ideas which we produce by our own wills, ideas we get from observing the workings of our own minds, and "perceptual" ideas. The latter are imprinted on the senses and are the kind of ideas in which we are particularly interested at the present.

We can, of course, make distinctions between one kind of perceptual idea and another. By the sense of sight we receive our ideas of color, by the faculty of hearing we experience various sounds, and so on. When various kinds of perceptual ideas come to us in a group or complex, we call this combination of ideas a "thing." For example, if we were to analyze what is called my desk, we would simply list its various perceptual properties. That is, the desk is of tan color, smooth and hard to the touch, and observed to emit a somewhat metallic sound when struck. (We can just as well remain in the dark concerning its smell and taste.) I suppose we might also include in our list of qualities which constitute my desk its shape, which appears rectangular when seen from above.

Now some philosophers who are materialists would try

---

[20] George Berkeley, *A Treatise Concerning the Principles of Human Knowledge* (1710), Part I. (Selections in anthologies AB, EP, F, MGAS, ST, TBO.)

to squeeze something else into the description of my desk. They would say that it is also composed of something they call "matter." They would, therefore, call my desk a *material* thing, and since matter is supposed to be different from mind, they would contend that my desk must exist in such a way that no one need be experiencing it in order for it to exist. However, this doctrine of materialism is wholly without foundation and hence is a philosophical prejudice. I shall explain why I say this.

Let us return to the list of perceptual properties which constitute my desk. Could its tan color exist outside of someone's perceiving the color? No. Could the hardness and smoothness of what we call the desk's surface exist apart from their being experienced in someone's mind? Again the answer is no. For what sense does it make to say that an idea could exist outside a mind in the first place? Perceptual ideas exist only in so far as they are perceived. Now see where this observation leads us. If each of the qualities which composes my desk exists if and only if someone is perceiving it, then the same thing must be said of the properties when they are grouped together in a complex which is referred to as my desk. Therefore, what materialists call material objects exist only in the mind perceiving them; they have no *independent* existence.

Admittedly, this is a hard pill to swallow, and it is bound to meet objections. For example, someone will surely say that such a view banishes everything from the world and leaves us with nothing but an elaborate group of illusions. Or it might be argued that if we accept this scheme of things, every time we shut our eyes or stop up our ears, the world goes out of existence, and then when we begin to receive perceptions again, things come back into existence. But both of these objections presuppose that there *are* material things outside our minds to banish away or to pop out of existence. The argument above has shown that what we call "things" are merely collections or combinations of certain perceptual ideas.

Our materialist friends will not be put down so easily. They admit that colors, sounds, tastes, touches and odors exist only as perceptual ideas in someone's mind. "But," they urge, "how about qualities like motion and extension or the ability to take up space? Surely, these qualities exist independently of our experience of them and material things are composed of these various qualities."

However, has the materialist ever perceived anything like "motion" or "extension" separated from the qualities of color, touch, etc.? Has he not always perceived something which, if in motion, was also colored and had certain tactile properties? There is no such thing as "motion" in general or in the abstract. One perceives motion *along with* the perceptions of color, sound, touch and so on. Therefore, whatever is true of qualities like colors and sounds will be true of qualities like motion and extension.[21] Since the former type of qualities exist only as perceptions in someone's mind, so the latter properties cannot exist apart from their being perceived.

One last refuge might be open to the materialist. He confidently asks us to explain why we have the perceptions we do. What *causes* them if material things do not? It should be noted that one supposed source of our perceptions is ruled out at the start. They could not be copies of something like a material

---

[21] It was common in Berkeley's days to refer to colors, sounds, tastes, touches and odors as "secondary qualities." The qualities of extension, figure, motion, rest, solidity, and number were called "primary qualities." It was thought that since the so-called "secondary" qualities (1) could not exist by themselves but required a perceiver to experience them, (2) varied greatly depending upon who was perceiving them and in what conditions, and (3) were incapable of objective measurement, these could not be the "real" properties of things. The "primary" qualities were believed by many to exist independently of any perceiving mind and were susceptible of exact scientific (or mathematical) measurement. The "primary" qualities were "real" properties of nature and consequently became the objects of investigation for early modern science. For a fascinating and provocative study of the role which this assumption (and others) played in the thinking of men like Galileo and Newton, see E. A. Burtt, *The Metaphysical Foundations of Modern Science* (New York: Crowell-Collier & Macmillan, Inc., 1955).

object, because ideas do not at all *resemble* what the materialist calls material things. Ideas are not like anything else and so could not stand for or copy anything else. Even if they could resemble something else, how could a material thing which is supposed to be so completely *unlike* an idea produce an idea in our minds?

But if ideas cannot be caused by material things (for the simple reason that they don't exist), then what (or who) produces them? Well, let's exclude another possibility right away. Perceptual ideas could not produce themselves, because ideas are completely passive; that is, they are effects but not causes. Furthermore, *we* do not produce our own perceptual ideas, because it is evident that they come when they do whether we want them or not. Could they be placed in our mind by other people? This is ruled out because no limited or finite mind would be capable of producing such a great number and variety of perceptions in such an orderly and purposeful way as we experience them. The only adequate explanation to account for the origin of our perceptual ideas is that an all-wise, all-powerful mind places them in our minds, and this being must be God. How else can we explain why a whole group of people at precisely the same time and place can have almost identical perceptions? How else do we account for the fact that when we have certain visual and tactile perceptions of fire, for example, they are accompanied by the perception of pain? By producing the proper ideas in our minds at the appropriate time, God mercifully warns us of impending danger and discomfort. What other explanation will do, since we have by a careful process of reasoning ruled out every other possible alternative?

Difficulties with This Argument

(1) Berkeley begins his argument by saying that what we know are ideas; in so doing he could be charged with assuming to be true the very thing his argument is intended to prove. That

is, he seems to be "begging the question," which is a fallacious way of reasoning.

(2) Berkeley does not appear to offer any grounds for the proposition that a material object could not cause a perceptual idea because the two are so unlike. Just because A might be very different from B, it does not follow that one of them cannot be the cause of the other. Berkeley does admit that our own wills cause our imaginary ideas, but yet there seems to be as great a difference between a person's act of will and an imaginary idea as there is between a so-called material object and a perceptual idea. In short, Berkeley has not shown that our perceptions cannot be caused by anything like a material object.

(3) Let us suppose for the moment that God directly produces our perceptions as Berkeley claims. What would count as a morally wrong act in such an arrangement? For example, what constitutes the act of murder? It seems to be little more than God's producing certain complexes of perceptual ideas. Admittedly, there would be some decisions and acts of will on the part of the agent, but what is the relationship between, on the one hand, an act of will to raise one's hand (which for Berkeley is a complex of perceptual ideas) in order to plunge a knife into someone's back (which is also a particular combination of perceptions), and on the other, God's producing these perceptions in the mind of the agent and in the minds of any witnesses there might be to the act? Since God produces these perceptions, in Berkeley's view, shouldn't God be held responsible for the act along with the agent? And for what is the agent to be held responsible, anyway? All the agent does is *will* certain things to happen, and it does not seem right to hold people responsible for what they merely will. In short, a major difficulty for someone who adopts Berkeley's viewpoint on perception is that of framing coherent concepts of "action" and "moral responsibility."

(4) If God is supposed to be morally perfect, why does he produce perceptual ideas which are painful? If we adopt Berkeley's explanation concerning the origin of our perceptual ideas, God would seem to be guilty of causing painful sensations

not only in cases where it is helpful for detecting some organic disorder. But he would have to be blamed for all the immense amount of suffering which serves no useful purpose. (Perhaps the major difficulty for Berkeley to overcome is the problem of evil which, you recall, was discussed in Chapter Two.)

PHENOMENALISM. There are some philosophers who believe that Berkeley made a fairly commendable start at answering the question, "What do we perceive?" But they are not so happy with the way he finished his analysis. As long as he confined himself solely to an analysis of what we actually experience in sense perception as opposed to what we *believe* we experience, he was making philosophical progress. But poor Berkeley was sidetracked by the question, "What *causes* our perceptual ideas?" The phenomenalist refuses to get dragged into the issue of what or who causes our sense perceptions. He is inclined to think that *any* proposed solution to that inquiry is strapped with difficulties which it would be better to avoid altogether. The phenomenalist believes that if we approach the problem of perception properly, we can show that we need not concern ourselves with the question of whether material objects exist. He will try to demonstrate that we can either think of material things as merely the "permanent possibilities of sensations"[22] or make clear the meaning of statements referring to material objects by translating them into statements about "sense data." Since the more recent phenomenalists have chosen the latter approach, we shall concentrate on their arguments and their use of this new phrase "sense data."[23] They would argue in the following way.

---

[22] J. S. Mill, *Examination of Sir William Hamilton's Philosophy* (London: 1865), Chap. XI, reprinted in R. J. Hirst, ed., *Perception and the External World* (New York: Crowell-Collier & Macmillan, Inc., 1965), pp. 274-82.

[23] A. J. Ayer, *The Foundations of Empirical Knowledge* (London: Macmillan and Co., Ltd., 1940), Chap. V. *The Problem of Knowledge* (Harmondsworth: Pelican Books, 1956), Chap. III.

In attempting to determine when we are justified in claiming to know something, or simply what we perceive, we must be careful not to go beyond what is actually experienced. This means that we should be aware of the distinction between that which we definitely experience in perception and what we are led to *believe* or *infer* on the basis of our perceptions. This is why, as phenomenalists, we will not be lured into any discussion about the *cause* of our perceptions. Any position concerning their ultimate origin would have to be an inference (and a very shaky one at that), and we had better not call beliefs in this area "knowledge" at all.

What do we actually *experience* in sense perception as opposed to that which we *believe* or *infer* that we experience? Put another way, what can we be certain of when we are having perceptual experiences? What we "directly experience" are various kinds of "sense data." (By this expression, "sense data," we mean the content of what is actually experienced in sense perception.) Various color patches, odors, sounds, touches, and tastes can all be classified as sense data. Where they come from and why they come to us as they do we neither know nor can know. One guess is as good as another when it comes to speculating on where our sense data originate. Berkeley, you remember, advanced a theory as to their origin because he thought he had found more evidence for the existence of God. Furthermore, he maintained that even if no human being was actually experiencing a certain collection of perceptions, God was always experiencing perceptual ideas. In this way he hoped to account for the relative permanence and order of what we call "nature."

However, we need not define material objects in terms of the *actual* perceptions which someone is having. More correctly, we can and should translate the meaning of material-object statements into statements about the actual and *possible* sense data which someone could have, given certain conditions. For example, suppose we consider the statement, "There is a desk in the other room." (This is a material-object statement because it makes some reference to a desk, which we classify as a material object.) What we want to do is to show what this statement about the desk *really* means, not what unreflective, naïve judgment takes it to mean. We can show that statements of this sort (about material objects) can be translated without loss of meaning into statements about actual or possible sense data.

The translation of the statement, "There is a desk in the other room," goes like this: "If someone with normal perceptual capacities were to go into the room and go through certain appropriate procedures, then he or she would experience various kinds of sense data." The procedures which would have to be gone through in order to experience certain sense data would be those of looking in the right direction, advancing to a certain part of the room, and placing one's hands at the appropriate position. Notice that the sense-datum statement also specifies that a person of *normal* perceptual abilities would have to go into the next room. If a person could not see, hear, or feel anything, he would not experience sense data (which we call the desk) in the other room. Other conditions for having sense data, such as having appropriate lighting available in the room, would also eventually have to be listed in the sense-datum statement so as to have a good translation of the material-object statement.

Let us keep in mind why the project of translating material-object statements into sense-datum statements is so important for us phenomenalists. It enables us to dispense with the category of "material object" and with it the whole untenable theory that there are some entities in existence which we cannot directly experience in sense perception but which we must nevertheless assume or believe to exist. The retention of material-object language is desirable for everyday affairs; it is certainly more convenient than supplying a complicated, extensive list of sense data in order to make references and communicate our desires. But in *philosophy* we should dispense with material-object statements because we do not actually *experience* anything like a material object—only sense data. The existence of

241

anything beyond our sense data is *inferred,* or *believed* to exist. If a person wants to be true to the empiricist approach, it is best that he stick to an analysis of only that which he directly experiences and forego the luxury of speculating about the source of his sense data.

A few points of explanation might be helpful concerning the use of the expression "sense data." We are certain there are such entities as sense data because we directly experience them (that is, we do not *infer* their existence); furthermore, they provide us with an explanation of such unusual experiences as illusions and hallucinations. If, for example, we see a stick "bend" when it is submerged in water, we are obviously not seeing a stick that is *really* bending. But we are experiencing *something,* and this something is a certain combination of sense data. Also, suppose on a certain occasion you think you see some green rats running around your room. After you check things out and find no evidence that real rats are paying a visit, you would probably conclude that you must have been having an hallucination. But you would still insist that you saw something which *appeared* to be green rats. What were you experiencing if not certain sorts of sense data? So the existence of the entities we phenomenalists call sense data is well substantiated, and *they* are what we perceive, not so-called material objects whose existence cannot be proved by argument.

Difficulties with This Argument

(1) Since the phenomenalist claims that material-object statements ("There is a desk in the other room") can be translated without loss of meaning into sense-datum statements ("If someone goes into the next room and goes through the appropriate operations, then he will have certain sense data"), we may ask whether there is mention of anything in this sense-datum statement which also needs to be reduced to sense data?

How does the phenomenalist propose to treat the terms "some-one" or "person"? Is a person nothing more than someone else's actual or possible sense data? Mention of time and location in his sense-datum statements raises further problems for the phenomenalist.

(2) If the statement, "There is a desk in the other room," is equivalent in meaning to the assertion, "If someone goes into the next room and looks in the right direction, then he will have sense data a, b, and c," then both of these assertions must be true under the same conditions. That is, one of them could not be true and the other false under any circumstances. Yet there seems to be one condition or set of circumstances which could make the material-object statement (the one above the desk) false but not the sense-datum statement (the one above beginning with the word "if"). Suppose that nothing except people's minds existed; although we might find this difficult to imagine, nevertheless it is a possibility. Now if such a set of circumstances or conditions existed, the assertion, "There is a desk in the other room," would be false if we take these words in their normal, accepted use. However, the statement, "If someone goes into the next room and looks in the right direction, then he will have sense data a, b, and c," would not be false given the condition that only minds and their contents exist. The reason such a statement would not be false under the condition is that the assertion is classified as "hypothethical." Such statements do not make claims concerning the actual existence of anything, as do categorical statements of which "There is a desk in the other room," is an example. Hypothetical statements such as the phenomenalist's sense-datum statements simply say that *if* such-and-such is the case, then something else is the case. In short, material-object statements are categorical propositions, and they would be false if only minds existed; sense-datum statements are hypothetical propositions, and they would not be false if only minds existed. Therefore, material-object statements cannot mean the same as sense-datum statements, because there

is at least one possible set of circumstances in which the one would be false and the other could be true.

(3) Has the phenomenalist really "discovered" some new "objects" or "entities" which he has named "sense data"? If a medical research scientist discovers a new virus, for example, he will undoubtedly specify how he discovered it and what procedures others should go through to verify his findings. Does the sense-datum theorist tell us anything like this about *his* "discovery"? Does he not rather present his case as though he is pointing out the necessary truth that whenever a person seems to be seeing a red apple, then he is having a red sense datum? He seems to be merely *defining* "seeing, touching, smelling, tasting, or hearing *X*" as "having sense data of *X*." If this is so, the phenomenalist is simply adopting another way of talking about the way physical things appear to us. The phenomenalist's seemingly "factual" discovery about what we perceive seems to boil down to a proposal on his part that we adopt a new mode of speech in certain circumstances. Then our question for the phenomenalist might come to this — in what way is talk about "sense data" superior to the ordinary use of expressions like "A penny looks elliptical when it is placed in a certain position," and "A straight stick appears to be bent when it is partly submerged in water"?

"Our Sense Data Are Caused by Material Objects Outside the Mind."[24]

The difficulties encountered in Berkeley's view and in that of phenomenalism have led some philosophers in a slightly different direction on the problem of perception. There is the

---

[24] Bertrand Russell, *The Analysis of Matter* (New York: Dover Publications, 1927), pp. 200-217, reprinted in Hirst, ed., *Perception and the External World*, pp. 209-23. A. O. Lovejoy, *The Revolt Against Dualism* (New York: W. W. Norton & Company, Inc., 1930), Chap. 8.

position which is sometimes called the "causal theory," since it maintains that our sense perceptions are the way they are and happen as they do because of their being produced by material objects which exist independently of our minds. The argument for the causal theory of perception goes something like this:

Berkeley and the modern phenomenalists were right up to a point. What we directly perceive or are immediately aware of in perception *are* various kinds of sense data. When we are having sense perceptions, we are very much like a telephone operator who must be content with receiving various telephone messages through a complex network of lines and exchanges; she cannot directly contact the sources of these messages. In like manner, we receive messages which are transmitted along a complex network of nerves. And, like the telephone operator, we can never get direct contact with that which we believe to be the source of our "messages." Nevertheless, Berkeley went wrong when he concluded that the only possible cause of our perceptual ideas was God, and modern phenomenalists likewise end up with a highly unsatisfactory view because they refuse to address themselves to the question, "What causes our sense data?"

Certain characteristics of the sense data we experience definitely stand in need of some explanation. For example, how is it that there is such a striking degree of orderliness and uniformity among our sense data? We are not being bombarded with all sorts of sense data in a chaotic fashion; they come for the most part in orderly combinations, as in the case where one perceives what is normally called a desk. Notice also that as long as a person continues to look in a certain direction, and the lighting conditions remain adequate, he continues to receive sense data of the desk and not sense data of the Taj Mahal. True, if a person begins to undergo an hallucination, or someone plays a trick on him by directing colored lighting onto the desk, his sense data will change. But in ordinary circumstances, there is a good deal of orderliness in what we perceive.

Because of this characteristic which our sense data have, we can predict with a high degree of accuracy what sense data we will receive under certain conditions. Didn't the phenomenalist himself include a prediction in his sense-datum statement which he took to be part of the translation of the statement about my desk in the other room? How is it that if someone else should enter the room I am now in, I can predict fairly accurately what sense data he will experience? Just because *I* am experiencing certain color patches, sounds and smells at the present time, what leads me to think that anyone else with similar perceptual faculties will experience roughly what I experience? The only reasonable explanation for this ability to predict the *content* of my own and other people's sense data as well as the *time* when they will have them is that material objects exist outside the mind and cause our sense data. Since many material objects remain relatively unchanged for an extended period of time, our predictions concerning what we will perceive in any given circumstance can attain a high degree of accuracy.

It would seem then that we must accept the proposition that material objects exist outside our minds and that they persist when no one is experiencing them. Their existence is not dependent upon anyone's being present and perceiving them. Now obviously, this proposition cannot be proved by appealing to what we directly experience. It *is* indeed an inference or belief, but yet a reasonable one. All that we *directly* experience are sense data when we are actually in the presence of the object. But just because we *believe* or *infer* that material objects exist and cause our sense data, this does not mean that we are not entitled to call such beliefs knowledge. The belief in material objects is so well confirmed that a reasonable man does not doubt it. The only disbelievers are philosophers who arbitrarily define "knowledge" as "that which we directly experience"; consequently, they are forced by their definition to deny that we can know whether or not material things really exist outside our minds.

Difficulties with This Argument

(1) If we can be in direct contact with our sensations only, how do we know that they represent material objects whose existence we must be content to infer? If our perceptions are supposed to be copies of material objects, how do we know we receive faithful copies when we never do have the original (the material object itself) before us to make the comparison?

(2) When we say that things like *A* cause other things like *B*, part of what we mean is that *A*-type things have been *observed* on occasion to accompany or precede *B*-type things. How can it be meaningfully said, then, that material objects (which, the theory states, are never observed) *cause* our sensation?

(3) How does this theory suppose we "receive" our sense data from the physical world "out there"? The sense organs and the nervous systems of the body would seem to be the logical candidates, but on what grounds can they be known to exist on the present theory?

(4) If we must admit the existence of material things in order to have an adequate explanation for the nature of the sensations we have, how are we to evaluate the adequacy of "explanations" in this area? How do such explanations resemble or fail to resemble those which are produced in the sciences? Would you regard the hypothesis that extremely intelligent beings from a remote planet cause our sensations by means of powerful and elaborate electronic radio signals to be a better or poorer "explanation" for the nature of our perceptual experience than the one offered by the theory just discussed? Why?

The Question, "Do We Perceive Material Things or Merely Sense Data?" Is Misleading.[25]

One of the leading practitioners of the philosophical method which has come to be known as "ordinary language"

---

[25] J. L. Austin, *Sense and Sensibilia* (Oxford: Clarendon Press, 1962), p. 1-32, especially.

analysis (or "conceptual geography") was the late J. L. Austin. He, like others who are sympathetic to this way of approaching philosophy, maintained that before we take sides in one of the age-old disputes of philosophy and begin throwing our philosophical blows, we would do better to find out what the dispute is all about. It is so easy in philosophy to march out arguments and spin theories of the strangest, most paradoxical sort before first analyzing the problem we have set out to solve. Austin maintained that the question, "Do we perceive material things or sense data?" is one of which some philosophers have been far too uncritical, and their failure to get clear on what the question presupposes has led them into troublesome tangles. He argued that the question is too simply put as it stands and is entirely misleading. Sliding over these shortcomings in the question itself has contributed to the difficulties in the positions of sense-datum theorists such as A. J. Ayer and H. H. Price. Austin's penetrating criticisms of all of the arguments advanced in support of the sense-datum theory cannot be summarized in the limited amount of space available. We shall follow his arguments only against the main pillars of the sense-datum theory and invite the more serious reader to pursue on his own the whole of Austin's work, *Sense and Sensibilia*. Austin's analysis proceeds along the following lines.

It is fairly clear that there is no one kind of thing we perceive. We perceive such diverse types of things as pens, desks, clouds, rainbows, after-images, and pictures on the movie screen. The question, "What do we perceive, sense data or material objects?" is an oversimplification and misleading for all that. Instead of trying to give an answer to this question (as many philosophers have done), we should attempt to rid ourselves of several fallacious arguments often advanced for the position that it is sense data which we perceive. And as sense-datum theorists put it, sense data are what we "directly perceive," not material objects.

Before we examine the two main arguments for the

sense-datum theory let's take a closer look at this phrase, "directly perceive." It is used rather freely by the sense-datum theorist and plays a hefty role in his view. But what does it mean to perceive something *directly*? The only way to tell what this would be like is to contrast it with *indirectly* perceiving something. When we see something through a periscope or by means of a mirror, we say we are seeing "indirectly." It seems that when we are not looking straight at the object in question with the naked eye we may properly be said to be perceiving "indirectly." But if we are looking dead ahead at a particular thing, it seems inappropriate to say that we are seeing the object in question "indirectly," as the sense-datum theorist would have it.

Perceiving "indirectly" makes sense only in certain limited cases of visual experience, and it certainly sounds odd when applied to perception through the other senses. What would it be like to smell or taste "indirectly"? Just where and how we are to use the expression "direct perception" is not spelled out by the sense-datum theorist, so it is no small point we are pursuing.

Furthermore, if we *do* want to speak of seeing something indirectly (by the use of a periscope or mirror) this object has to be the sort of thing which we could perceive without the aid of these devices. But the believer in sense data claims that *all* of our perception of material things is "indirect," that all we ever perceive "directly" are sense data. Clearly, the philosopher here is stretching the ordinary use of words to such a point that we cannot be sure how he wants his expression "direct perception" to be taken.

Now we can proceed to the two principal pillars of the sense-datum theory. The first one is usually called "the argument from illusion," and we had better refresh our memories on its main points. First of all, the sense-datum theorist parades various examples before us of what he calls cases of "illusions." The stick that "bends" when partly submerged in water is the old standby, so let's take a closer look at this example. Normally, the stick "appears straight," but when partly submerged in water it looks bent. Now at least one of the visual appearances of the stick must be "delusive," argues Ayer, one of the leading proponents of the sense-datum theory. The stick cannot actually *be* both straight and bent, but nevertheless we do really see *something* when we see the stick "bend" in water. This "something" we perceive is a sense datum — and in this case a "delusive" one. Other examples in the parade of illusions which are called to our attention are mirages and reflections in mirrors. The same point is made about them that is made concerning the "bent" stick in water. The desert traveler "sees" *something* when he sees a mirage, but it is merely an illusion; all he sees are various sense data which look like a real oasis. So goes the argument from illusion which we must now dissect.

The argument contains two crucial presuppositions: first, that the cases just mentioned are genuine examples of illusions, and second, that illusions and delusions are the same. Both of these assumptions are mistaken. A *genuine* case of illusion would result from the work of professional conjurors and ventriloquists where something *not totally unreal* is conjured up. The dummy on the ventriloquist's knee does not talk on its own, but it is certainly real in its own right. A delusion, on the other hand, is a grossly disordered belief, such as a delusion of grandeur or of persecution, and such beliefs have little or nothing to do with perception. A delusion suggests that something totally unreal is conjured up. Delusions, consequently, are private disorders in someone's personality, whereas illusions are quite public in the sense that anyone can see them if they happen to be in the right place.

How does the sense-datum theorist make capital out of the erroneous assumption that illusions and delusions are the same? Well, he argues that *something* is being perceived in the cases of "illusion" he mentions, but he then calls this something (the "bent" look of the stick) *delusive* because of the non-real, immaterial nature of the bend of the stick in water. Since the stick is not *really* bent, one must be perceiving "delusory" sense data in such a case, he concludes.

But is anybody really deluded when he sees a stick "bend" when partly submerged in water? Is anyone taken in? The changed appearance of the stick is precisely what we would expect in such circumstances, so why call it "delusory"? If a cover on one of my books becomes warped because of contact with moisture, must I now call the "warped look" of the book "delusive"? An object is not going to look the same in all circumstances regardless of what is done to and with it, so why call some of these ways of appearing "delusory" and some "veridical"?

The other main prop of the sense-datum theory attempts to support a stronger claim. The argument from illusion merely sets us up for the knockout blow. So far, all the sense-datum theorist has tried to prove is that *sometimes* (in cases of illusion) we perceive sense data and not anything we could call material objects. The following argument by the sense-datum theorist is intended to prove that we *always* directly perceive only sense data.

Ayer, for example, maintains that there is no intrinsic difference in kind between veridical perceptions and those which are delusive. By "veridical" perceptions he presumably means those which we take to be genuine presentations of material objects, such as the normal appearance of a straight stick. And by "delusive" perceptions he means those which do not correctly present material things, as in the case of the "bent" look of the stick in water. Ayer argues that if we were to compare (a) our normal sense data of a crooked stick with (b) the abnormal crooked sense data of a straight stick (submerged in water), we would find the two complexes of sense data qualitatively indistinguishable. Taken by themselves, that is, the veridical sense data could not be distinguished from the delusive. He then draws the conclusion dear to the heart of every sense-datum theorist: (a) and (b) above *both* must be of the same kind. Therefore, if we perceive only sense data when we see the stick "bend" in water,

251

then we must perceive only sense data *whenever* we claim to see a stick, regardless of where it is or in what condition it happens to be.

In answer to this argument, we might first point out that delusive and veridical perceptions *are* qualitatively different, and that the difference is obvious. We can, for example, readily tell the difference between the content of dreams and experiences in waking life. Don't we refer to some of our experiences on occasion as having a "dream-like" quality?

Second, what about the sense-datum theorist's apparent acceptance of the principle that "if A and B look identical, then they belong to the same type"? Just because a bar of soap may look like a lemon, it does not follow that they belong to the same type of category. The sense-datum theorist argues that because the bent look of the stick in water and the straight appearance of the stick in normal situations are alike in that, considered by themselves, one can't tell the correct from the delusory, then the two must be of the same type. But again, two objects which are alike in many different ways could still be quite different in kind.

The sense-datum theorist's argument is built upon another erroneous principle. He argues that delusive and veridical sense data are not qualitatively distinguishable, because if they were distinguishable, we would never be deluded. But it seems perfectly clear that from the fact that one has failed to distinguish between A and B, it does not follow that A and B are indistinguishable. An uninstructed child or a primitive person might not be able to distinguish between a stick's "being refracted" and its "being crooked." All sorts of explanations can be given for the fact that we sometimes fail to distinguish veridical from non-veridical perceptions. We often make hasty judgments; some of us don't see or hear well to start with; and sometimes we see what we hope or expect to see, not what is actually there. But it is obvious that failure to distinguish on occasion between A and B does not imply that A and B must be "indistinguishable" or of the same kind generally.

CONCLUDING COMMENTS

It is a curious fact that in spite of the immense differences which usually exist between the rationalist and empiricist approaches, they are not always so far apart. Some empiricists are just as much dedicated to the quest for the unquestionable as any rationalist ever was. Consider, for example, the phenomenalist who seems to give the impression that he regards his philosophy as the most orthodox form of empiricism; he insists that a philosophical analysis of knowledge stay close to exactly what is experienced through the senses. He will have nothing to do with the "guesswork" involved in trying to prove that there is a real world outside of our experience which in some way is supposed to account for the content of experience. He argues that the existence of any objects beyond our sensory experience is not verifiable, but the reality of our sense data (those color patches, sounds, tastes, etc., which make up the content of perceptual experience) cannot be doubted. Here you have some "hard data" which cannot be washed away by an effort of doubt. As long as we confine our philosophical utterances to statements which can somehow be reduced to statements about our indubitable sense data, we shall be on solid, unassailable ground.

It is clear that the attraction of an absolutely certain starting point for knowledge has had its effects outside the rationalist camp. Admittedly, what the hard-headed empiricist takes to be unquestionable is quite different from the data with which the rationalist begins. For the phenomenalist, as we have just seen, the "quest for the unquestionable" ends with his "discovery" of sense data. For the rationalist, on the other hand, the indubitable is discovered in those ideas and principles which have always been lying dormant in his mind waiting to be awakened and put to work. We have only to recall the way Descartes put the supposedly "innate ideas" concerning God and causal relationships through their paces.

253

It is easy to appreciate the motives which lead a particular philosopher in quest of the unquestionable. When we say
that we *know* that X is the case, there is a certain force to our
claim that is not able to be captured by saying that we *believe*
that X is the case. It seems that we should reserve the word
"know" for those circumstances in which we have the very best
reasons for making a particular knowledge-claim. And what
better reason could we have for claiming to know that X is the
case than the fact that it is not possible to doubt X? This is the
sort of reasoning that has led some philosophers to define
"knowledge" in terms of being *certain* and "being certain" in
terms of "not being open to any possible doubt."

Having stated how understandable the quest for the
unquestionable is, we may ask, however, whether philosophers
engaged in this program have not been led down the garden
path? Two considerations especially may throw the whole
project open to question. First of all, if we accept for the moment
the philosopher's definition of "certainty" as "being beyond any
possibility of doubt," where will this eventually lead us? Suppose we consider a case where a person has a certain sense
datum such as a red color patch and he reports the event by
means of the statement, "I am seeing a red color patch." Can
such a person rightly claim that he has made a statement the truth
of which it is not possible to doubt? At least the individual
making the statement must admit that he remembers what the
word "red" means and what it means to "see" something. But
surely no sensible person would claim that one's memory is an
infallible faculty. Even if it is reliable a good share of the time,
one can never be *absolutely* certain that on any given occasion
its deliverances are wholly trustworthy. So what happens to the
absolute certainty which is usually claimed for reports about
one's sense experiences? Must we not admit (on the sense-datum
theorist's own definition of "certainty") that even sense-datum
statements are in principle open to theoretical doubt? It would
seem that if one insists on defining knowledge in terms of

certainty, and certainty is taken as being incapable of doubt, no knowledge is possible at all, which is a conclusion the phenomenalist would hardly find very attractive.

The second consideration which throws some doubt upon the quest for the unquestionable as it is conceived by the philosophers we have been discussing centers around the normal, everyday use of the words "certain" and "being sure." If I were to claim there was a copy of Immanuel Kant's *Critique of Pure Reason* on my bookshelf, and my claim were challenged, what would I do? I would probably check my bookshelf again and see whether the book I was referring to was still there, or look it over again to see that I had not misread the title on the cover. I would probably also invite the person challenging my claim into my study, show him the book and have *him* page through it to see that it really is a copy of Kant's classic work. But if, after having done all this, my sceptical friend were to ask, "But can you be certain that this object is what you claim it is?" I should be at a loss to know what he was asking. What more could be done to make sure that there really was a copy of the work in question on my bookshelf? Going through the various verification processes just mentioned is what we *mean* by the expression, "making sure." I would have the *best* reasons for claiming that a copy of Kant's *Critique of Pure Reason* was on my bookshelf, because there *are* no other reasons which I could appeal to in order to make sure of my claim. It could always be said that I could be dreaming the whole episode or that my perceptions and those of my sceptical friend could have been produced by some powerful malicious being or an elaborate projector operated by an extremely intelligent race of creatures on the planet Kroton. But I would probably take such a suggestion as a feeble attempt at jest and not as a possibility worthy of serious consideration.

SUGGESTIONS FOR FURTHER STUDY

Anthologies:

AB, Parts 5 and 6; BKW, Chap. 1 and 5; EP, Parts 1, 6, and 7; F, Part 2; MGAS, Parts 2 and 3; SA, Part 3; ST, Part 1; TBO, Part 7; TH, Part 1.

Others:

Hirst, R. J., ed., *Perception and the External World.* New York: The Macmillan Company, 1965.

Hospers, John, *An Introduction to Philosophical Analysis*, Chapter 6. Englewood Cliffs, N.J.: Prentice-Hall, Inc. 1953.

Swartz, R. J., ed., *Perceiving, Sensing and Knowing.* New York: Doubleday & Company, Inc., 1965.

INDEX
